KT-420-689

(1

]

12

THE SOMME

Ruins of Flers, September 1916. (Q.4272)

THE SOMME

The Day-by-Day Account

CHRIS McCARTHY

Introduction by Peter Simkins

ARMS AND
ARMOUR

Arms & Armour Press
A Cassell Imprint
Villiers House, 41–47 Strand, London WC2N 5JE

Distributed in the USA by Sterling Publishing Co. Inc.,
387 Park Avenue South, New York, NY 10016-8810

Distributed in Australia by Capricorn Link (Australia) Pty Ltd,
P.O. Box 665, Lane Cove, New South Wales 2066

British Library Cataloguing-in-Publication data:
A catalogue record for this book is available from the British Library.

ISBN 1 85409 206 5

Edited by Michael Boxall
Designed by Roger Chesneau/DAG Publications
Printed in Great Britain by The Bath Press

CONTENTS

INTRODUCTION

The Somme offensive of 1916 is implanted deeper in the folk-memory of the British people than any other First World War battle—with the possible exception of Passchendaele. The reasons are not far to seek. It was the first major offensive of the war against the main enemy, the Germans, in which British troops played the leading part instead of a supporting or diversionary role. It was also the first great battle to involve the bulk of Britain's first-ever mass citizen army. Unique among the principal armies on the Western Front in being composed of volunteers, the British Expeditionary Force of the summer and autumn of 1916 was drawn from all levels of society in Britain and the Dominions and, moreover, had been recruited on a peculiarly parochial basis.

The character of the 1916 army was symbolized by its 'Pals' battalions, units raised by local civilian committees rather than the War Office and made up of workmates, friends or men with a shared geographical or social background, who had enlisted together on the understanding that they would be permitted to train and fight together. Precisely because so many formations were closely identified with particular communities at home in Britain or the Dominions, the psy-chological impact of the lengthening casualty lists was all the more marked during that summer and autumn.

It was the intention of General Sir Douglas Haig, the Commander-in-Chief of the BEF, that on the opening day of the offensive—1 July 1916—Lieutenant-General Sir Henry Rawlinson's Fourth Army should take the German front-line defences from Montauban in the south to Serre in the north. In addition, the attacking troops were to secure the German second position on the ridge stretching from Pozières to the River

Battle of Albert. British troops attacking German trenches near Mametz, 1 July 1916. (Q.86)

Battle of Ginchy. Supporting troops moving up to the attack, near Ginchy, 9 September 1916. (Q.1302)

Ancre and on the slopes before Miraumont. After that, if all went well, Haig hoped to break through the second position on the right, on the high ground between Pozières and Ginchy. This might, in turn, facilitate the capture of the German third position in the Morval–Flers–Le Sars sector, uncovering Bapaume and allowing the Reserve Army, commanded by Lieutenant-General Sir Hubert Gough, to wheel northwards and roll up the German lines in the direction of Arras.

In the event, the results of the offensive—at least in terms of 'breakthroughs' or ground gained—fell far short of hopes and expectations. Of the 142 days of the Battle of the Somme, none was more traumatic than the opening day, the bloodiest twenty-four hours in the entire history of the British Army. By nightfall on 1 July the only real British successes had been on the right flank, where Montauban and Mametz were captured and the Fourth Army had managed to advance about a mile on a sector some 3½ miles wide. On other sectors, from Mametz northwards, the gains were negligible. The 36th (Ulster) Division, part of X Corps, succeeded initially in overrunning the formidable Schwaben Redoubt on the Thiepval plateau—one of the toughest German strongholds on the Western Front—but were compelled to pull back in the afternoon and evening, partly because of the failure of the divisions on their flanks. A similar fate befell 56th (London) Division in the diversionary attack on the Gommecourt Salient by VII Corps of General Sir Edmund Allenby's Third Army. The modest first-day gains cost 57,470 British casualties, including 19,240 killed and 35,493 wounded.

The scale of the collective tragedy and of the personal and family grief represented by this appalling total is still mind-numbing more than 75 years later. Yet it could be argued that the story of 1 July currently exerts too powerful a hold upon our emotions and imagination, leading many students of the First World War to pay less attention than they should to the remaining 141 days of the battle. One of the most obvious benefits of Chris McCarthy's painstaking summaries of each day's operations is that they help to correct this imbalance and remind us of what John Terraine has called 'the true texture of the Somme'.

It is possible for the historian, luxuriating in the comfort of hindsight, to divide the rest of the British offensive into a number of distinct phases while recognizing, of course, that the pattern of operations would have seemed much less neat and clear-cut to the 'poor bloody infantry' who actually fought on the Somme. From 2 to 13 July 1916, as Gough's Reserve Army started to assume responsibility for the battle north (or left) of the Albert–Bapaume road, the principal thrust of operations was on Rawlinson's Fourth Army front, with the British trying to exploit their rare first-day successes on the right. During this period Fourth Army strove to secure Mametz Wood, Contalmaison and Trônes Wood so that the flanks of an assault on the German second main position would be covered. The assault took place early on 14 July. Following a potentially difficult but skilfully accomplished night assembly in no man's land, and a sudden intensification of the three-day preliminary bombardment in the five minutes before zero hour, the infantry attacked at dawn under a creeping barrage, swiftly capturing some 6,000 yards of the German second position between Longueval and Bazentin-le-Petit. Compared to 1 July the attack was, in several respects, a more accurate reflection of the capabilities of the New Army formations, given imaginative operational planning. However, opportunities to exploit the initial gains were missed and the overall result of the 14 July assault was less impressive than it might have been. Delville Wood, immediately adjacent to Longueval, was not completely in British hands until 27 August, and High Wood, to the north-west, defied capture until 15 September.

The British official historian describes the period from 15 July to 14 September as one of 'heavy losses, great hardships, and tremendous physical and moral strain' for troops of all armies. The siege-type oper-

ations of early July began to give way to semi-open warfare, with the Germans often holding lines of shell-holes rather than continuous trenches. Although, in essence, he had little real choice in the matter, Haig himself, for a time, cast aside thoughts of an imminent break-through, acknowledging to an increasing extent that the BEF was engaged in a dour battle of attrition. Haig correspondingly came to regard the operations of late July and August as part of a 'wearing-out' phase of the battle in preparation for another big set-piece assault in mid-September, an attack which he hoped would indeed prove decisive. During this 'wearing-out' phase, Rawlinson's Fourth Army continued to play the leading role. Besides repeated efforts to take High Wood and Delville Wood, Rawlinson also tried to ease the progress of the French Sixth Army on his right by seizing Guillemont and Ginchy, but neither of these objectives was in his grasp be-

fore early September. Meanwhile the Reserve Army's operations were growing in importance. From 23 July to 5 August the Australians of I Anzac Corps were involved in a bitter fight for Pozières on the Albert–Bapaume road and for the ruined mill on the crest of the ridge beyond the eastern end of the village. The Australian success here, bought at a high price in casualties, gave the BEF good observation over the surrounding terrain. Nevertheless it was merely a curtain-raiser to the long, hard slog which the Reserve Army had still to face in order to overcome the various German trench lines and strongpoints north-west of the Albert–Bapaume road, on the slopes and spurs of the Morval–Grandcourt ridge, thereby threatening the defences of Thiepval from the rear. In the ensuing operations the names of these trenches and strongpoints—Fabeck Graben, Mou-

British RAMC dresser tending a wounded German, near Carnoy, 30 July 1916. (Q.4059)

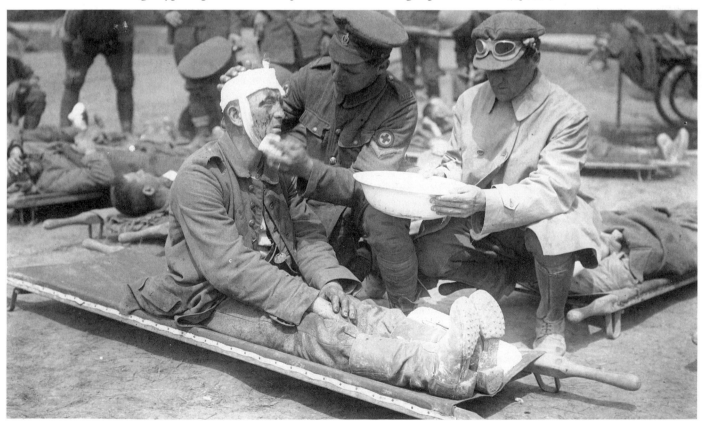

SOMME CHRONOLOGY

July		
1–13	Battle of Albert	
1	Capture of Montauban	
1	Capture of Mametz	
2	Capture of Fricourt	
2–4	Capture of La Boisselle	
3	Capture of Bernafay Wood	
7–11	Mametz Wood	
10	Capture of Contalmaison	
7–13	Fighting in Trônes Wood	
14–17	Battle of Bazentin Ridge	
14	Capture of Trônes Wood	
14–18 and 29	Capture of Longueval	
15 (until 3 Sept)	Battle of Delville Wood	
17	Capture of Ovillers	
20–30	Attacks on High Wood	
23 (until 13 Sept)	Battle of Pozières Ridge	
27–28	Capture and consolidation of Delville Wood	

August		
6 (until 3 Sept)	Fighting for Mouquet Farm	
8–9	Attack on Waterlot Farm–Guillemont	

September		
3–6	Battle of Guillemont	
9	Battle of Ginchy	

14	Capture of the Wonder Work	
15–22	Battle of Flers-Courcelette	
15	Capture of Flers	
15	Capture of High Wood	
15	Capture of Martinpuich	
25–28	Battle of Morval	
25	Capture of Lesboeufs	
26	Battle of Thiepval Ridge	
26	Capture of Combles	
26	Capture of Grid Trench and Gueudecourt	
26	Capture of Mouquet Farm	

October		
1–18	Battle of Transloy Ridges	
1 (until 11 Nov)	Battle of the Ancre Heights	
1–3	Capture of Eaucourt l'Abbaye	
7	Capture of Le Sars	
7 (until 5 Nov)	Attack on the Butte de Warlencourt	
9	Capture of Stuff Redoubt	
14	Capture of Schwaben Redoubt	
21	Capture of Regina Trench and Redoubt	
21	Capture of Stuff Trench	

November		
3–11	Battle of the Ancre	
13	Capture of Beaumont Hamel	
14	Capture of Beaucourt	
13–18	Battle of the Ancre	

quet Farm, Zollern Graben, Stuff Trench, Stuff Redoubt, Regina Ridge—would become depressingly familiar to Gough's divisions.

Many of the relatively small-scale attacks delivered in July, August and early September were intended to push forward the British line at different points, win local tactical advantages and so improve the jumping-off positions for the next *major* assault. The less convoluted the start-line, the greater were the chances of ensuring an accurate preliminarty bombardment or supporting barrage, but the broader tactical benefits were not always instantly apparent to the officers and men who saw the strength of their battalions progressively eroded by minor yet costly 'line straightening' operations. As Robin Prior and Trevor Wilson have shown in their recent study of Rawlinson's generalship, *Command on the Western Front*

(Blackwell, 1992), Fourth Army advanced barely 1,000 yards on a five-mile front in the 62 days between 15 July and 14 September, incurring approximately 82,000 casualties in the process. Only on some five occasions out of some ninety operations during these weeks did Fourth Army employ twenty or more battalions and only four attacks were launched across the whole of its front.

The set-piece assault against the German third position on 15 September—which began the next phase of the British Somme offensive—marked the battlefield debut of the tank. It also coincided with attacks by French Sixth Army to the south and Allied offensives in Salonika, in Transylvania and on the Italian front, a potent reminder that the struggle on the Somme was but part of a wider coalition war. Fourth Army's objectives on 15 September included the

German third position in front of Flers and the subsequent capture of Morval Lesboeufs and Gueudecourt, while Courcelette was to be seized by the Canadian Corps of the Reserve Army. On the day, the British advanced about 2,500 yards, securing the German third position on a front of 4,500 yards. Flers was captured by XV Corps with the aid of four of the tanks allotted to 41st Division, and Courcelette, Martinpuich and High Wood were also seized. In square miles, the territory won by the BEF on 15 September was about twice that gained on 1 July and at about half the cost in casualties. Even so, it was not the decisive blow which Haig and Rawlinson had sought.

The offensive was renewed on 25 September as Fourth Army fought to secure the objectives that had remained out of reach a few days earlier. In some ways the operations in the last week of September were among the most fruitful since the dawn assault on 14 July. In the Battle of Morval, as Fourth Army's operations between 25 and 28 September became known, the preliminary bombardment and initial creeping barrage were particularly effective in XIV Corps' sector on the right. Morval and Lesboeufs were taken on 25 September, Combles and Gueudecourt the following day. At the same time, in the Battle of Thiepval Ridge, Gough's Reserve Army launched the biggest operation it had yet undertaken and attacked on a front extending from the Schwaben Redoubt to Courcelette. The German garrison of Mouquet Farm surrendered to the 11th Division on the first day of Gough's attack, and Major-General Maxse's 18th Division took much of Thiepval itself, completing the clearance of the village on 27 September. But, as was so often the case in the middle years of the Great War, the offensive lost momentum. It was not

Dugouts and ammunition dumps in the Arrow Head Copse position. Trônes Wood in background. (Q.53169)

until 14 October that the last German defenders were ejected from the Schwaben Redoubt and the Canadian Corps was still fighting for parts of Regina Trench as late as the second week of November.

The failure to achieve a breakthrough in these large-scale and co-ordinated assaults of the second half of September could, and probably should, have been reason enough for Haig to halt the offensive. That he continued with it was partly a consequence of the over-optimism of his Intelligence chief, Brigadier-General Charteris, who helped to persuade him that, if the BEF kept up the pressure, the Germans would eventually crack. Between 1 and 20 October, as Fourth Army inched towards Le Transloy—capturing Le Sars on 7 October—the weather deteriorated and the battlefield became a morass. Even the protests of a Corps commander, Lord Cavan, that his men were exhausted, did not bring the ordeal of the front-line troops to an end. In the hope that a late British success might create a good impression at a forthcoming inter-Allied conference at Chantilly, Fifth Army

(as the Reserve Army was now called) delivered a well-organized attack astride the Ancre, after several postponements, on 13 November.

This final phase of the Somme offensive saw Beaumont Hamel and Beaucourt pass into British possession, but Serre, which had been an objective on the very first day, 4½ months before, was still occupied by the Germans when the battle petered out on about 19 November 1916. Together, since 1 July, Rawlinson's and Gough's formations had wrested from the Germans a strip of territory measuring approximately twenty miles wide by six miles deep, yet Fourth Army remained three miles from Bapaume while the French, farther south, had been stopped short of Péronne. The offensive cost Britain and the Dominions the enormous total of 419,654 casualties. French losses were 204,253 while estimates of German casualties range from 437,000 to 680,000.

Even if one does not subscribe to the view that all senior commanders were 'butchers' and 'bunglers', it is difficult to escape the conclusion that British generalship was not at its best

on the Somme in 1916. For example, prior to 1 July, the basic divergence of concept between Haig, who envisaged a breakthrough, and Rawlinson, who favoured step-by-step 'bite and hold' operations, was never properly resolved. The inevitable outcome was that the final plan for the initial assault was riddled with contradictions and false assumptions, yet these differences in approach re-surfaced before the attack of 15 September. As Prior and Wilson remark in their recent work, Fourth Army managed, on at least two occasions (11–14 July and 24–25 September), to organize artillery bombardments sufficiently intense in terms of weight of shell per yard of trench attacked to ensure success in the subsequent assault. However, having apparently grasped the significance of this factor, Rawlinson did not consistently apply the formula in the late summer and autumn of 1916. Both he and Gough can also be

Salvaged rifles—mostly Lee Enfields—at Aveluy, September 1916. (Q.1446)

accused of launching too many attacks on narrow fronts, allowing the Germans, in most cases, to concentrate more of their defensive firepower on the threatened sector.

By no means all the mistakes were committed by one side. Shortly after the start of the British offensive, General Erich von Falkenhayn, the Chief of the German General Staff, decreed that any ground lost should be retaken 'by immediate counter-attack, even to the use of the last man'. General Fritz von Below, commanding German Second Army, similarly demanded that 'the enemy should have to carve his way over heaps of corpses'. The self-inflicted policy of stubbord linear defence and relentless counter-attacks only served to increase the rate at which the life blood of the German Army was draining away in the late summer of 1916, given that the Germans were simultaneously embroiled in a titanic attrition battle at Verdun. German troops reaching the Somme front swiftly recognized that the Allies were obvi-

ously winning the war of *matériel*. When Falkenhayn fell from grace and Hindenburg and Ludendorff came to power at the head of the German Army on 29 August, significant changes were made in German strategy and tactics. A fresh doctrine of flexible and mobile defence in depth, with the forward positions held more thinly, began to replace the expensive linear tactics of previous months and years. Work commenced in the early autumn on the construction, 25 miles to the rear, of a major new defensive position—the *Siegfried Stellung* or Hindenburg Line—which embodied the revised tactical doctrine and enabled the Germans to economize on manpower. On 21 September Hindenburg asserted that the Somme front was 'all-important' and must now have first call on available divisions. That the British attacks were hurting was confirmed by those reliable barometers of the state of the German Army, Crown Prince Rupprecht of Bavaria and his chief of staff General von Kuhl, both of whom

View of the battlefield showing German dead. Somme, 1916. The man in the centre appears to have his hands tied together. (CO.940)

noted the decline in the strength and morale of their forces on the Somme and expressed doubts whether they could withstand a similar offensive in 1917. Captain von Hentig, a staff officer with the Guard Reserve Division, graphically described the Somme as 'the muddy grave of the German field army'.

One should be careful not to exaggerate the deterioration in the Imperial German Army at the end of 1916. The battles of 1917 would reveal only too clearly that it had a great deal of resilience left. It should also be remembered that, although the Allied blockade of Germany was beginning to bite and cause genuine hardship by the second half of 1916, the slack in German industry was only taken up that autumn when the 'Hindenburg Programme' was initiated to expand

munitions production, and an Auxiliary Service Law was passed to make better use of the country's human resources. It is therefore extremely doubtful whether the German Army could have been beaten in 1916, wherever the Allies had attacked on the Western Front. The Somme offensive was a necessary if painful stage in the process of weakening a skilful, courageous and highly professional enemy. There was no real alternative to doing it the hard way.

Another problem was that the BEF was not yet a properly balanced force in 1916. Its tactical knowledge, experience and ideas—and even, to some extent, its equipment—were still inadequate to achieve the desired breakthrough. Having said that, there were unmistakable signs of improvement. Commanders such as General Maxse of the 18th Division were now urging greater use of Lewis-guns so that infantry battalions could be more self-supporting in firepower in an at-

tack. In the artillery sphere, the creeping barrage was becoming standard; progress in flash-spotting and sound-ranging was helping to make counter-battery work more effective; guns and ammunition were becoming more numerous and reliable; and the development of devices such as the instantaneous '106' fuze would soon increase the ability of the artillery to cut German barbed wire without turning the whole of the neighbouring terrain into a cratered lunar landscape. The results of these improvements were manifest on the first day of the Battle of Arras in April 1917, when the Canadian Corps stormed Vimy Ridge and British XVII Corps advanced some 3½ miles at a comparatively light cost in casualties. The true gains of the BEF from the Somme offensive might therefore be best judged by examining the story of 9 April 1917 rather than the bloody assaults of 1916.

Peter Simkins

Site of Montauban, July 1916. (Q.4003)

JULY

Saturday 1 July

Temperature 72°F; clear sky

THE BATTLE OF ALBERT (1–13 July)

XIII CORPS

CAPTURE OF MONTAUBAN

30th Division

The wire had been cut successfully. The Germans were mostly caught in dugouts, so little resistance was encountered.

89 Brigade: Starting from four lines of assembly trenches at 7.30 a.m., 17th and 20th King's met little resistance and moved on to Casement and Alt Trenches. The 2nd Bedfordshires were in support and mopping-up. The attack pressed on to Dublin Trench. At 8.30 a.m. the right of the line joined with the French and the left, in the east end of Glatz Redoubt; simultaneously, 3rd Battalion of the French 153rd Regiment entered Dublin Redoubt at the east end of Dublin Trench. The position was consolidated.

21 Brigade: The enemy here was also caught in its dugouts so little resistance was encountered.

Leading, with 19th Manchesters, 18th King's went forward until they caught up with British barrage at Alt Trench, where they had to wait until the barrage lifted at 7.45 a.m., before occupying it. The Manchesters had few losses but the King's were caught in enfiladed machine-gun fire from the west side of Railway Valley. Fire from The Warren caused severe casualties among 2nd Green Howards who were in support, and few managed to cross no man's land. A party of Germans came out of a deep dugout and proceeded eastwards but were out-bombed by a party of moppers-up. This enabled 18th King's to advance along Train Alley to Glatz Redoubt, reaching it at 8.35 a.m. and joining with 89 Brigade.

90 Brigade: At 8.30 a.m. 90 Brigade began its advance on Montauban, passing through 21 Brigade with 16th and 17th Manchesters. The 2nd Royal Scots Fusiliers were in close support. Despite machine-gun fire from Breslau Alley, they continued their advance, and the German machine-gun was finally wiped out by a Lewis-gun of 16th Manchesters. Under cover of a smoke-screen, the Manchesters and Royal Scots Fusiliers entered the village of Montauban at 10.05 a.m., to find it deserted. By 11 a.m. the second objective in Montauban Alley was entered. The Germans were pulling back in large numbers. The 16th Manchesters rushed the battery in Caterpillar Valley and captured the first three field guns of the Battle. Montauban was consolidated.

At 12.30 p.m. No. 4 Company, 20th King's (89 Brigade) attacked La Briqueterie from Dublin Trench under cover of a bombardment. Simultaneously, bombers moved up Nord Alley and cut off the retreat of the garrison. By 12.35 p.m. La Briqueterie was taken, as were all objectives, and the position was consolidated. By 6 p.m. the road to Maricourt–Montauban had been repaired 200 yards beyond the old German front line.

The 30th Division had taken all its objectives.

18th Division

At 7.27 a.m. two mines—one of 5,000, the other of 500 pounds—laid by 183 Tunnelling Company, RE, were exploded: one at Casino Point and the other at the west end of the front to be attacked. Six Russian saps were dug across no man's land. The badly cratered area by the Carnoy–Montauban road was covered by a flame-thrower and the wire was cut.

55 Brigade: The Brigade advanced across no man's land on a front some 200 yards wide. One company of 7th Buffs making up the clearing party was unable to force an entry to the cratered section. A machine-gun in no man's land raked 7th Queen's on the left and 7th Royal West Kents in support, delaying 8th East Surreys on the right beyond the support line, even though they had crossed the

Battle of Albert: assault on Beaumont Hamel, 7.45 a.m. 1 July 1916. 16th Middlesex Regiment, 29th Division retiring after having reached the crater on Hawthorn Ridge with heavy losses. The crater can be seen in the centre of the horizon. (Q.750)

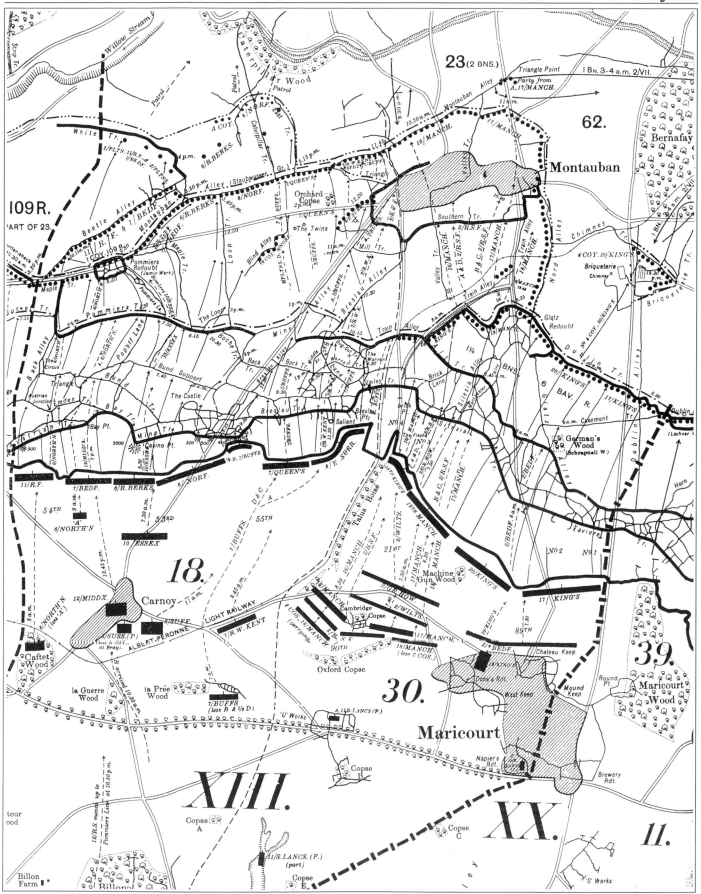

enemy front line.★ Not until half an hour later, when 30th Division had pushed on and were threatening to cut off the Germans, were 8th East Surreys and two companies of 7th Buffs able to bomb forward to Train Alley. The 7th Queen's were still held up at Breslau Support Trench.

At 9.30 a.m. 7th Buffs managed to clear the Carnoy crater area. The 7th Royal West Kents went to reinforce 8th East Surreys and by noon both battalions had reached the Montauban road. At 10 a.m. 7th Queen's sent parties along communication trenches, cleared The Loop and entered the west end of Train Alley, held by part of the East Surreys; the

east end being dealt with by 8th Norfolks (53 Brigade).

Back Trench still held out and continued to do so until 2 p.m. when, after bombing attempts forced the garrison to surrender, it was occupied by 7th Queen's and 8th Norfolks. The Queen's, now reinforced by a company of 7th Buffs, moved to the Montauban–Mametz road where, at 3 p.m., they joined 7th Royal West Kents and other Buffs. They pressed on to take Montauban Alley by 5.15 p.m.

53 Brigade: With 8th Norfolks on the right and 6th Royal Berkshires on the left, 53 Brigade was able to get through with little resistance thanks

to the mine at Casino Point and the flame-thrower. Resistance was first experienced at The Castle and then in Back Trench where a party held up the right of the Norfolks. The Castle quickly fell, however, and the left of the Norfolks and the Berkshires pushed on to their next objective of Pommiers Trench. This was defended by three machine-guns which checked the advance until rushed by bombers working along Popoff Lane.

At 7.50 a.m. Pommiers Trench was occupied, but The Loop still held

★The Eighth East Surreys had advanced kicking footballs supplied by Captain W. P. Neville, who was killed shortly after leaving the British front line.

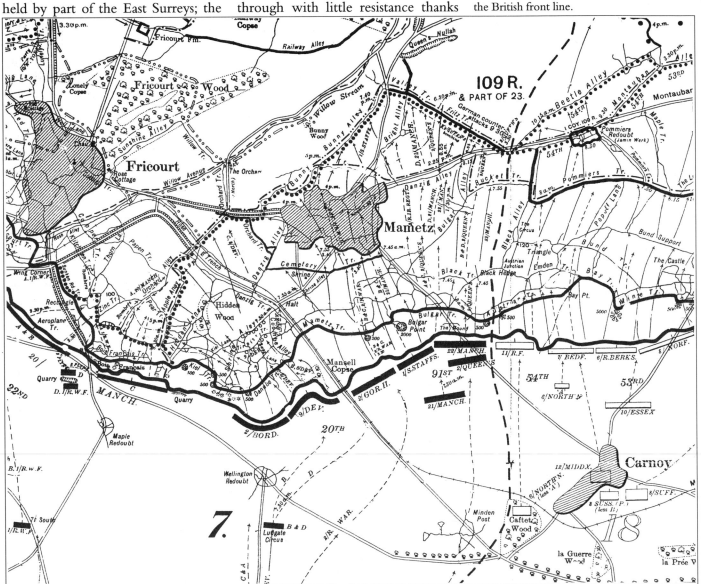

Battle of Albert. British troops resting in captured mine crater, July 1916. The man in the soft cap would appear to be a Royal Artillery signaller with a field telephone slung on his back. (Q.97)

out. A company of 10th Essex were sent to reinforce but the trench leading to The Loop was blocked.

54 Brigade: At 8.30 a.m. 10th Essex, with 7th Bedfordshires and 11th Royal Fusiliers carried out an attack against Pommiers Redoubt. The Fusiliers sent Lewis-gunners to Maple Trench to enfilade the Redoubt. This surprised the Germans, and the Royals and Berkshires (53 Brigade) rushed the Redoubt, carrying it after hand-to-hand fighting. Maple Trench was also taken.

The Royal Fusiliers and Bedfordshires pushed on to Beetle Alley which was entered at 10.15 a.m. with reinforcements of 6th Northamptonshires.

Attempts to push further eastward along it and Montauban Alley were strongly resisted and no further progress was made by the centre and left brigades of 18th Division until 3.30 p.m., when a bombing party of 10th Essex reached White Trench, having cleared 400 yards of Montauban Alley

starting from Pommiers Redoubt. At 5.40 p.m. it met parties of 6th Royal Berkshires and 8th Norfolks (53 Brigade) which had come from Loop Trench with great difficulty, because of snipers. The entire Alley, the second objective of 18th Division, was now in British hands.

The Norfolks now sent parties along Caterpillar Trench and set up posts with the Berkshires in the third objective overlooking Caterpillar Wood. On 54 Brigade's front, 7th Bedfordshires and 11th Royal Fusiliers had taken White Trench by 4 p.m. The entire Division then spent its time consolidating its positions. At 9.30 p.m. a small German counter-attack was launched from a quarry in Caterpillar Valley, north of Montauban, but was driven off.

XV CORPS

At 7.26 a.m. three mines of 25,000, 15,000 and 9,000 pounds were placed by 178 Tunnelling Company, RE under the salient. The 'Tambour' at Bulgar Point was completely destroyed by a 2,000-pound mine and a sap west of it by one of 200 pounds. Four 500-pound mines were also placed under the line, south of Hidden Wood.

7th Division
CAPTURE OF MAMETZ

91 Brigade: The 22nd Manchesters and 1st South Staffordshires led the attack across the 100–200 yards of no man's land. Despite machine-gun fire from Mametz and Danzig Alley, they progressed some 700 yards. By 7.45 a.m. the Staffords had taken Cemetery Trench and by 8 a.m. parties of the Manchesters had entered Bucket Trench. The Staffords were now in the ruins of Mametz. There was some opposition from a few machine-guns but basically little resistance was encountered. From west and north Mametz and Danzig Alley, however, opposition brought the attack to a halt. The Staffords fell back to Cemetery Trench and the hedges south of the village, leaving only a few troops in the village itself. Just after 9.30 a.m. the two supporting battalions were sent up. The two front companies of 2nd Queen's reached the Manchesters in Bucket Trench, and 21st Manchesters reinforced the Staffords. Soon after 1 p.m. Danzig Alley (East) was taken by 2nd Queen's after a barrage. Bombers now moved west along Danzig Alley and then north up Bright Alley,

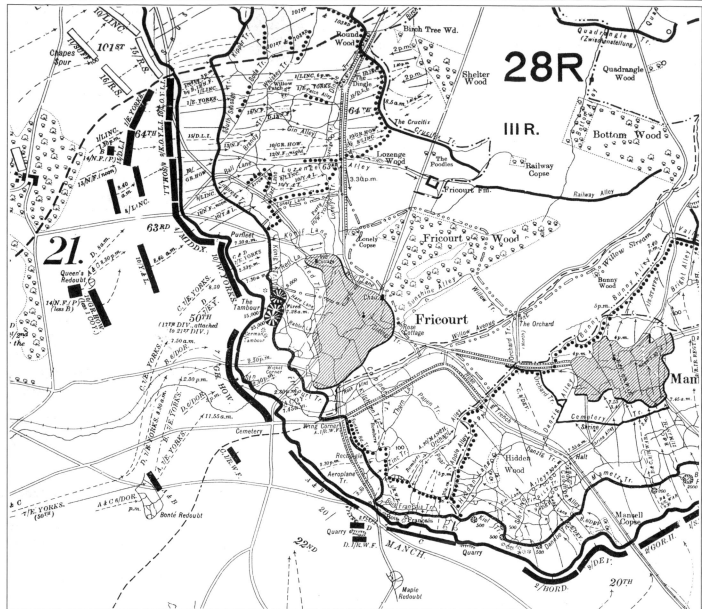

which was taken by 1.40 p.m. At the same time, the Queen's entered Fritz Trench from the east end of Danzig Alley, mainly with bombers. The 1st South Staffords, supported by three companies of 21st Manchesters from Cemetery Trench, occupied the southern houses of Mametz, reinforcing troops already there in the ruins and then moving on to the centre of the village to occupy Danzig Alley (East), which ran along the main street. At 3 p.m. 2nd Queen's entered the east end of Fritz Trench and by 6.30 p.m. Bright Alley had been taken. At 7.30 p.m. the Staffords

moved from Mametz up Bunny Alley to its junction with Fritz Trench. Positions were consolidated.

20 Brigade: The 9th Devonshires'★ attack suffered badly from machine-gun fire from Fricourt Wood, mostly before they reached Mansel Copse, but they pushed on and entered the front line, some reaching the support trench 250 yards behind, and cleared the adjoining communication trench. At 7.40 a.m. their 4th Company was sent to reinforce, but no further progress could be made. Later two companies of 8th Devons were also sent up, but sustained heavy casualties

in no man's land although they gained touch with 2nd Gordon Highlanders and 9th Devons.

The Gordons were at first held up on wire and suffered heavy casualties before the trench in front was cleared from the flank. Heavy fire was directed at them from The Shrine. By 7.55 a.m. Shrine Alley had been taken and, in places, the Mametz–

★Whilst on leave, Captain D. L. Martin, an officer of 9th Devonshires, made a plasticine model of the ground to be attacked, correctly predicting that they would suffer from machine-gun fire from the Shrine. He himself was killed, as was the poet William Hodgson.

Halt road. The left of 2nd Gordons and one company of 8th Devons cleared the dugouts in the cutting on the south side of the Maricourt road (here parallel to the light railway), which took most of the morning. The remainder of the Gordons were still at Shrine Alley.

On the left, 2nd Border Regiment advanced to the front line, wheeled left and advanced on Hidden Lane which was taken by 9.30 a.m. Machine-gun fire from Mametz Wood–Hidden Wood was stopped by an attack across the open and simultaneously by a bombing raid down Hidden Lane. Parties then went forward to Apple Alley.

At 3.30 p.m., after a 30-minute bombardment, two companies of 2nd Royal Warwicks (Division Reserve) were to push forward to Bunny Trench. They were to co-operate with 1st Staffords and 21st Manchesters (both 91 Brigade). By 4–5 p.m. Mametz was in British hands and Bunny Trench was occupied.

Gordon Highlanders, believed to be 2nd Battalion, 7th Division, on the Albert–Bapaume Road near Ovillers, July 1916. The fact that they are carrying two extra cloth bandoliers suggests that they are moving up to the line. Note the branch used as a splint on the German prisoner on the wheeled stretcher. (Q.818)

21st Division

50 Brigade (attached from 17th Division): The two attacking companies of 10th West Yorkshires pushed through to Red Cottage on a frontage of 600 yards, and with little loss. But by the time their 3rd and 4th Companies advanced, the machine-guns in the Tambour and Fricourt were in action, virtually annihilating them in their attacking waves, and only a few small groups reached the German front line where they remained until after dark. The troops at Red Cottage were overcome later in the morning, except a few who joined up with the right of 63 Brigade to their north.

63 Brigade: Two companies of 4th Middlesex on the right attempted to crawl forward into no man's land five minutes before zero hour, but were forced back by machine-gun fire. One minute before zero hour, they attacked in earnest and despite machine-gun fire reached the German support line. Small parties, totalling 40 men in all, reached the sunken road. The survivors of the rear company of the Middlesex only got as far as the German front line, but consolidated their position and repelled three German bombing attacks. The 8th Somerset Light

Infantry on the left also suffered heavily in the assault, but also managed to reach the support trench and beyond.

At 8.40 a.m. 10th York & Lancasters and 8th Lincolns went forward in support. Both suffered from the machine-gun in Fricourt. On the right, the York & Lancs advanced through the Middlesex in the front line and on to the sunken road, but were stopped by machine-gun fire from Fricourt Wood. On the left, the Lincolns reinforced the Somerset LI and, led by bombers, cleared Lozenge Alley as far as the sunken road, but could not get to Fricourt Farm. They were later forced to retire. Small detachments advanced north along the sunken road into Crucifix Trench. German bombers counter-attacked up Lonely Trench but were repulsed and the York & Lancs blocked the trench with sandbags.

64 Brigade: The attack was led by 9th and 10th KOYLI in the last five minutes of the bombardment. They crawled into no man's land where they met with heavy machine-gun fire from Fricourt and were enfiladed by fire from south of La Boisselle, but pushed on with the attack. The 15th Durham LI and 1st East Yorkshires' supporting battalions following close behind, joined the KOYLI and all

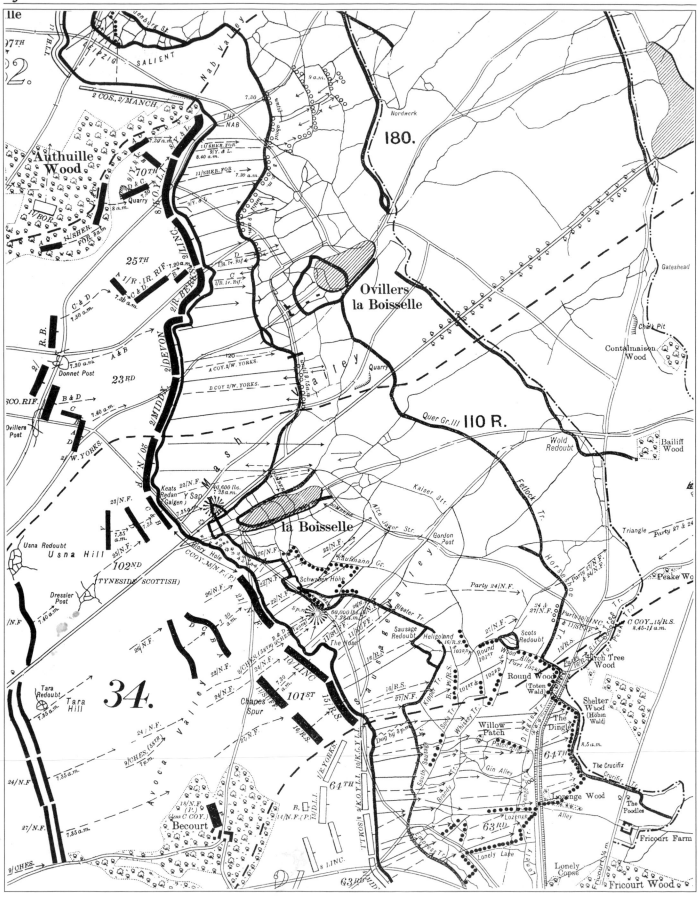

four battalions pressed on together to the support trench. At 8 a.m. the sunken road was reached and some parties got as far as Crucifix Trench. Lewis-gun detachments moved to hold Lozenge Wood to the south. Round Wood was occupied at 9.45 a.m. by a company of 1st East Yorks.

A counter-attack was forced back. The 10th Green Howards and 1st Lincolns (62 Brigade) were sent to re-inforce. At 2.30 p.m. 10th KOYLI and 15th DLI tried to take Shelter Wood from Crucifix Trench but failed. At 4.35 p.m. the order to consolidate was given.

ATTACK ON FRICOURT

7th Division

22 Brigade: South of the village, 22 Brigade sent 20th Manchesters, bomb-ers and two companies of 1st Royal Welsh Fusiliers to attack the village. The Manchesters suffered under heavy machine-gun fire. In the centre a small party entered The Rectangle, but was bombed out of the support trench.

The Welsh Fusiliers bombed their way up Sunken Road Trench and both sides of the Rectangle to Apple Alley, taking the pressure off the Manchesters who held on. That evening they consolidated.

50 Brigade (21st Division attached from 17th Division): North of Willow Stream, 7th East Yorks and three companies of 7th Green Howards★ attacked at 2.30 p.m. There were only four small gaps in the wire. The attack was covered by Lewis-gun fire from railway embankment. Whole lines of Green Howards fell in the first 50 yards and, within three minutes, they had 351 casualties. A few reached the village but were soon killed or captured. The East York-shires shared a similar fate, losing 155 men in the first few yards, and the attack was brought to a halt.

III CORPS
34th Division

At zero hour the entire infantry of the Division, consisting of 101, 102 Brigade (Tyneside Scottish) and 103 Brigade (Tyneside Irish), attacked in four columns; the front line leaving the British front-line trench, and the rear lines leaving from Tara and Usna Hills.

★One company of Green Howards attacked in error at 7.45 a.m. and was practically des-troyed in twenty yards by a single machine-gun.

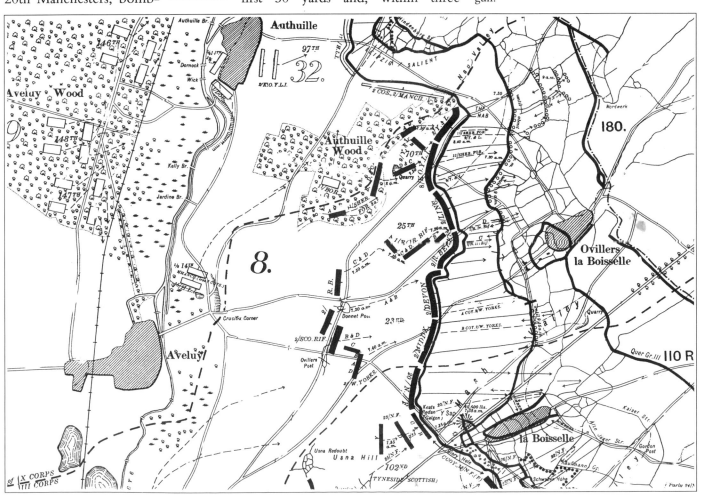

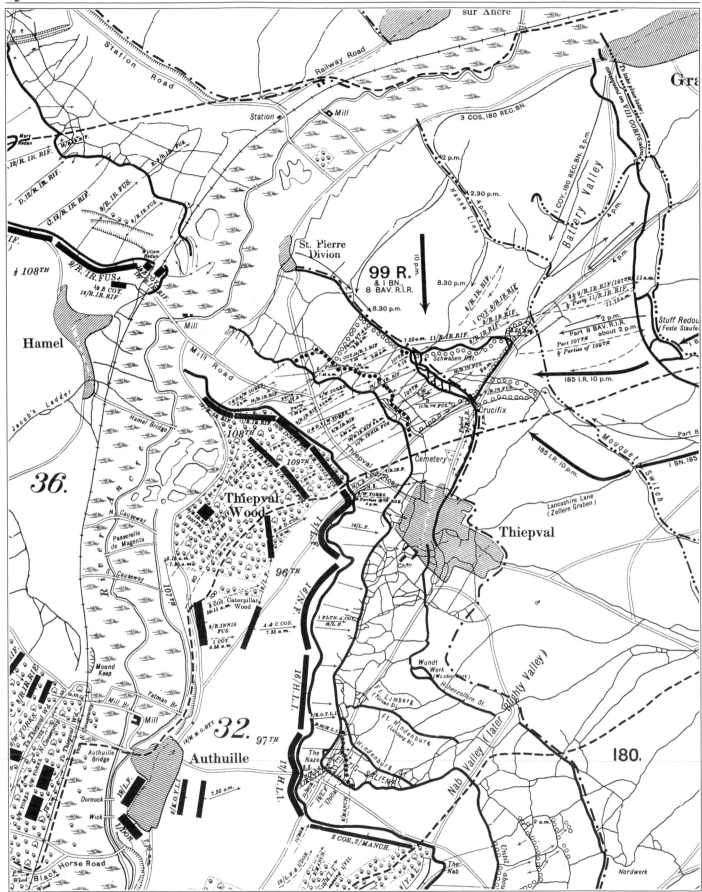

101 Brigade: Two mines were exploded two minutes before zero hour: at Lochnagar south of La Boisselle (60,000 pounds) and Y sap (40,600 pounds) north of the village.

There was no surprise and, ten minutes after zero, 80 per cent of the men in the leading battalion of the first column were casualties. The 15th Royal Scots were in no man's land some 200 yards from the German front line at zero hour and were forced to the right by machine-gun fire from Sausage Valley and La Boisselle, as were 16th Royal Scots who were in support, leaving parties of 15th Royal Scots to clear the trench in the north.

The Scots reached Birch Tree Wood beyond the sunken road in 21st Division's area and, in meeting some units of the same, veered back northwards to correct their drift. A counter-attack stopped an advance up Birch Tree Trench. The 16th Royal Scots, 27th Northumberland Fusiliers (103 Brigade) and 11th Suffolks pressed on and attacked Scots Redoubt and Wood Alley, and both objectives were taken. Other parties got through to Acid Drop Copse but not in any numbers. The position was consolidated.

The 10th Lincolns with 11th Suffolks following, received machine-gun fire from Sausage Valley, La Boisselle and the German front-line trench, which inflicted severe casualties. On the extreme right a party which tried to storm Sausage Redoubt was burnt to death by flame-throwers and the Lincolns and Suffolks were unable to cross the 500 yards of no man's land. The 24th Northumberland Fusiliers (103 Brigade) following, were ordered to stay in the British front-line trench. Some men from all three battalions consolidated a position in Lochnagar Crater. The 15th Royal Scots, left to deal with Sausage Redoubt, tried to bomb north. Various attempts were made to reinforce the Scots but to no avail. The isolated parties withdrew after dark.

102 Brigade: The 21st and 22nd Northumberland Fusiliers and 26th Northumberland Fusiliers (103 Brigade) tried to pass south of La Boisselle and north of Lochnagar. They started the moment the mine was fired, crossing the 200 yards of no man's land and reaching the trench of Schwaben Hohe, they continued down the west side of Sausage Valley and crossed both Kaufmanngraben and Alte Jugerstrasse. Bombers were sent out to La Boisselle but could not make progress.

Machine-gun fire from La Boisselle started to cause heavy casualties, but Quergraben III was reached in places and a few men were reported in Bailiff Wood. A German counter-attack forced the defenders back to Kaufmanngraben where they consolidated.

The Glory Hole was held by a company of 18th Northumberland Fusiliers (Pioneers) and no attack was made.

103 Brigade: After the firing of Y sap mine, 20th, 23rd and 25th Northumberland Fusiliers following, attacked down Mash Valley across some 800 yards of no man's land. The attack was cut down by machine-gun fire from Ovillers, La Boisselle and trenches on the right of the attack. A few isolated parties made the front-line trench, but were all killed.

Various relief attacks by 21st Division (XV Corps) and 34th Division were proposed during the day, but the 21st were too weak to continue the attack. The 34th Division attack lost 23 out of 30 men as soon as they left the trench. Two communication trenches were dug that evening on either side of Sausage Redoubt: one on the right for 15th and 16th Royal Scots at Birch Tree Wood, the other on the left for access to a party of Tyneside Scots south of La Boisselle.

8th Division

23 Brigade: The Brigade was to attack up Mash Valley towards Pozières, leading with 2nd Middlesex and 2nd Devonshires. They suffered very heavy casualties from machine-gun fire from Ovillers and La Boisselle but a few, 70 in all, managed to get into the German trench and held 300 yards of it for two hours, after which they were driven out by counter-attacks from both flanks. The 2nd West Yorkshires in support, suffered similar casualties and only small parties joined the Middlesex and Devons.

The 2nd Scottish Rifles' advance was halted in the British front line.

25 Brigade: The 2nd Royal Berkshires and 2nd Lincolns received the same fire as 23 Brigade. By 7.50 a.m. parties of the Lincolns reached the German front line and, at 9 a.m., attempted an assault on the second line but were forced to withdraw to the British front line. The 1st Royal Irish Rifles, in support with the survivors of the initial attack, tried to renew the assault but machine-gun fire from the front and flanks stopped them in their tracks; only ten men managed to get across no man's land.

70 Brigade: Two leading waves of 8th KOYLI and 8th York & Lancs managed to cross no man's land and press on to the second trench, some even reaching the third line. Very few of the third and fourth waves, however, managed the 400 yards of no man's land. The 9th York & Lancs in support received machine-gun fire from Thiepval Spur and very few men reached the German front trench. The 11th Sherwood Foresters also advanced, only to share the same fate. A further attempt was made by 50 bombers down the sunken road

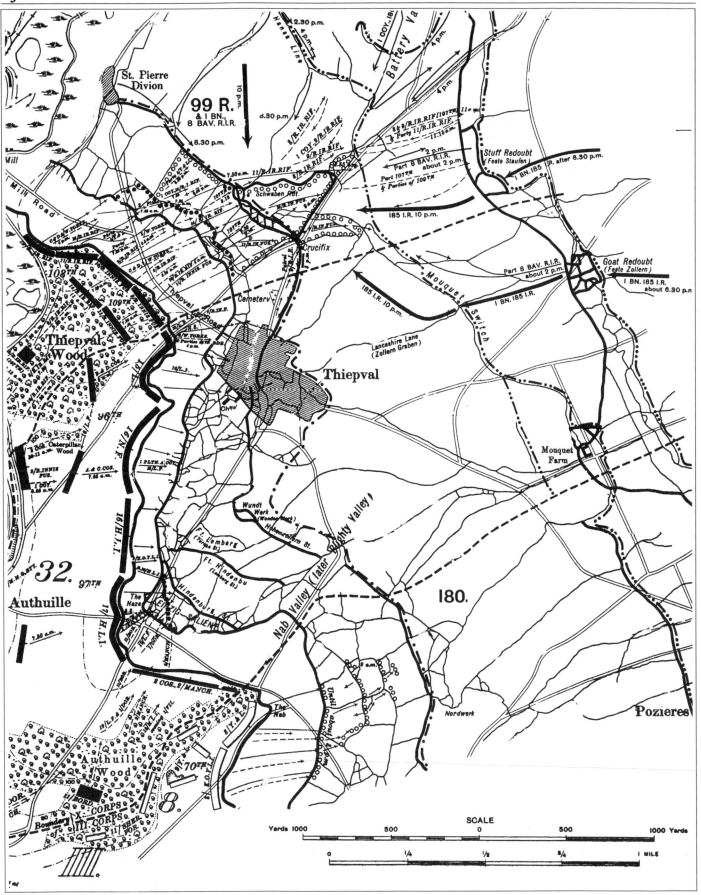

leading from the Nab to Mouquet Farm, but a single machine-gun checked them 80 yards from the German trench.

X CORPS
32nd Division
97 Brigade: At 7.23 a.m. 17th Highland Light Infantry crept forward to 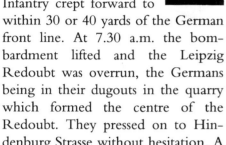 within 30 or 40 yards of the German front line. At 7.30 a.m. the bombardment lifted and the Leipzig Redoubt was overrun, the Germans being in their dugouts in the quarry which formed the centre of the Redoubt. They pressed on to Hindenburg Strasse without hesitation. A machine-gun in the Wonder Work, however, forced them back to the Redoubt. The right of 2nd KOYLI, in support, helped to consolidate the position in the Redoubt. Bombers attempted to advance along Hindenburg and Lemburg Strassen.

At 8.30 a.m. 11th Border Regiment, in reserve, left Authuille Wood and came under heavy machine-gun fire from the Nord Werk, sustaining very severe casualties, although small parties on the left joined those in the Redoubt. The rest lay in no man's land. On the left 16th HLI with 2nd KOYLI in support failed to take the German front line. The wire was not cut and as the HLI took up their position in no man's land they came under fire from the front-line trench and château. Small groups on the right joined up with 17th HLI in Leipzig Redoubt, but the centre and left were marooned in no man's land. Later in the day the survivors in no man's land crawled back and reassembled in Authuille Wood.

96 Brigade: Following a football kicked in advance, 16th Northumberland Fusiliers and 15th Lancashire Fusiliers only managed to reach no man's land where the survivors were pinned down by machine-gun fire

from Thiepval Fort. The 15th Lancashire Fusiliers managed to get a few survivors into the enemy front line north and east of the village but were cut off by Germans coming out of deep dugouts. The survivors managed to join with 36th Division, south of Schwaben Redoubt.

At 9.10 a.m. 2nd Royal Inniskilling Fusiliers and two companies of 16th Lancashire Fusiliers at Johnson's Post were ordered to attack Thiepval to reinforce 15th Lancashire Fusiliers and link with 36th Division at the Crucifix. As soon as they left Johnson's Post (eastern corner of Thiepval Wood), they came under fire from the Fort and were forced back to their start-line.

14 Brigade (Reserve Brigade): On leaving the shelter of Authuille Wood, 1st Dorsets received machine-gun fire from the Nord Werk. Only six officers and 60 men reached the Leipzig Redoubt from the first two companies. The remaining companies stayed in the Wood and British front-line trench. Three companies of 19th Northumberland Fusiliers, following the Dorsets under cover of smoke, suffered a similar fate and only two officers and 40 men reached the Redoubt.

At 1.30 p.m. two companies of 2nd Royal Inniskilling Fusiliers, plus various other companies of 96 Brigade, left Thiepval Wood to attack Thiepval but were stopped in no man's land by machine-gun fire. The remaining companies on the right of 2nd Manchesters approached the Redoubt by the left of the line and, by 1.45 a.m., had reinforced 97 Brigade in the Redoubt with little loss. Attempts to bomb forward from Hindenburg and Lemburg Strassen met with no success.

At 4 p.m. a further attempt was made from Johnson's Post by 1/6th and one company of 1/8th West

Yorkshires, but, once again, wire and fire from Thiepval Fort and village stopped the attack in no man's land.

36th Division

109 Brigade: At 7.30 a.m. buglers sounded the advance on the right, and 9th and 10th Royal Inniskilling Fusiliers crossed the 300–450 yards of no man's land. The wire had been cut and they pushed through to the reserve trench some 500 yards beyond the front face of the Schwaben Redoubt; an advance of nearly a mile. By 8.30 a.m. the advance had reached the Mouquet Switch and the east salient of the Schwaben Redoubt.

108 Brigade: The right battalion, 11th Royal Irish Rifles, was equally successful, reaching part of the Hansa Line under cover of smoke. The remainder of 108 Brigade on either side of the swampy Ancre valley, came under very heavy machine-gun fire from St Pierre Divion.

The 9th and 12th Royal Irish Rifles on the right side of the river suffered severe losses crossing the 600 yards of no man's land and the attack failed.

107 Brigade: At 9.15 a.m. 107 Brigade, in support, crossed no man's land with considerable loss. They pushed on, however, and got to within 100 yards of the Grandcourt Line when they ran into their own barrage and were forced to take cover in no man's land, coming under machine-gun fire from Beaucourt Redoubt and Grandcourt. At 10.10 a.m., however, some fifty men entered Stuff Redoubt which was found unoccupied. Another group entered the position 300 yards further north, working along the trench and blocking it towards Grandcourt. On the left 200 men reached a German battery position in the upper part of Battery Valley.

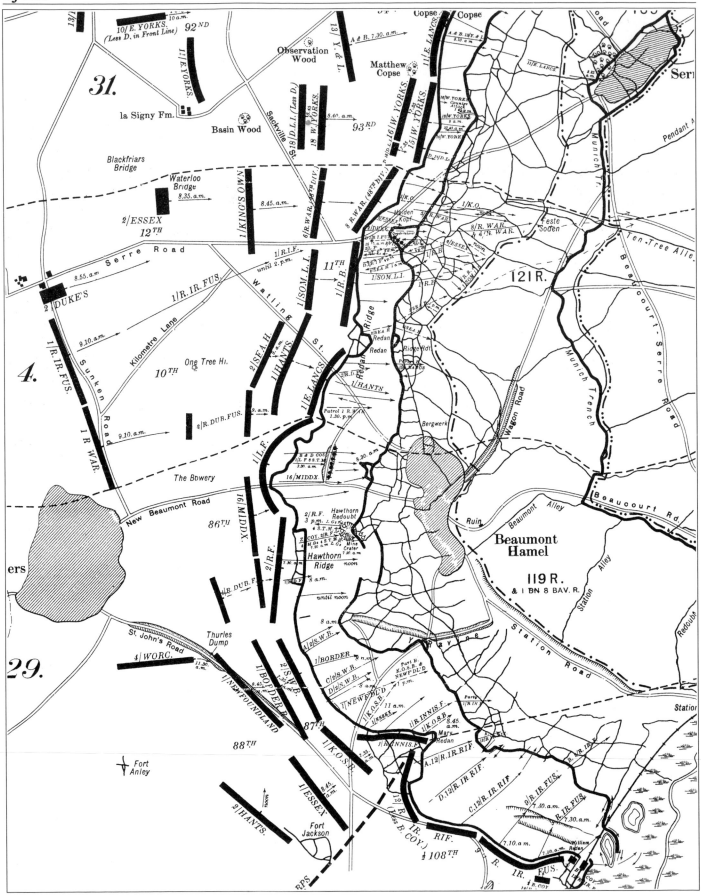

Lancers on the move in a side track off the Albert–Amiens road, July 1916. The British officer in the front is wearing a French steel helmet. (Q.4054)

The Division held out all day, but owing to numerous counter-attacks and running short of bombs and small-arms ammunition, they fell back. By 10.30 p.m. only a few small parties remained in the original German front lines.

The 49th Division, who were in reserve, sent two companies of 1/7th West Yorkshires to support the troops attacking the Schwaben Redoubt. They wandered too far to the left and took possession of some trenches in the reserve line, northwest of the Redoubt.

VIII CORPS
29th Division

The wire was cut in places. The whole Corps artillery was ordered to lift its barrage to the second and third lines at 7.20 a.m., ten minutes before zero hour.

At 7.20 a.m. Hawthorn Redoubt mine—40,000 pounds of ammonal placed by 252 Tunnelling Company, RE—was blown. Two platoons of 2nd Royal Fusiliers with four machine-guns and four Stokes mortars moved to occupy the crater.

87 Brigade: The 1st Royal Inniskilling Fusiliers attacked south of Y Ravine. The majority were held up on uncut wire. Some men of 2nd South Wales Borderers, opposite the Ravine on the left, managed to get within 100 yards of the front line but the majority were caught by three machine-guns. At 8.05 a.m. 1st KOSB, with 1st Border Regiment in support, met with a similar fate.

86 Brigade: Of the 2nd Royal Fusiliers (less half a company at the crater), some 30 or 40 diverged left and entered the mine crater; the rest of the battalion making no progress on the left. The 1st Lancashire Fusiliers had 100 bombers (two companies, A and D), with four Stokes mortars★ and two machine-guns in a sunken lane in no man's land. The rest of the battalion assaulted from the front line.

Of the men in Sunken Lane, only 50 reached the low bank beyond it.

The 1st Royal Dublin Fusiliers and 16th Middlesex in support found the wire uncut and received machine-gun fire from the Bergwerk. Apart from the 120 men in the crater, 86 Brigade did not reach the German front line.

88 Brigade: The Brigade attacked at 9.05 a.m. The 1st Newfoundland Regiment met severe fire from Y Ravine and lost 710 men. The 1st Essex, delayed by dead and wounded in the communication trenches, shared a similar fate. By noon the crater party had been driven out. Efforts were made to reinforce them by 1st Lancashire Fusiliers but they were cut down by machine-gun fire in no man's land.

★The Lancashire Fusiliers' History states eight Stokes mortars.

4th Division

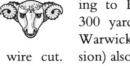

10, 11, 12 Brigades: The 1st East Lancs and 1st Rifle Brigade found the wire cut. Two machine-guns on the parapet fired until the last minute and two machine-guns in Ridge Redoubt dominated no man's land. Some reached the front line but did not hold. The 1/8th Royal Warwicks (attached from 48th Division) and the left company of The Rifle Brigade entered the Quadrilateral Redoubt★ and the support trench behind it on a front of 600 yards.

At 7.40 a.m. the support battalion started On the right 1st Hampshires were stopped by machine-gun fire. In the centre 1st Somerset LI moved right as no man's land was being swept by machine-gun fire, and reinforced the Quadrilateral, penetrat-ing to Feste Soden and occupying 300 yards of it. The 1/6th Royal Warwicks (attached from 48th Division) also supported the Quadrilateral, but the left flank was enfiladed from Serre by machine-gun fire and was forced to fight off a bombing counter-attack, also from the direction of Serre.

The order to halt the attack was not received and at 9.30 a.m. 2nd Royal Dublin Fusiliers (10 Brigade) received fire from Ridge Redoubt and Beaumont Hamel. Seeing that only a few men had reached the German position and that most of the East Lancashires and Hampshires were still in no man's land ahead of them, the rear companies stayed in the British front line.

The 2nd Seaforth Highlanders (10 Brigade) and 2nd Lancashire Fusiliers (12 Brigade) inclined left and reinforced the Quadrilateral. The 2nd Essex and 1st King's Own (both 12 Brigade) got to the German position, reinforced the furthest troops in Munich Trench, and pressed on to Pendant Copse. By 11 a.m. they had been forced back to the Quadrilateral by bombing counter-attacks; one company of 2nd Duke of Wellington's (12 Brigade) and two companies of Lancashire Fusiliers were sent to reinforce the redoubt and the adjac-

★The Quadrilateral was known to the Germans as 'Heidenkopf'. The Germans, realizing that it would be difficult to defend, mined the position. It was defended by one machine-gun and some engineers who were to blow the mine. At 7.30 a.m. the machine-gun jammed and the crew and engineers were blown up by their own mine; the explosion blocked dugouts and stopped the enemy from taking their positions.

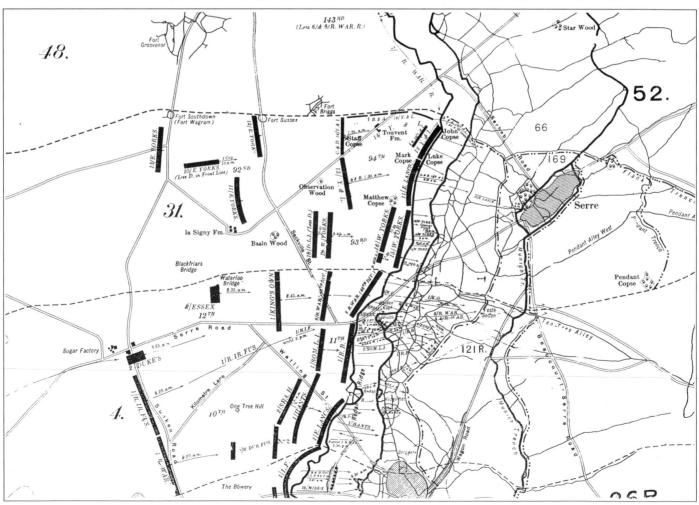

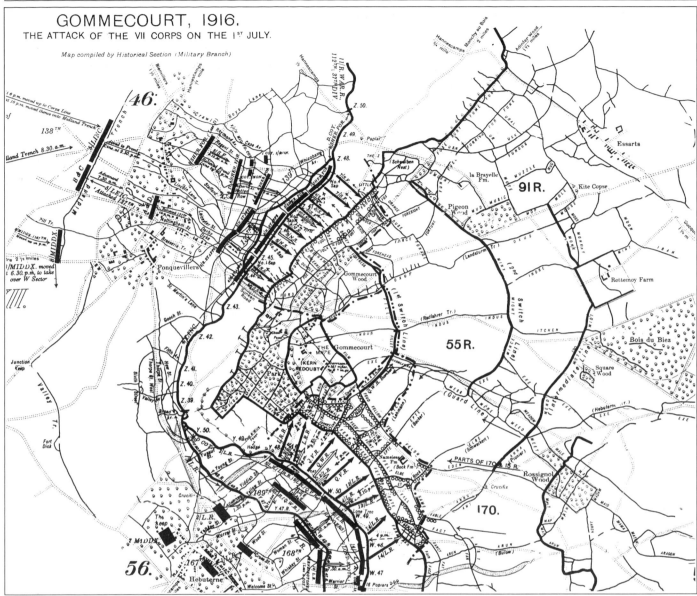

GOMMECOURT, 1916.
THE ATTACK OF THE VII CORPS ON THE 1ST JULY.

Map compiled by Historical Section (Military Branch)

ent front-line trench. (The position was finally abandoned at 11.30 a.m. on the following day.)

31st Division

At 7.20 a.m. the attack waves passed through gaps in the British wire and lay down in no man's land. At 7.30 a.m. the men stood up and were mowed down before crossing 100 yards of no man's land.

93 Brigade: The 15th West Yorkshires were stopped in no man's land by rifle and machine-gun fire. The wire was cut in places. The 16th West Yorkshires and one company of 18th Durham LI suffered heavy losses but some Durhams reached Pendant Copse. The 18th West Yorkshires in support made no headway and the remaining 18th DLI, in reserve, were held back.

94 Brigade: The Brigade assaulted with 11th East Lancs and 12th York & Lancs who met heavy fire from the left flank. The right company of East Lancs entered Serre, but was lost, together with a few men from the right company of 12th York & Lancs. The rest were held up in no man's land. The 13th and 14th York & Lancs tried to reinforce but were stopped short. The attack was then suspended.

VII CORPS

ATTACK ON GOMMECOURT

56th Division

At 7.20 a.m. smoke was released from the left of the line and under cover of this the attacking troops formed up in no man's land.

168, 169 Brigades: At zero hour 168 Brigade attacked with 1/14th London (Scottish), 1/12th London (Rangers), 1/13th London (Kensington) and 1/4th London in support; 169

Destroyed German trenches at Ovillers, looking towards Albert, July 1916. The man on the right is wearing the badge of 6th Division on his arm. (Q.4044)

Brigade attacked with 1/9th London (Queen Victoria's Rifles), 1/5th London (Rifle Brigade) and 1/16th London (Queen's Westminster Rifles) in support.

The wire was cut sufficiently to cause the attacking troops little trouble. The first two lines of trenches were taken with comparatively little loss. Nameless Farm, however, stayed in German hands and the third line was gained only after a fight. Bombers of 1/16th London reached it via the cemetery, but were wiped out.

The attacking troops, and two companies of 1/4th and 1/16th London sent up to support them, were now cut off by the German counter barrage on their old front line and no

man's land, and carrying parties could not reach them.

The Germans continued to counter-attack with an intense artillery barrage and bombs. Most damaging was the fire from a single or pair of light field guns 3,000 yards away in Puisieux Valley. At approximately 9 a.m. half a company of Kensingtons with a London Scottish machine-gun crew managed to reach the London Scottish. These were the last reinforcements received. At 9.30 a.m. a large party of bombers was sent to help the Queen's Westminsters in attacking the Quadrilateral. They ran into the German counter barrage in no man's land and mostly became casualties. At 2 p.m. two companies of 1/2nd London (169 Brigade) attempted to reinforce but were cut down by machine-gun fire from the Park.

By 2 p.m. 168 and 169 Brigades were holding the first and second

lines. By 4 p.m. the second line had fallen. At 9.30 p.m. the last of the Londoners withdrew, suffering heavy casualties in no man's land.

46th Division

137 Brigade: The attack was carried out by 137 Brigade consisting of 1/5th and 1/6th South Staffords, and 1/5th and 1/6th North Staffords in the front line, and 1/5th Lincolns (attached from 138 Brigade) in reserve.

At first the covering smoke was so thick that many men lost their way. Moreover, no man's land was cut up and muddy and the wire was intact or repaired.

The 1/6th South Staffords and 1/6th North Staffords were met at the wire by hand-grenades and fierce rifle fire. A few managed to reach the German front-line trench but were soon driven out. Behind them the second and third waves were caught in a fierce barrage and machine-gun crossfire from the 'Z'—a salient to the north of the attack.

139 Brigade: The Brigade were on the left with 1/5th and 1/7th Sherwood Foresters in the lead, 1/6th Sherwood Foresters in support and 1/8th Sherwood Foresters in reserve. The first three waves reached and entered the German front-line trench at some considerable cost, and some even managed to make the second line. But after the British barrage lifted the Germans came up from deep dugouts and prevented reinforcements from coming up.

In the afternoon various plans were made to renew the attack with the rear waves of 1/5th South Staffords, 1/5th North Staffords (both 137 Brigade) and 1/5th Leicesters (138 Brigade), but all were aborted. During that evening the few survivors of the 1/5th and 1/7th Sherwood Foresters (139 Brigade) filtered back.

Sunday 2 July

Temperature 75°; clear sky

XIII CORPS

30th Division

The Germans attacked twice between 3 a.m. and 4 a.m. at Bernafay Wood. They were repulsed by a shrapnel barrage laid by 30th Divisional artillery, which later made an unsuccessful attempt to set the wood on fire with a Thermite barrage (this being the first trial of Thermite).

XV CORPS

CAPTURE OF FRICOURT

17th Division

At midnight 7th Division sent a patrol into Fricourt and the village was occupied in the early morning by a patrol of 8th Staffords (51 Brigade)

who took more than 100 prisoners. By noon Fricourt was fully occupied and eleven enemy stragglers had been captured.

Movement continued slowly behind the barrage through Fricourt Wood and machine-gun fire caused the 7th Lincolns some losses. The Lincolns and South Staffords, reinforced by 10th Sherwood Foresters, held the old German front line, and 200 yards of Railway Alley was captured at 11 p.m. by the Foresters' bombers.

Before dawn the ground in front of Mametz was reported clear. At 7.30 a.m. 91 Brigade was ordered to occupy White Trench and Queen's Nullah. By 11 a.m. 2nd Queen's were in possession, taking a few prisoners and a machine-gun. The 8th Devons linked up with 17th Division on their left by reaching Orchard Trench North. The new line was consolidated and wired before

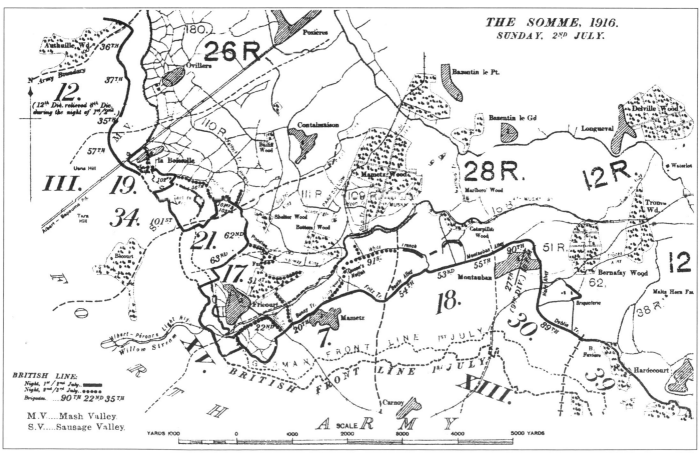

dark; 22 Brigade advanced from the old German support line south-east of Fricourt and cleared trenches as far as the light railway cutting. Twenty-five prisoners were taken.

21st Division

Patrols towards Fricourt Farm were pushed out by 62 Brigade, and 75 men and two machine-guns were captured. By 2 p.m. 10th Green Howards were near the copse called 'Poodles', and eventually linked with 17th Division.

III CORPS

CAPTURE OF LA BOISSELLE

19th Division

A night attack on La Boiselle scheduled for 10.30 p.m. on 1 July had not taken place, and congestion stopped 57 and 58 Brigades from getting forward. By dawn on the 2nd only 9th Cheshires (58 Brigade) had relieved the men of 34th Division at Schwaben Hohe (crater).

It was decided that 58 Brigade should attack alone at 4 p.m. Two companies of 7th East Lancs (on loan from 57 Brigade) were to capture Sausage Redoubt and attack with 34th Division, capturing the trenches beyond the Redoubt, occupying and consolidating a front of 1,000 yards and taking 58 prisoners.

At 4 p.m. 58 Brigade's attack started, after a 30-minute bombardment of Ovillers and a smoke-screen released at zero hour. This ruse worked, drawing the German artillery. The 6th Wiltshires and 9th Royal Welsh Fusiliers captured the German front line west of the village with little loss and were joined by 9th Cheshires on the right. Searching and bombing with artillery assistance, the western half of the village was cleared by 9 p.m. The line was consolidated

along the road just short of the church.

X CORPS

12th Division

The Division relieved 8th Division at Ovillers. The dawn attack was cancelled and the day was spent in reconnaissance and preparation for the attack next day.

36th Division

The Division still held the ground north of Thiepval. The artillery put a box barrage around the village; 107 Brigade sent 360 reinforcements from various battalions and carrying parties. After 6 p.m. the enemy made repeated bombing attacks on this position and at the Leipzig Redoubt. The 29th Division took over from 36th Division north of the Ancre; 49th Division relieved the rest of 36th Division at dusk.

Monday 3 July

Temperature 68°F; fine, with some cloud and thunderstorms to the south-east

---

XIII CORPS

CAPTURE OF BERNAFAY WOOD

9th Division

After a 20-minute bombardment of the near edge, 27 Brigade attacked Bernafay Wood at 9 p.m., occupying it almost unopposed and sustaining only six casualties. The 6th KOSB and 12th Royal Scots covered 500 yards of open ground and took 17 prisoners, three field guns and three machine-guns. The east end of Montauban Alley was consolidated. Patrols sent out towards Trônes

Wood found it held by some machine-gun detachments.

18th Division

The 10th Essex (53 Brigade) occupied Caterpillar Wood. At 4 a.m. they found five field guns and took possession of a length of trench flanking the valley and left rear of the wood.

XV CORPS

7th Division

The 1st Royal Welsh Fusiliers and 2nd Royal Irish Regiment were to have occupied the south of Mametz Wood, Wood Trench and Quadrangle Trench after dark, but got lost.

17th Division

At 9 a.m. 7th Borderers (51 Brigade) advanced, coming under machine-gun fire at once with the result that Railway Alley was not captured until 11.30 a.m. The 7th Lincolns and bombing detachments of 8th South Staffords and 10th Sherwood Foresters were involved. One company of the Border Regiment went up the slope and entered the west part of Bottom Wood. It was almost surrounded by the enemy until 21st Division on the left captured Shelter Wood. The Borderers pressed on and captured Bottom Wood, forestalled by 21st Manchesters (91 Brigade, 7th Division) who occupied the east end without a fight. Two batteries of XIV Brigade Royal Horse Artillery (7th Division) were brought up to Queen's Nullah and began to cut the wire of Mametz Wood with the assistance of a howitzer battery south of Mametz.

21st Division

The 1st Lincolns (62 Brigade) sustained losses from machine-gun fire before reaching Shelter and Birch Tree Woods, where stubborn resistance was met. The 12th Northumberland Fusiliers were moved in support and were soon deployed. German columns could be seen moving forward from Contalmaison. The 13th Northumberland Fusiliers were brought up and succeeded in securing the Woods.

At 2 p.m. a German counter-attack against Bottom and Shelter Woods was repulsed and 800 prisoners were taken. Patrols sent out at 3 p.m. discovered that Mametz Wood and Quadrangle Trench were both empty.

A light railway in Caterpillar Valley was used for the evacuation of wounded.

III CORPS

CAPTURE OF LA BOISSELLE

34th Division

Three bombing attacks were made in an attempt to link with 19th Division, but these failed. The 23rd Division relieved the 34th Division that night.

19th Division

57 Brigade came up on the left of 58 Brigade and, at 2.15 a.m., 8th North Staffords together with bombers of 5th South Wales Borderers led an advance between La Boisselle and the Albert road, with 10th Worcesters covering their outer flank.

At 3.15 a.m. both brigades attacked and captured the village of La Boisselle and also the German trenches 400 yards beyond, taking 153 prisoners. Following a severe bombardment and counter-attack by the enemy from the direction of Pozières, they gained the east end of the village where they were reinforced by 10th Royal Warwicks and 8th Gloucesters.

In the end the Germans held the line running through the church, representing a British gain of 100 yards.

12th Division

At 2.15 a.m. the opening bombardment started with two brigades of artillery from 19th Division. 12th Division attacked Ovillers at 3.15 a.m. Assembly trenches had been dug in no man's land, reducing its width from 800 yards to 500 yards. On the right were 5th Royal Berkshires and 7th Suffolks (35 Brigade), and on the

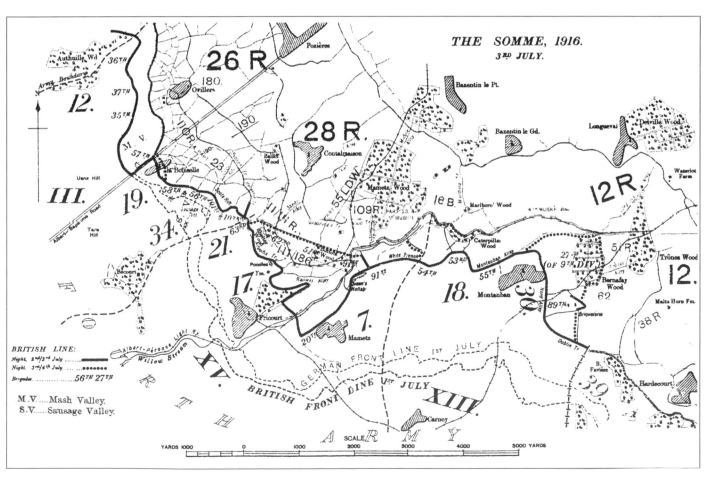

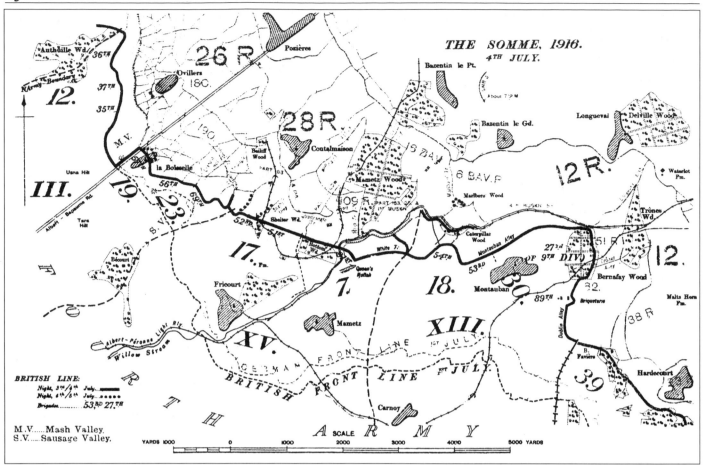

THE SOMME, 1916.
4TH JULY.

BRITISH LINE:
Night, 3rd/4th July.........
Night, 4th/5th July.........
Brigade.............. 53RD 27TH

M.V.....Mash Valley.
S.V.....Sausage Valley.

YARDS 1000   0   1000   2000   SCALE   3000   4000   5000 YARDS

left 6th Queen's and 6th Royal West Kents.

By 9 a.m. the Division reported total failure, at a cost of 2,400 casualties. One company of 9th Essex, in support of the Berkshires, drifted towards La Boisselle where it cut off 220 Germans.

X CORPS
32nd Division

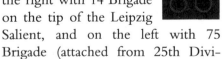

The Division attacked on the right with 14 Brigade on the tip of the Leipzig Salient, and on the left with 75 Brigade (attached from 25th Division).

There was confusion over the starting time so the attack received little or no artillery support. The 14 Brigade attack consisted of no more than two companies of 15th Highland LI advancing from the Leipzig Salient. At 6.15 a.m. they entered the German front line only to be forced out; they tried again later with the same result.

Tuesday 4 July

Temperature 70°F; overcast with thunderstorms

XIII CORPS
18th Division

Marlboro' Wood was occupied at night, unopposed.

The 9th Division was relieved by 30th Division.

XV CORPS
17th Division

A number of advances were made by 17th Division along the trenches towards Contalmaison.

III CORPS
CAPTURE OF LA BOISSELLE

19th Division

Starting at 8.30 a.m., with support fire from Stokes mortars and machine-guns, 56 Brigade with 7th King's Own leading, had cleared La Boisselle by 2.30 p.m. except for a few ruins at the end of the village.

X CORPS
49th Division

From 9.30 a.m. onwards 49th Division counter-attacked towards German bombing parties around the north of Thiepval, but was unsuccessful. Two night attempts to take some machine-gun nests near St Pierre Divion were also abortive.

32nd Division was relieved by 25th Division.

Wednesday 5 July

Temperature 72°F; low cloud

XV CORPS
7th, 17th Divisions

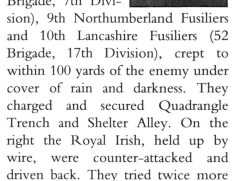

At 12.45 a.m., after a 30-minute bombardment, 2nd Royal Irish Regiment and 1st Royal Welsh Fusiliers (22 Brigade, 7th Division), 9th Northumberland Fusiliers and 10th Lancashire Fusiliers (52 Brigade, 17th Division), crept to within 100 yards of the enemy under cover of rain and darkness. They charged and secured Quadrangle Trench and Shelter Alley. On the right the Royal Irish, held up by wire, were counter-attacked and driven back. They tried twice more under heavy machine-gun fire but with no success, so neither Mametz Wood nor Wood Trench was gained. That night 7th Division was relieved by 38th Division.

III CORPS
23rd Division

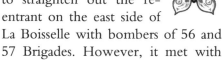

At 4 a.m. bombers of 9th Green Howards attacked on the left. The 11th West Yorks and 10th Duke of Wellington's (69 Brigade) advanced on the right at 6.45 a.m.

Fighting was continuous in Horseshoe Trench until 10 a.m. when the enemy made a strong counter-attack, winning back much of the gained ground.

The enemy attacked again in the afternoon, causing most of the Brigade to be involved in the fighting, but at 6 p.m. 10th Duke of Wellington's and 8th and 9th Green Howards cleared both Horseshoe Trench and the west end of Lincoln Redoubt in an attack over the open. Ground was gained to the east on the other flank but no contact was made with 17th Division in Shelter Alley.

19th Division

The Division attempted to straighten out the re-entrant on the east side of La Boisselle with bombers of 56 and 57 Brigades. However, it met with little success.

X CORPS
25th Division

One company of 1st Wiltshires (7 Brigade) attacked at 7 p.m., obtaining a foothold in Hindenburg Trench and

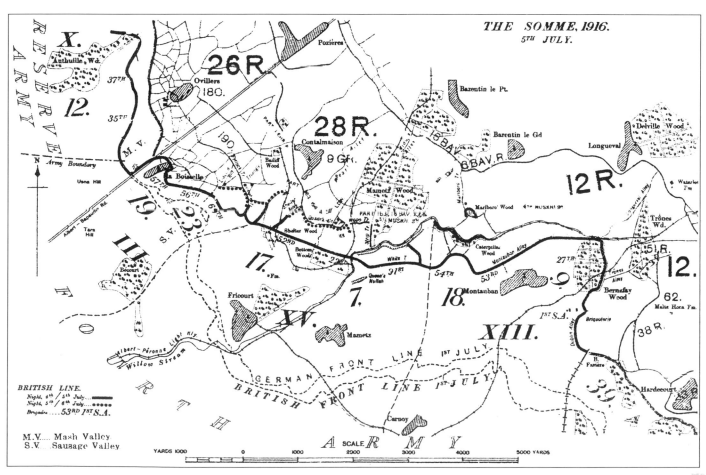

THE SOMME, 1916.
5TH JULY.

BRITISH LINE.
Night 4th / 5th July _____
Night 5th / 6th July ....
Brigades ..... 53RD 1ST S.A.

M.V. ... Mash Valley
S.V. ... Sausage Valley

improving their grip on the Leipzig Salient.

Thursday 6 July

Temperature 70°F; overcast with intermittent showers

During the day the German bombardment became more general but some areas were shelled with tear-gas that night.

III CORPS
23rd Division
That night 68 Brigade relieved 69 Brigade and 12th Durham LI (68 Brigade) then occupied Triangle Trench unopposed.

19th Division
At 7.30 p.m. 7th East Lancs (56 Brigade) tried to clear the re-entrant be-

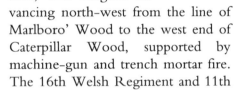

tween 19th Division in La Boisselle and 23rd Division in Horseshoe Trench, which was still occupied. This bombing attack was unsuccessful, but a direct assault over the open was, and three later counter-attacks were repelled.

Friday 7 July

Temperature 70°F; overcast and showery (13mm rain)

XV CORPS
MAMETZ WOOD
38th Division
The Division attacked Mametz Wood at 8.30 a.m., 115 Brigade advancing north-west from the line of Marlboro' Wood to the west end of Caterpillar Wood, supported by machine-gun and trench mortar fire. The 16th Welsh Regiment and 11th

South Wales Borderers were soon held up by machine-gun fire, but tried again at 10.15 a.m. At 3.15 p.m., reinforced by 10th South Wales Borderers, they tried once more but could not get within 250 yards of the Wood because of enfilading machine-gun fire from further up the valley. The Brigade was not ready to attack again, so was withdrawn, leaving two companies of the 17th Royal Welsh Fusiliers to hold Caterpillar Wood–Marlboro' Wood.

17th Division
At 2 a.m., after a 35-minute bombardment, 9th Northumberland Fusiliers and 10th Lancashire Fusiliers (52 Brigade), with 10th Sherwood For-

Bomb-carrying party going up to the front line at La Boisselle, 6 July 1916. The sergeant has 1914-pattern pistol, equipment and binoculars. (Q.780)

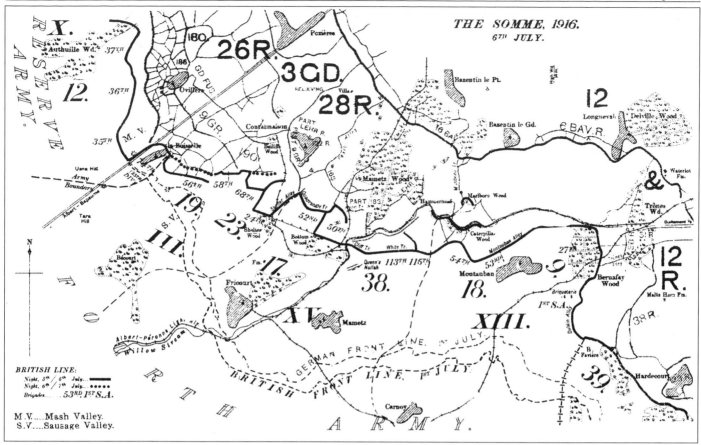

THE SOMME, 1916.
6TH JULY.

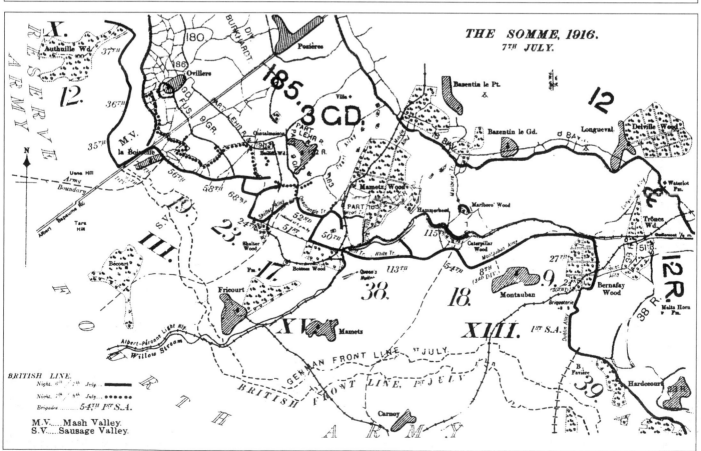

THE SOMME, 1916.
7TH JULY.

esters (51 Brigade) in support, made a night advance on two trenches. The Northumberland Fusiliers and the right of the Lancashire Fusiliers were held up by British shells falling short and then found the wire uncut. They retired and later attacked again. This was also unsuccessful and they withdrew. The left of the Lancashire Fusiliers, however, entered Pearl Alley and some even reached Contalmaison.

The Germans counter-attacked causing the Lancashire Fusiliers, who were few in number, to be driven back. A counter-attack from the eastern side of Contalmaison raged until 7 a.m., disrupting preparations for the main attack. At 8 a.m., after some confusion over the start time, 12th Manchesters and 9th Duke of Wellington's (52 Brigade) attacked Quadrangle Support in broad daylight. The delay in starting had meant that the barrage had lifted before the troops were within assaulting distance and they were cut down by machine-gun fire from Mametz Wood.

On the right, 50 Brigade attacked with 7th East Yorks bombing up Quadrangle Alley, but they were driven back. A company of 6th Dorsets attempted to take the west face of Mametz Wood but were caught by machine-gun fire from Strip Trench, losing 50 men. After various postponements they attacked again at 8 p.m. The Dorsets, East Yorks and 10th Sherwood Foresters (51 Brigade) were machine-gunned and caught by the enemy's artillery barrage while struggling forward through the mud, and so, with no hope of success, the attack was abandoned with nearly 400 casualties.

At 8 p.m. 17th Division was scheduled to advance on Contalmaison again, but the mud, German barrage and lack of fresh troops ruled out any chance of continuing the attack.

III CORPS
23rd Division

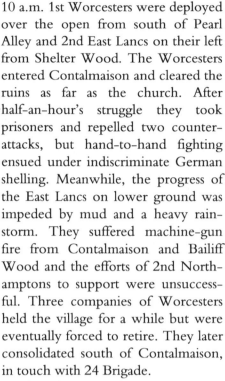

24 Brigade's objective was Contalmaison. Soon after 10 a.m. 1st Worcesters were deployed over the open from south of Pearl Alley and 2nd East Lancs on their left from Shelter Wood. The Worcesters entered Contalmaison and cleared the ruins as far as the church. After half-an-hour's struggle they took prisoners and repelled two counter-attacks, but hand-to-hand fighting ensued under indiscriminate German shelling. Meanwhile, the progress of the East Lancs on lower ground was impeded by mud and a heavy rainstorm. They suffered machine-gun fire from Contalmaison and Bailiff Wood and the efforts of 2nd Northamptons to support were unsuccessful. Three companies of Worcesters held the village for a while but were eventually forced to retire. They later consolidated south of Contalmaison, in touch with 24 Brigade.

The objective of 68 Brigade was Bailiff Wood. The 11th Northumberland Fusiliers reached the southern edge of the Wood and captured some Germans, but machine-gun fire from Contalmaison, forced them to retire 400 yards to link with 19th Division. To achieve this, 12th Durham LI were brought up under heavy fire to occupy a trench on higher ground on the left.

19th Division

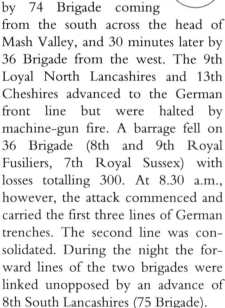

The objectives were one trench running south-west from Bailiff Wood, and then west, and one towards the north-east end of La Boisselle. At 8.15 a.m., after a 15-minute delay, the 9th Welsh (58 Brigade) and 7th King's Own (56 Brigade) moved forward behind a barrage in an attempt to get as close as possible to the objective—more than 300 yards away—before the barrage lifted.

The bombardment was successful, but through some error in timing, the infantry immediately ran into it, causing considerable loss and disorganization. They reorganized quickly and the advance was re-started at 9.15 a.m. with reinforcements from 6th Royal Wiltshires (58 Brigade). The three battalions rushed their objectives, capturing 400 prisoners from six regiments and five divisions. The 9th Royal Welsh Fusiliers (58 Brigade) were brought up to secure the right flank. Consolidation started with the assistance of 56th Machine-gun Company.

X CORPS
12th Division

The first assault on Ovillers was to be at 8 a.m. by 74 Brigade coming from the south across the head of Mash Valley, and 30 minutes later by 36 Brigade from the west. The 9th Loyal North Lancashires and 13th Cheshires advanced to the German front line but were halted by machine-gun fire. A barrage fell on 36 Brigade (8th and 9th Royal Fusiliers, 7th Royal Sussex) with losses totalling 300. At 8.30 a.m., however, the attack commenced and carried the first three lines of German trenches. The second line was consolidated. During the night the forward lines of the two brigades were linked unopposed by an advance of 8th South Lancashires (75 Brigade).

25th Division

At 1.15 a.m. the Germans tried to rush the Leipzig Salient which was held by 7 Brigade. Aided by artillery fire, 1st Wiltshires beat off the attack but spent the next two hours in a bombing contest which continued intermittently until 5.30 a.m. A pre-arranged attack was made by two companies of Wiltshires who captured the German front line and held it with 3rd Worcesters under heavy bombardment.

49th Division

The Division suffered a heavy bombardment from 12.30 to 2.30 a.m. which centred on the Ancre and eventually focused on the position north of Thiepval. The Germans launched a furious assault using the new light 'egg' grenades—which could be thrown 50 yards—on two companies of 1/4th KOYLI (148 Brigade) who were later reinforced by two companies of 1/5th KOYLI. Bombers of 1/5th York & Lancs were sent forward, but soon after 6 a.m. the survivors were forced to withdraw to their old front line.

Saturday 8 July

Temperature 73°F; overcast (8mm rain)

FIRST ATTACKS ON TRONES WOOD

In the early hours the objectives were bombed by XIII Corps' artillery and batteries of 30th Division. The artillery of 18th Division fired on the southern edge of Longueval.

XIII CORPS
30th Division

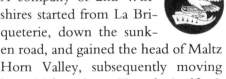

A company of 2nd Wiltshires started from La Briqueterie, down the sunken road, and gained the head of Maltz Horn Valley, subsequently moving into Maltz Horn Trench itself. A counter-attack was repulsed in the afternoon and a company of 19th Manchesters reinforced.

At 1 p.m. the remaining company of Wiltshires made a fresh advance from Bernafay Wood and managed to reach and entrench on the south-eastern edge of Trônes Wood which

was a thick tangle of undergrowth and branches brought down by the bombardment. Two companies of 18th King's and one of 19th Manchesters helped to consolidate the position. They were joined that night by 18th Manchesters (90 Brigade).

9th Division

The 2nd Green Howards (21 Brigade) left Bernafay Wood at 8 a.m. to assault Trônes Wood to the east. The attack failed because of fire from two field guns as they reached the crest of the rise and machine-gun fire from Trônes Wood.

An attempt to bomb down Trônes Alley was also unsuccessful. Some gallantly made an attack across the open and reached the Wood but were not seen again. The Green Howards were withdrawn and 2nd Wiltshires were ordered to renew the attack at 10.30 a.m., but it was postponed until 1 p.m.

XV CORPS
MAMETZ WOOD
38th Division

The Division was ordered to occupy the southern salient of Mametz Wood under cover of darkness. One platoon of 14th Royal Welsh Fusiliers (113 Brigade) started out at 2 a.m. but was stopped by mud and wire before reaching the starting point.

17th Division

From 6 a.m. bombers of 50 and 51 Brigades had tried to advance from Quadrangle Trench and Pearl Alley. Little progress was made, the Germans fighting vigorously in trenches knee-deep in mud, and at 10 a.m. the Division was ordered to co-operate with the III Corps attack that

afternoon. In the event, they attacked alone at 5.50 p.m. after a 25-minute bombardment, with parties of 7th East Yorks, 7th Green Howards and 6th Dorsets (all 50 Brigade) together with the bombers. However, they met with little success.

The division was then ordered to gain a footing in Wood Trench. Advancing at 8.50 p.m., a company of Dorsets secured two-thirds of the trench and then dug back to Quadrangle Trench.

III CORPS
23rd Division

The Division was ordered to take Contalmaision. The 1st Worcesters (24 Brigade) were stopped by machine-gun fire, as were 2nd Northamptons as they emerged from Peake Wood.

19th Division

Only bombers were engaged during the day and at 6 p.m. a German counter-attack was repelled with rifle and machine-gun fire. Later the left were ordered to co-operate with 12th Division's (X Corps) attack on a trench which ran into the north end of Ovillers. It fell after little opposition, following a 1,000-yard dash by 13th Royal Fusiliers—one of the two battalions of 111 Brigade (34th Division) attached to 56 Brigade—as a step towards its relief. Consolidation proceeded.

X CORPS
12th Division

From 3.45 a.m. onwards the Division tried to bomb forward, but was handicapped by mud. At the edge of Ovillers, 36 Brigade had been reinforced by 7th East Surreys (37 Brigade) and 9th Essex (35 Brigade) during the night. After great ex-

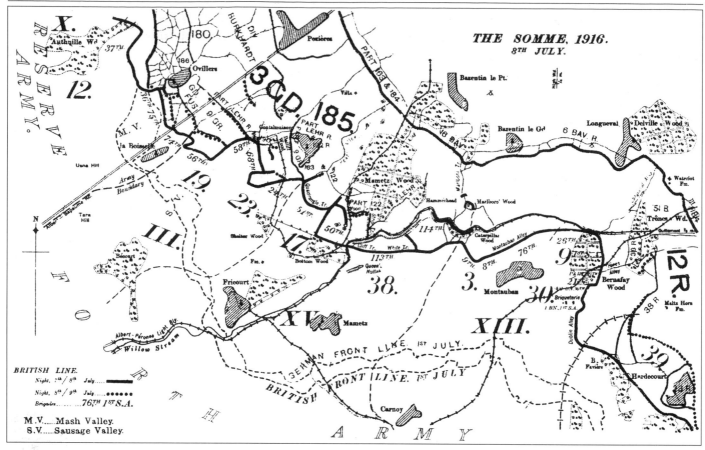

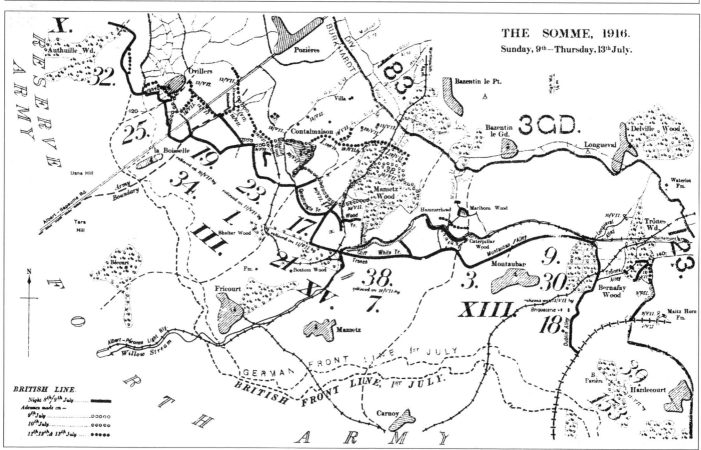

ertions, a distance of 200 yards into the ruins was achieved. From the valley to the south-east 2nd Royal Irish Rifles and 13th Cheshires (74 Brigade), with 8th South Lancs (75 Brigade) on the left, bombed forward and then, turning right, secured the trench which ran to Ovillers church. At 8 p.m. 74 Brigade renewed its attack. One company of 11th Lancashire Fusiliers went 600 yards too far, but held despite being under a British barrage. One company of 2nd Royal Irish Rifles was then sent to help consolidate them, and 13th Cheshires went to man the trench that had been passed over. That night 14 Brigade of 32nd Division completed the relief of 12th Division.

Sunday 9 July

Temperature 70°F; cloudy but fine

XIII CORPS
30th Division

The Division renewed its attack on Trônes Wood. At 3 a.m., after a 40-minute bombardment by divisional artillery, 2nd Royal Scots Fusiliers (90 Brigade) formed the right of the attack. After successfully reaching Maltz Horn Trench by the sunken road from La Briqueterie, they reached the ruins of Maltz Horn Farm. They then bombed northwards along Maltz Horn Trench, taking 109 prisoners. By 7 a.m. the entire trench as far as the intersection with the track leading to Guillemont from the east side of the Wood was in British hands.

The 17th Manchesters were to advance from the Wood. An attack astride the light railway, scheduled for 3 a.m., was delayed by gas and the density of the Wood itself so did not start until 6 a.m. After a struggle in the undergrowth, shell-holes and fallen trees, they made the eastern edge of Trônes Wood by 8 a.m., where they linked with the Royal Scots Fusiliers and sent patrols northwards. The Wood was largely now in British hands. In retaliation, the Germans began a systematic barrage at 12.30 p.m. causing the 17th Manchesters to retire to Bernafay Wood at 3 p.m. All but one company of 18th Manchesters in the south-eastern corner of the Wood fell back on La Briqueterie, and the Royal Scots withdrew from Maltz Horn Trench, blocking it just clear of the Wood.

When, at 3.30 p.m., the Germans counter-attacked the whole front line, from the north end of Trônes Wood to Maltz Horn Farm, the Royal Scots and the one remaining company of 18th Manchesters drove off the enemy. The north-west of the Wood was penetrated, however. At 6.40 p.m. 16th Manchesters successfully attacked from the sunken road east of La Briqueterie and dug in 60 yards from the south-western edge.

By the 9th, 18th Division on Montauban Ridge had been relieved by 3rd Division.

XV CORPS
17th Division

At 11.20 p.m. 7th Green Howards (50 Brigade) and 8th South Staffords attacked Quadrangle Support Trench, assisted by bombers of 7th Lincolns (both 51 Brigade). On the left, the Staffords reached and occupied the trench, but, unsupported on the flanks, were forced to fall back with the loss of nineteen officers and 200 other ranks. The Green Howards on the right did not reach the trench and the attack came to a halt. Despite reinforcements of one company of 7th East Yorks and one company of 6th Dorsets (50 Brigade), a renewed attack was also stopped.

III CORPS
23rd Division

24 and 68 Brigades were sent to improve their position south and west of Contalmaison. The 10th Duke of Wellington's (attached to 24 Brigade) sent bombers out to establish machine-gun posts south of the village.

Patrols of 12th Durham LI (68 Brigade) entered Bailiff Wood, but came under fire from British artillery and could not stay. Two companies were to have advanced from the west at 6.15 p.m., but an attempted German counter-attack delayed them. At 8.15 p.m. two companies of the Durhams captured Bailiff Wood and trenches either side.

X CORPS
32nd Division

The fighting for Ovillers continued with 15th Highland LI, 1st Dorsets and 2nd Manchesters (14 Brigade, 32nd Division) on the west side of the village.

25th Division

On the southern edge, 11th Cheshires and 3rd Worcesters (75 Brigade) and 8th Loyal North Lancs (7 Brigade) gained little ground on 9/10 July.

Monday 10 July

Temperature 82°F; thick cloud, very hot, with no wind

XIII CORPS
30th Division

At 4 a.m., assisted by a company of 4th South African Regiment (9th

Division), the Division began to move through Trônes Wood. To the west bombing parties occupied a portion of Longueval Alley. There was fighting in a small redoubt in Central Trench, which ran up the centre of the Wood.

The Germans advanced from the east and occupied the western edge. By 8 a.m. only the south-eastern portion of Trônes Wood remained in British hands.

XV CORPS
MAMETZ WOOD
38th Division

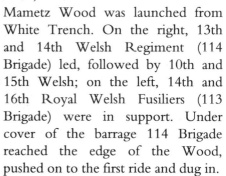

At 4.15 a.m., after a 45-minute bombardment, an attack on Mametz Wood was launched from White Trench. On the right, 13th and 14th Welsh Regiment (114 Brigade) led, followed by 10th and 15th Welsh; on the left, 14th and 16th Royal Welsh Fusiliers (113 Brigade) were in support. Under cover of the barrage 114 Brigade reached the edge of the Wood, pushed on to the first ride and dug in.

The Hammerhead (an oddly shaped projection on the eastern edge) held out. On the left, 16th Welsh Fusiliers lost the protection of the barrage, but, supported by 14th Welsh Fusiliers, rallied and pushed on to the first objective. The 15th Welsh Fusiliers, in reserve at Queen's Nullah, sent two companies initially, then followed with the rest of the Battalion. A gap between the two battalions was filled by 10th Welsh who also reinforced the Fusiliers near the Hammerhead, and positions were consolidated.

After 6.15 a.m. the infantry advanced to the second ride. Two companies of 15th Welsh were sent to clear the Hammerhead but were driven back. On the left of Quadrangle Alley the attack was stopped by enemy fire.

Indecisive fighting took place until 2.30 p.m. when three companies of 17th Welsh Fusiliers (113 Brigade) arrived in support—13th Welsh Fusiliers having been ordered to capture Wood Support—while bombers from 50 Brigade (17th Division) had advanced from the western end of the trench. The attack was successful and the trench was captured.

At 4.30 p.m. there was an advance by 10th South Wales Borderers to clear the Hammerhead with 14th and 15th Welsh Regiment and 13th Royal Welsh Fusiliers, with 13th Welsh Regiment in support. As the movement progressed, 17th Royal Welsh Fusiliers joined in. After two hours Mametz Wood was cleared to within 40 yards of the northern edge.

A machine-gun from the trench beyond the Wood stopped further progress, despite efforts of 14th Welsh Regiment and 17th Royal Welsh Fusiliers. A line was occupied 200 yards back, its flanks thrown back—the left flank to the light railway. In the early hours of 11 July, 11th South Wales Borderers and 16th Welsh Regiment (115 Brigade) relieved the line.

17th Division

With the fall of Contalmaison in the afternoon, parties of 51 Brigade bombed their way from the sunken road, east of the village, into Quadrangle Support Trench. Others of 50 Brigade worked up Strip Trench into Wood Support. After stubborn hand-to-hand fighting it was cleared and 17th Division was left in possession; touch was gained with 38th Division in Mametz Wood and 23rd Division in Contalmaison.

III CORPS
23rd Division

The 8th and 9th Green Howards (69 Brigade) assembled in and near the

northern part of Horseshoe Trench on a front of 1,000 yards; some 2,000 yards west of Contalmaison. Two companies of 11th West Yorks (69 Brigade) were sent to Bailiff Wood to make a flank attack. At 4.30 p.m., under fire of all kinds, the Green Howards captured the village of Contalmaison, the numbers of the 8th having been reduced to five officers and 150 men. A flank attack by the West Yorks caught the retreating Germans with rifle fire, and they joined with the Green Howards at 5.30 p.m., the attack having taken one hour in all. The 10th Duke of Wellington's, 101st Field Company, RE and 11th West Yorks helped to consolidate. At 9 p.m. a counter-attack was repulsed by bombers.

X CORPS
25th Division

The 11th Cheshires (75 Brigade) launched a daylight attack with little result. The 8th Loyal North Lancs (7 Brigade) tried to get round the rear of Ovillers from the Albert–Bapaume Road, but met with repeated counter-attacks which they repelled with the help of 3rd Worcesters, but made little progress.

That night 2nd Royal Inniskilling Fusiliers (96 Brigade, attached 14 Brigade) attacked the north-west of the village with some success.

Tuesday 11 July

Temperature 68°F; overcast

XIII CORPS
30th Division

At 1 a.m. 90 Brigade were relieved by 89 Brigade. At 2.40 a.m. a fierce British barrage was laid on Trônes Wood. At 3.27 a.m. 20th King's bombed northwards along Maltz Horn Trench, while 2nd Bedfords advanced north-east to the Wood. The two companies of Bedfords on the right swerved under machine-gun fire to occupy the south-eastern edge, while the other two companies entered it between Trônes Alley and the light railway. The fighting continued indecisively. At noon the Germans cleared the north end of the Wood. At 10.30 p.m. 17th King's attacked the Wood from the sunken road east of La Briqueterie. Two companies entered without opposition along the south-eastern edge, wired and dug in.

XV CORPS
MAMETZ WOOD
38th Division

115 Brigade was ordered to clear the rest of Mametz Wood. An attack arranged for 3 p.m. was delayed until 3.30 p.m. The 15th South Wales Borderers and 10th, 15th and 16th Welsh encountered little resistance, although 16th Welsh, on the left, suffered from machine-gun fire and flame-throwers, and fell back slightly. The line was fixed 60 yards inside the Wood with both eastern and western edges held, but a German night bombardment forced a withdrawal to the former position.

III CORPS
23rd Division was relieved by 1 Brigade (1st Division) before noon.

Wednesday 12 July
Temperature 68°F; fine but overcast

XIII CORPS
30th Division

A line was dug to link the King's with the Bedfords on the left. At 8.30 p.m.

the German counter-attack on Maltz Horn Trench and Trônes Wood was checked by artillery.

XV CORPS
21st Division
Between dawn and 9 a.m. 62 Brigade relieved 38th Division. During the morning patrols of 10th Green Howards, 12th and 13th Northumberland Fusiliers finally cleared the Wood, consolidating and linking with 7th Division on the right and 1st Division (III Corps) on the left. (62 Brigade held until it was relieved on 15–16 July, having lost some 950 officers and men.)

X CORPS
On the night of 12/13 July, 10th Cheshires (7 Brigade), 8th Border Regiment and 2/5th Lancs (both 75 Brigade) attacked Ovillers from the south-east and south, in conjunction with 96 Brigade which attacked from the west. Considerable progress was made.

Thursday 13 July
Temperature 70°F; overcast, with strong wind and a little rain

XIII CORPS
Before dawn on the 13th, 30th Division was relieved by 18th Division.

18th Division

At 7 p.m., 7th Buffs bombed along Maltz Horn Trench, but they failed to reach the strongpoint after several attempts.

The 7th West Kents, attacking across Trônes Wood, lost direction and came under fire from Central Trench, but 150 men reached the

eastern edge of the Wood, south of the Guillemont track. The 7th Queen's, forming the left, attacked across open ground from Longueval Alley but did not get within 100 yards of the Wood and retired in darkness at 8.45 p.m.

X CORPS
32nd Division
96 and 97 Brigades made a bombing attack and improved their position a little.

Friday 14 July
Temperature 70°F; fine but overcast

XIII CORPS
CAPTURE OF TRÔNES WOOD
18th Division
The Division had been ordered to make a last desperate attempt to secure Trônes Wood before the main attack; 12th Middlesex (54 Brigade) to lead and 6th Northamptons to clear up and form the defensive flank. The 11th Royal Fusiliers and 7th Bedfords were in support. By 2.30 a.m. the Northamptons were ready in the sunken road east of La Briqueterie, but the Middlesex had only one company in position and so their roles were reversed. By 4.30 a.m. they had entered the south-western edge of Trônes Wood. The redoubt in the southern part of Central Trench resisted strongly but was rushed at 6 a.m. The advance continued but lost direction and a projection on the eastern side was mistaken for the northern end of the Wood. At 8 a.m. the Middlesex were in the Wood, together with parties of 7th Royal West Kents who had been there all night. Colonel Maxwell collected all the troops he could find in the south-eastern corner. One

company of Middlesex attacked a strong-point on the Guillemont road in conjunction with 7th Buffs (55 Brigade) in Maltz Horn Trench and, shoulder-to-shoulder, they cleared the Wood by 9.30 a.m., rushing the strongpoint at the railway and consolidating the position.

DAWN ATTACK – BATTLE OF BAZENTIN RIDGE (14–17 July 1916)

9th Division

At 3.25 a.m. the Division assaulted with 8th Black Watch and 10th Argylls (26 Brigade), with 7th Seaforths (26 Brigade) in support in Montauban Alley. The 5th Camerons (26 Brigade) were in reserve south of Montauban. The 11th Royal Scots and 9th Scottish Rifles led, with 12th Royal Scots behind (all 27 Brigade).

The leading wave reached Delville Wood before a shot had been fired. A counter-barrage fell on Caterpillar Valley. On the right 26 and 27 Brigades carried two lines of trenches. There was some delay to the south of Longueval, but by 10 a.m. the Scots had captured all their immediate objectives including the edge of Delville Wood (except for a strongpoint to the south-east of Longueval and the northern part), but they could not take Waterlot Farm (a sugar refinery). Parties of Seaforths and Camerons, therefore, occupied Longueval Alley.

3rd Division

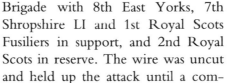

The Division was deployed in a sunken road. In the front line were 8 Brigade with 8th East Yorks, 7th Shropshire LI and 1st Royal Scots Fusiliers in support, and 2nd Royal Scots in reserve. The wire was uncut and held up the attack until a company of 2nd Royal Scots broke through and bombed along the front line. 9 Brigade, however, had no trouble with wire. The 1st Northumberland Fusiliers passed through and, despite heavy machine-gun fire from the village, captured Bazentin-le-Grand.

XV CORPS
7th Division

As no man's land was some 1,200 yards wide, 7th Division moved forward at night to 300–500 yards from the German trenches with their assaulting battalions, 2nd Border

Below: Battle of Bazentin Ridge, 14–17 July 1916. An officer observing from the ruins of Longueval Church. Note the private purchase trench coat. (Q.4418)
Below right: Battle of Bazentin Ridge (capture of Longueval). Refreshments caravans for the walking wounded, 14 July 1916. On the left-hand vehicle can be seen 9th Scottish Division's sign. (Q.164)

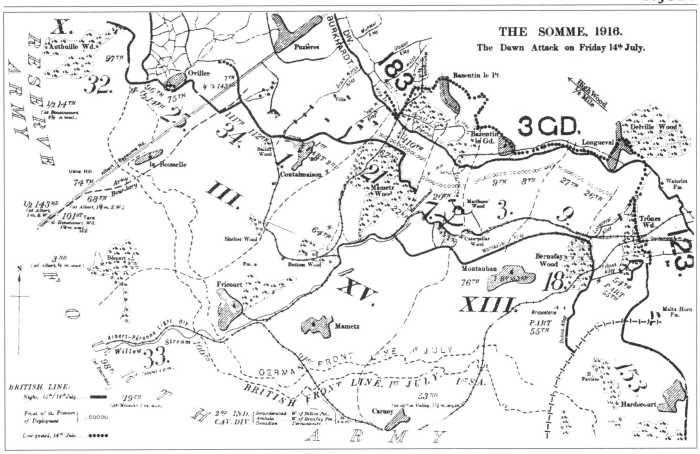

THE SOMME, 1916.
The Dawn Attack on Friday 14th July.

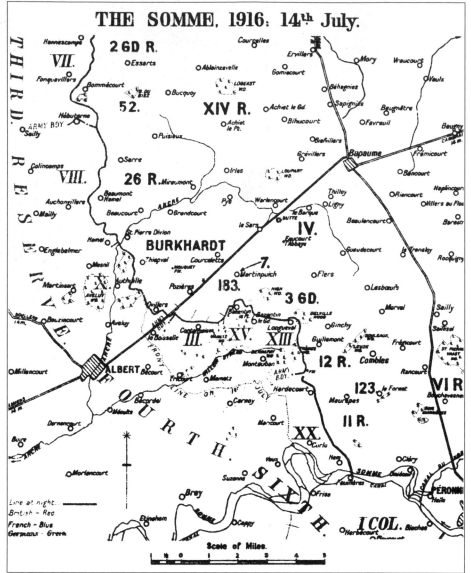

THE SOMME, 1916: 14th July.

21st Division

Like 7th Division, 21st Division moved forward at night to 300–500 yards from the German trenches. The assault was to be made by 110 Brigade: 6th and 7th Leicesters plus one company of 8th Leicesters; the rest of the Battalion were in support. The 9th Leicesters and 1st East Yorks were in reserve. After a minor hold-up on its left centre caused by machine-gun fire, 110 Brigade had possession of Bazentin-le-Petit Wood by 4 a.m., except the north-west corner which was not taken until 7 p.m.

CAVALRY CORPS

The Cavalry were brought up at this time—one squadron each of 7th Dragoon Guards and 20th Deccan Horse. They moved to the high ground between Delville Wood and High Wood, where they came under shellfire. The Dragoons charged some infantry and machine-guns hidden in the crops and, at 9.30 p.m., took up a line from near Longueval to the southern corner of High Wood. A bank beyond a rough road provided cover for the horses.

III CORPS
34th Division

At 7 p.m. strong patrols went forward to just south of Pozières (which was reported to be evacuated), but were soon driven back.

21st Division

That evening the Division was relieved by 1st Division on the western edge of Bazentin-le-Petit Wood.

X CORPS

The 10th Cheshires failed in a daylight attack, as did 1/7th Warwicks (143 Brigade, attached from 48th

Regiment and 9th Devons. Held by two companies, 9th Devons (20 Brigade) occupied the covering trenches 200 yards in front of Caterpillar Wood, since the Wood was under shellfire. The 2nd Borderers and 8th Devons (20 Brigade) were at Flat Iron Copse—the left boundary of the Division—and 22 Brigade were in reserve in Mametz Wood.

After a successful bombardment, all the Germans in the Snout (a German-held salient north-east of the Hammerhead) were killed and the wire destroyed. The infantry captured the German front line without difficulty and moved on to the second line which also fell early.

20 Brigade waited until 4.25 a.m. for the barrage to stop, then cleared Bazentin-le-Grand Wood and consolidated. The 2nd Royal Warwicks (22 Brigade) passed through the consolidating troops and covered the attack of 2nd Royal Irish Regiment on Bazentin-le-Petit, reaching the southern edge of the village at 6.30 a.m. An hour later, with the assistance of 6th Leicesters (110 Brigade), the Royal Irish cleared the village. They were driven out of the northern part at 8.30 a.m. but held the cemetery on the eastern side. Reinforced by 2nd Gordons (20 Brigade), the Irish recaptured and consolidated Bazentin-le-Petit, fighting off counter-attacks.

Division) later. At 11 p.m. the Cheshires tried again, took their objective, but had to withdraw because of casualties.

Saturday 15 July

Temperature 72°F; morning mist clearing to a bright day

THE BATTLE OF DELVILLE WOOD (15 July–3 September)

FOURTH ARMY
XIII CORPS
9th Division

At daybreak one company of 5th Camerons (26 Brigade), with later support from two companies of 4th South African Regiment, made repeated attempts to carry Waterlot Farm. Eventually they succeeded but the place was soon so heavily shelled by the Germans, that it could not be occupied and consolidated until the morning of the 17th.

After a bombardment, 12th Royal Scots (27 Brigade) attacked Longueval soon after 8 a.m., by bombing up North Street. An attempt to advance north through the orchards on the west side made little progress and all gains were eventually recaptured. At 7.30 p.m. the Royal Scots made another unsuccessful attempt.

The South African Brigade were ordered to take Delville Wood. At 6.15 a.m., after a preliminary bombardment, the South Africans left the 26 Brigade line on the south-western edge of the Wood. They cleared the southern half in less than two hours. Another advance then secured the remainder of the Wood, apart from the north-west portion which the Germans held strongly and from which they had to be expelled by a fresh attack.

Consolidation was attempted under heavy machine-gun fire from the north and east, and nearly every man was put into action to repel

Above: Newly hollowed-out shelters for reserves at Mametz, July 1916. Note the large screw pickets on the left. (Q.3968)
Below: Battle of Bazentin Ridge. Men of 26 Brigade, 9th Division returning from the trenches with 8th Black Watch piper after the attack on Longueval. Montauban, 14 July 1916. (Q.4012)

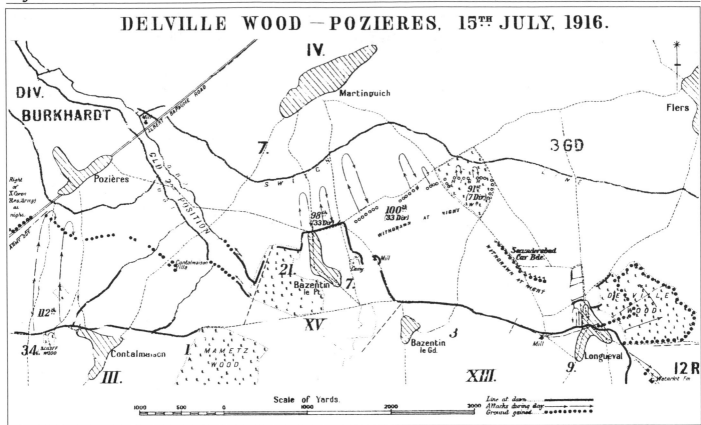

DELVILLE WOOD — POZIERES, 15TH JULY, 1916.

counter-attacks delivered in succession from the south-east, east and north-east during the early afternoon. The British barrage put down behind the Wood proved effective.

Later in the day the troops in Delville Wood were reinforced by 1st South African Regiment, and 9th Seaforths (Pioneers) sent a company to wire the north-eastern edge of the Wood. The German bombardment increased prior to an advance of German infantry; this was stopped but the bombardment continued all night.

XV CORPS
7th Division

At 9 a.m., having reinforced 2nd Queen's and 1st South Staffords with 21st Manchesters the previous evening, 91 Brigade began the first of several efforts to clear High Wood, but were stopped by machine-gun fire from the part of the Switch Line which ran through it.

At 2.30 p.m. the enemy counter-attacked after a heavy barrage and gained ground which was only recovered by using the Brigade Reserve. At 4.45 p.m., after a barrage, 91 Brigade attempted another attack, but met with no better result. At 11.25 p.m. a complete withdrawal by 91 Brigade was ordered and the entire Wood was to be kept under fire by divisional artillery.

33rd Division

On the evening of the 14th, 1/9th Highland LI and 1st Queen's (100 Brigade) had taken up position between High Wood and Bazentin-le-Petit.

After a 30-minute bombardment they attacked the Switch Line at 9 a.m. on 15 July. Simultaneously a further effort was made to clear the western side of the Wood with three platoons of 1/9th HLI, but this was unsuccessful, a machine-gun in the

Wood taking the entire assault in enfilade. Even after 16th KRRC and 2nd Worcesters had been brought forward to reinforce, 100 Brigade was back to its starting position by 4 p.m. During the night it was withdrawn to the Mill and Cemetery east of Bazentin-le-Petit.

The left of the attack was formed by 98 Brigade. At 9 a.m. 1st Middlesex, advancing on a 1,000-yard front, led the way. As soon as they left Bazentin-le-Petit they were machine-gunned and shelled. Further attempts were made to get forward, but between 4 and 5 p.m. the attack was abandoned.

III CORPS
1st Division

In the evening of the 14th, 1st Division had relieved 21st Division at the western edge of Bazentin-le-Petit Wood.

At 9 a.m. 1st Loyal North Lancs (2 Brigade) attacked north-westwards along the trench of the German second position, gaining 400 yards of front-line trench and 200 yards of support. Machine-gun fire prevented further advances. At 5 p.m. 2nd Welsh Regiment (3 Brigade) made an unsuccessful attempt which was also stopped by machine-gun fire, but after dark 3 Brigade linked with 34th Division 60 yards to the north-west, forming a line of posts.

34th Division

After a bombardment lasting an hour, an attack on Pozières started at 9.20 a.m. from the Contalmaison area. The 8th East Lancs (112 Brigade) started their 1,300-yard advance across no man's land, but some 300 yards from Pozières they were largely brought to a halt by machine-gun fire. At 6 p.m., after another hour's bombardment, they made a little more ground which was consolidated by 112 Brigade and one battalion of 111 Brigade.

CAVALRY CORPS

The 7th Dragoon Guards and 20th Deccan Horse withdrew from their overnight position at 3.40 a.m.

X CORPS

ATTACK ON OVILLERS

At 2 a.m. 25th Division attacked Ovillers from the north-east, east and south, while 32nd Division attacked from the south-west but with little success. The troops of 32nd Division were relieved after dark by 144 Brigade (48th Division).

49th Division

The Division, on the left of the Corps, on the Ancre, fought off an attack of bombs and flame-throwers at the Leipzig Salient.

Sunday 16 July

Temperature 73°F; dull and overcast (4mm rain)

XIII CORPS
9th Division

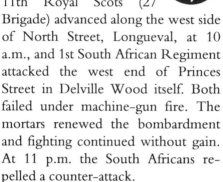

After a heavy trench mortar barrage of Longueval, 11th Royal Scots (27 Brigade) advanced along the west side of North Street, Longueval, at 10 a.m., and 1st South African Regiment attacked the west end of Princes Street in Delville Wood itself. Both failed under machine-gun fire. The mortars renewed the bombardment and fighting continued without gain. At 11 p.m. the South Africans repelled a counter-attack.

XV CORPS
7th Division

By 8 a.m. 91 Brigade had concentrated behind Bazentin-le-Grand, having extricated themselves from High Wood with little difficulty.

III CORPS
1st Division

The 2nd Welsh Regiment made another unsuccessful bombing attempt on the German second position at 2 a.m. A frontal attack by 3 Brigade was ordered for midnight. The artillery spent the whole day cutting wire. After an intense 10-minute bombardment 1st Gloucesters and 2nd Royal Munster Fusiliers attacked north-east while 2nd Welsh bombed in from the right.

The stormers reached some 300 yards beyond their objective to which they retired at dawn. Strong-posts were established some distance up the communication trenches, now called Welch Alley and Gloster Alley. On the left, 1st South Wales Borderers formed a defensive flank in Black Watch Alley.

X CORPS
25th Division

At 1 a.m. on the 16th, 1/5th Royal Warwicks (143 Brigade attached to 25th Division) attacked from the north-east with 74 Brigade (25th Division) and 144 Brigade from the east and south. Fighting continued all day and by evening Ovillers was reported to be in British hands. The Division was relieved by 48th Division (145 Brigade) that night and consolidation continued.

Monday 17 July

Temperature 70°F; misty and overcast

XIII CORPS
9th Division

At 2 a.m., after an hour's bombardment, an attack was launched: 27 Brigade astride North Street, the South Africans north from Princes Street and west from the ride called the Strand. The machine-guns had not been destroyed by the bombardment and the attack failed, with heavy losses on both sides. The Germans bombarded Delville Wood and Longueval village all night with gas and HE.

21st Division

The Division handed over Bazentin-le-Petit to 33rd Division and went into reserve. The 7th Division relieved 3rd Division (XIII Corps) eastwards from Bazentin-le-Grand Wood.

III CORPS
23rd Division

At 8 p.m. 12th Durham LI (68 Brigade), which had relieved 112 Brigade on

34th Division's front, delivered an assault on a trench south of Pozières after a bombardment but was stopped by machine-gun fire at an early stage.

X CORPS

The next morning 144 Brigade took 300 yards of the original German front line on the north side of Ovillers village.

Tuesday 18 July

Temperature 72°F; overcast

XIII CORPS

35th Division

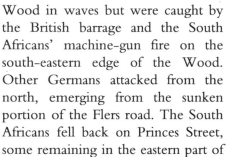

The Division relieved 18th Division during the night, taking over from Maltz Horn Farm to Longueval. One battalion, 16th Cheshires (105 Brigade), was already in the line holding Waterlot Farm. During the day they repelled three counter-attacks. In the early hours of the 20th, two more attempts to capture Munster Trench were defeated by machine-gun fire.

9th Division

At 3.30 p.m. the Germans north of Givenchy road advanced towards Delville Wood in waves but were caught by the British barrage and the South Africans' machine-gun fire on the south-eastern edge of the Wood. Other Germans attacked from the north, emerging from the sunken portion of the Flers road. The South Africans fell back on Princes Street, some remaining in the eastern part of the Wood until early next morning. The Germans reached the southern edge but were stopped by artillery and machine-gun fire from Longueval.

Meanwhile another German attack against Longueval had been launched from the north and north-west and 27 Brigade were forced back to the southern edge of the village. At 6 p.m. 5th Camerons attacked and regained the line of Clarges Street in the centre of Longueval.

3rd Division

The German bombardment had slackened by 3.45 a.m. when 1st Gordons, supported by two companies of 8th King's Own (76 Brigade), moved out from a trench near the Windmill and assaulted Longueval from the

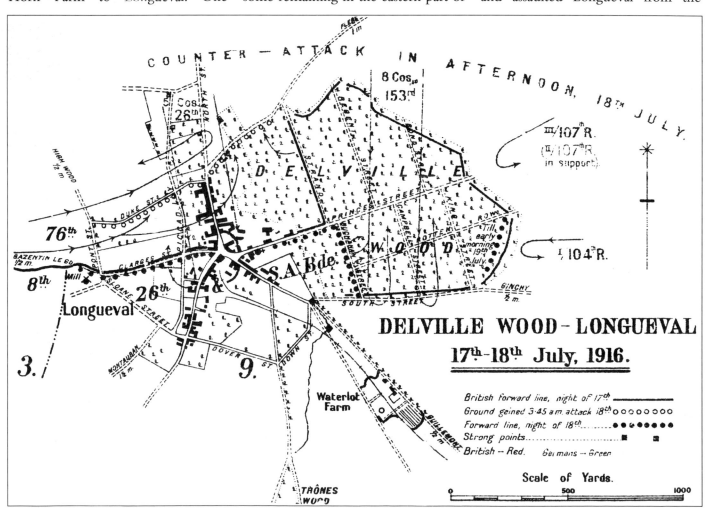

DELVILLE WOOD – LONGUEVAL
17th–18th July, 1916.

British forward line, night of 17th ————
Ground gained 3·45 a.m. attack 18th ∘∘∘∘∘∘∘∘
Forward line, night of 18th ……••••••••
Strong points ……………………■ ▣
British – Red. Germans – Green.

Scale of Yards.

0   500   1000

Battle of Bazentin Ridge. A German prisoner helps a dispatch rider to push his motorcycle through the mud at Mametz Wood, 17 July 1916. The bike is a Triumph, the rider is in the Royal Engineers. Note the saddle bags on the petrol tank. (Q.3972)

west. Longueval was occupied as far as Duke Street, but not the orchards north of the village. A line was taken north-west of Delville Wood in contact with the South Africans who had advanced to the northern edge of the Wood.

After a very severe German barrage 76 Brigade were withdrawn westwards to their assault trench near the Mill.

III CORPS
1st Division
South of Pozières 2nd Royal Munster Fusiliers (3 Brigade) briefly captured the junction of Munster Alley and OG2 (OG1 = old German front-line trench; OG2 = old German support trench). The Division also established, at little cost, a line of outposts and strongpoints along the crest of Pozières Ridge, running north-west from Bazentin-le-Petit Wood and parallel to and half-way between OG2 and the Switch Line.

Wednesday 19 July
Temperature 70°F; cloudy

XIII CORPS
18th Division
Having been lent to 9th Division, 53 Brigade attacked with 8th Norfolks at 7.15 a.m., advancing from the southwest edge of Longueval. After a struggle they claimed the southern portion of Delville Wood. Later 10th Essex, 6th Royal Berks and 8th

Suffolks renewed the attack without much success. Fighting continued all day.

Thursday 20 July
Temperature 75°F; fine morning, clear sky

ATTACKS ON HIGH WOOD
(20–30 July)

XIII CORPS
35th Division
At 5 a.m., after a 30-minute bombardment, one company of 15th Sherwood Foresters (105 Brigade) attacked just south of Arrow Head Copse and another at Maltz Horn Farm, suffering heavy losses from shell and machine-gun fire. Parties that did enter the trenches were shelled out. After a second bombardment 23rd Manchesters (104 Brigade) attempted an attack at 11.35 a.m., with some results.

3rd Division
Early in the morning the Division made another attack on Delville Wood and village using 2nd Suffolks and 10th Royal Welsh Fusiliers (76 Brigade). At 3.35 a.m. the Suffolks advanced from the west, but the two leading companies were almost entirely wiped out. The Fusiliers went astray and came under fire from a British machine-gun barrage, losing most of their officers, only to press home a fruitless attack. In the evening 76 Brigade relieved the South Africans.

XV CORPS
5th, 7th Divisions
The first objective was a track known as Black Road which ran north-north-west to the southern corner of High Wood. After a barrage 8th Devons and 2nd Gordons (20 Brigade, 7th Division), started crawling towards their objective at 20 minutes before zero hour at 3.25 a.m.

They had no trouble in taking either the track or the corner of High Wood, after the barrage had lifted at 3.25 a.m. The 5th Division came up in line. The attack continued to the second objective, Wood Lane. The Germans, in strength with machine-guns, took the gardens in rear from High Wood. Both battalions attempted to dig-in 25 yards short of the Lane, but after an hour the survivors fell back to Black Road which was then consolidated. After dark, 13 Brigade (5th Division) relieved 7th Division's troops.

33rd Division

At dusk 2nd Worcesters (100 Brigade) pushed out posts from Bazentin-Le-Petit in the direction of the west corner of High Wood to protect the flank in the assault. The 1st Cameronians and 5/6th Scottish Rifles (19 Brigade) crept forward before the barrage lifted at 3.25 a.m. The Scots forced their way into the Wood where they came under fire from a machine-gun in the part of Switch Line which was in the Wood and also from a strongpoint on the western corner.

The 20th Royal Fusiliers (19 Brigade), following close on the right flank, joined the fight and the southern part of the Wood was cleared. Early in the afternoon 2nd Royal Welsh Fusiliers came up in support and reached the northern edge of the Wood. Losses had been heavy and relief was requested. The 1st Queen's and 16th KRRC (100 Brigade) were sent up. At dusk a German bombardment forced the evacuation of the north portion of the Wood. German infantry re-occupied the Wood in the vicinity of Switch Line. Both sides dug-in. The relief was accomplished by next morning. The posts put out by 2nd Worcesters were withdrawn.

III CORPS
1st Division

In the early hours of the 20th, two more attempts to take Munster Trench were defeated by machine-gun fire.

Friday 21 July

Temperature 75°F; fine, with clear skies

XV CORPS

During the night 51st Division relieved the troops of 33rd Division in and about High Wood.

ANZAC
1st Australian Division

On the morning of the 21st, 1st Australian Division was established in

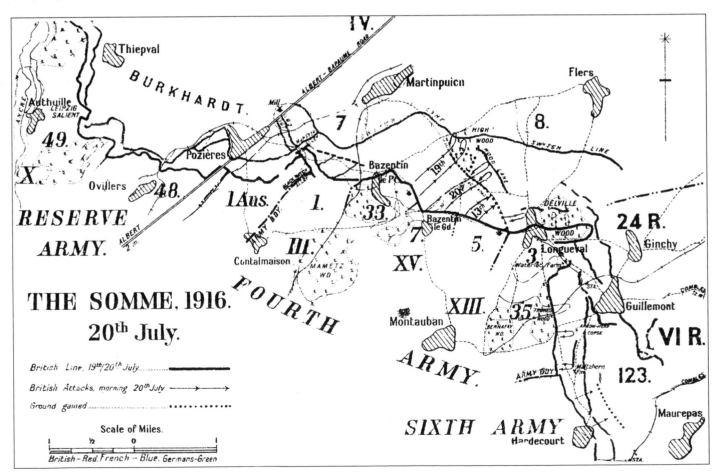

THE SOMME, 1916.
20th July.

British Line, 19th/20th July ....
British Attacks, morning 20th July ....→ →
Ground gained ....

Scale of Miles.

British – Red. French -- Blue. Germans–Green

Black Watch Alley and had taken over the part of OG1 that lay beyond the Alley, almost back to back with 1st Division.

Saturday 22 July

Temperature 77°F; clear sky, although dull early on (rain-trace)

XIII CORPS
35th Division
At 1.30 a.m. a battalion of 35th Division unsuccessfully assaulted the trench between Maltz Horn and Arrow Head Copse.

3rd Division
The Division, which had relieved the left of 35th Division as far as the Trônes Wood railway, advanced on Guillemont railway station from

Waterlot Farm but was forced back by machine-gun fire.

ANZAC
1st Australian Division
At 2.30 a.m. 9th (Queensland) Battalion (3 Brigade) tried to push forward up OG1 and OG2, but were stopped by bombers and machine-gun fire.

Sunday 23 July

Temperature 68°F; overcast

BATTLE OF POZIERES RIDGE (23 July–3 September)

XIII CORPS
30th Division
The Division came up from reserve and attacked Guillemont with 21 Brigade at 3.40 a.m. The 19th Manchesters were to assault Guillemont

Site of Waterlot Farm, July 1916. (Q.4261)

from Trônes Wood; 2nd Green Howards went further north. The Manchesters reached the German wire which they found uncut, but managed to get into the village from which they were forced to withdraw, some of them not until 2 p.m. however. Meanwhile the Green Howards had lost direction in the smoke-screen* and half-light. This led to parties going in all directions. One party took one trench south of the railway, but fell back to Waterlot Farm (most others falling back to Trônes Wood), disorganizing the advance of 3rd Division.

Two strong bombing parties of 7th Shropshire LI and a company of 8th East Yorks (8 Brigade) which was to clear the ground south of the railway, made little headway and also fell back

*Special Brigade RE fired 210 smoke bombs from a position near Waterlot Farm.

55

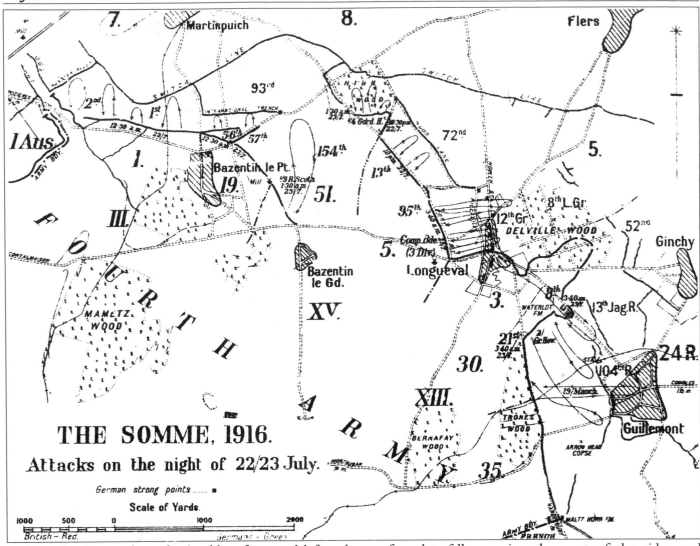

THE SOMME, 1916.

Attacks on the night of 22/23 July.

German strong points ...... ■

Scale of Yards.

British – Red.
German – Green

to Waterlot Farm where the jumble of units repelled a counter-attack later in the morning. The 2nd Royal Scots (8 Brigade) tried to bomb down trenches from Waterlot Farm on either side of Guillemont road and railway, but none of the ground could be held.

3rd Division

An attack was made on Delville Wood. The 5th Division were to deal with the strongpoints in the orchards north of Longueval. At 3.40 a.m. 1st Northumberland Fusiliers advanced, followed by 13th King's and 12th West Yorkshire (9 Brigade). They made considerable progress, but were met by machine-gun fire from the front and left and were forced to fall back, first to Piccadilly and eventually to their starting-place in Pont Street. The 1st East Surreys and 1st Duke of Cornwall's LI (95 Brigade) captured a strongpoint, but after a counter-attack fell back to Pont Street.

XV CORPS
5th Division

As a preliminary to the attack on the Switch Line east of High Wood, Wood Lane had to be taken. The 14th Royal Warwicks and 1st Royal West Kents (13 Brigade) made considerable ground before the barrage had lifted at 10 p.m. They were, however, spotted by the light of German flares while they were crossing the crest of the ridge and caught machine-gun fire in enfilade from the eastern corner of High Wood, where a strongpoint defied the assaults of a platoon of the 1/4th Gordons (154 Brigade). Further fire from Wood Trench brought the attack to a standstill. The 2nd KOSB and 15th Royal Warwicks were sent to reinforce the attack and another attempt was made at 1.30 a.m. with the same result. By dawn all were back in their old positions, having lost more than a thousand men.

51st Division

At 1.30 a.m. 1/4th Gordons and 1/9th Royal Scots (154 Brigade) were to complete the capture of High

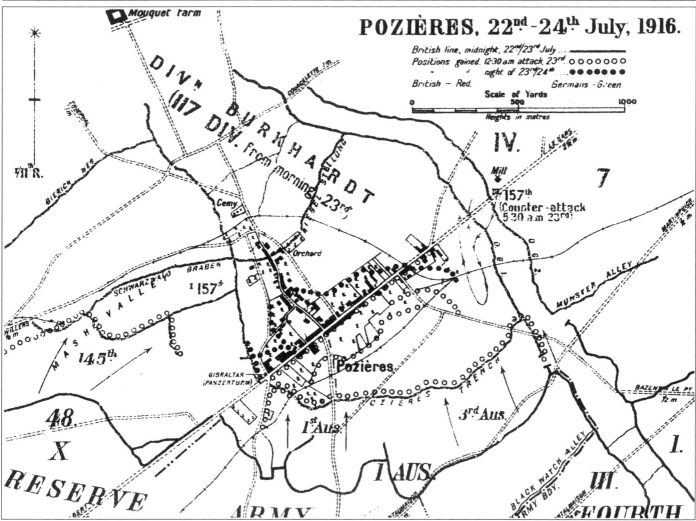

POZIÈRES, 22nd-24th July, 1916.

British line, midnight, 22nd/23rd July ————
Positions gained 12.30 a.m. attack 23rd OOOOOO
"   "   night of 23rd/24th ●●●●●●
British – Red.   Germans – Green.

Scale of Yards
0   500   1000

Heights in metres

Wood and secure 600 yards of Switch Line. The Gordons lost direction in the Wood and machine-gun fire caused heavy casualties. The Royal Scots were shelled as they advanced up the depression south-west of the Wood and also came under machine-gun fire from the eastern end of Intermediate Line. By 3 a.m. both battalions were back at their starting-point having taken 450 casualties.

III CORPS
19th Division
The Division attacked at 12.30 a.m., 57 Brigade creeping forward to within 75 yards of the German trenches. The 10th Royal Warwicks relieved 10th Worcesters at the last moment and were not ready in time. Next on the

left, 8th Gloucesters were halted by machine-gun fire. The 7th South Lancs and 7th Loyal North Lancs (56 Brigade) could do no better, and between 3 and 4 a.m. were withdrawn.

1st Division
The Division was formed up on the right, outside the British wire. The 1st Camerons and 10th Gloucesters (1 Brigade) were caught by machine-guns hidden by the long grass, and failed to reach the Switch Line. A similar fate befell 2nd KRRC and 2nd Royal Sussex (2 Brigade), whose objective was the re-entrant formed by the Switch Line and Munster Alley. At 2.30 a.m. 1st Loyal North Lancs (2 Brigade) was sent to attack Munster Alley, but had no success.

X CORPS
48th Division
The 1/6th Gloucesters (144 Brigade) attacked at dawn and were mown down, only a few bombers entering the German line by the railway. The 1/4th Gloucesters bombed forward on the left flank. The 1/5th Gloucesters on the left of the Battalion (145 Brigade) shared the same fate. On the right 1/4th Ox and Bucks LI and 1/4th Royal Berks captured the trench south of the railway.

At daybreak a counter-attack from the cemetery was checked. At 6.30 a.m. 145 Brigade repeated its attack on the left with 1/1st Bucks taking the railway track and the trench to the east of it. On the right the Germans still held the trenches running into Pozières. During the day the village was taken and consolidated by the Australians.

ANZAC
1st Australian Division
After the bombardment of Pozières, which had begun on the 19th and increased in volume until 23 July, 9th and 11th Battalions (3 Brigade), on the right, and 1st and 2nd Battalions (1 NSW Brigade) attacked at 12.30 a.m. and secured Pozières Trench. Only on the right at OG1 and OG2 was there any hold-up. The remainder of the line went forward to the second objective. By dawn only OG1 had been secured as far as the junction with Pozières Trench.

At 1 a.m. the attack continued on the gardens bordering the Bapaume road. By 3 a.m. 3rd and 4th Battalions on the left and 10th and 12th Battalions on the right were on the road itself and dug-in. Five howitzers and 100 prisoners were taken. On the right, the OG trenches required 3 Brigade to throw back its flank to the left railway to face OG1 some 300 yards away. At 5.30 a.m. a counter-attack was launched from the OG trenches near the Bapaume–Albert road, but was repulsed.

Monday 24 July
Temperature 70°F; overcast but hot

Before dark, the heavy guns of Fifth Army opened up on OG1, and those of III Corps on OG2.

X CORPS
48th Division
had a few bombing encounters during the day but made no advance. The Germans shelled Pozières all day.

Tuesday 25 July
Temperature 66°F; overcast

III CORPS
3rd Division
were relieved by 2nd Division.

ANZAC
1st Australian Division
At 2 a.m. 5th Battalion on the right seized OG1. When the barrage lifted, OG2 was entered but the Battalion

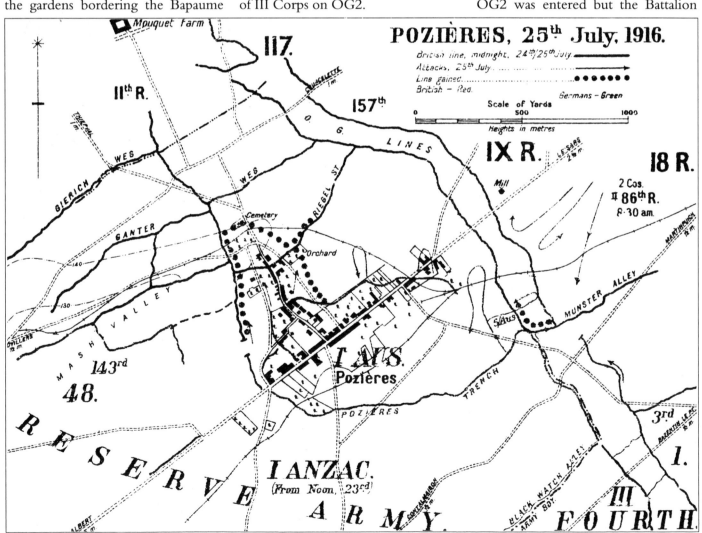

POZIÈRES, 25th July, 1916.

was bombed from both flanks and had to fall back to OG1. After a bombing exchange, the Germans kept possession as far as the railway.

On the right, 10th and 19th Battalions, assisted later by two companies of 7th Battalion, were trying to clear a trench connecting the OG lines. A strongpoint in OG1 was captured by 10th Battalion. The Germans remained near the junction of OG2 and Munster Alley.

At 3.30 a.m. the securing of Pozières began. On the right 12th Battalion was exposed to heavy fire from OG1 which prevented it from forming the link with 11th Battalion, who had reached the Light Railway but had come under fire from 8th Battalion, causing some confusion. At daylight 11th Battalion was so heavily

shelled that it was withdrawn back to its old line.

The 8th Battalion (2 Brigade, lent to 1 Brigade), went through Pozières and consolidated a position at the cemetery and also put out a line of posts to the orchard. The 4th Battalion bombed up the trench on the west side of the village, capturing 700 yards of trench and linking up with 8th Battalion at the cemetery.

At 8.30 a.m. a large force of Germans appeared southwards over the crest near the Pozières windmill, but the artillery of 1st Australian Division and 25th Division, together with the machine-gun fire from 3 Australian Brigade, brought the attack to a halt.

During the night 2nd Australian Division relieved 1st Australian Division.

Wednesday 26 July

Temperature 75°F; windy

X CORPS
48th Division

In the early hours 1/7th Royal Warwicks (143 Brigade) linked up with the Australians to the north-west of the village. At 3 a.m. a company of 20th Battalion (5 Brigade) attempted a raid on OG1 to the north of the railway, but this was unsuccessful. During the afternoon 17th Battalion and bombers of the 18th became involved in the fighting for Munster Alley.

Two companies of the Welsh, left behind by 1st Division, attacked to-

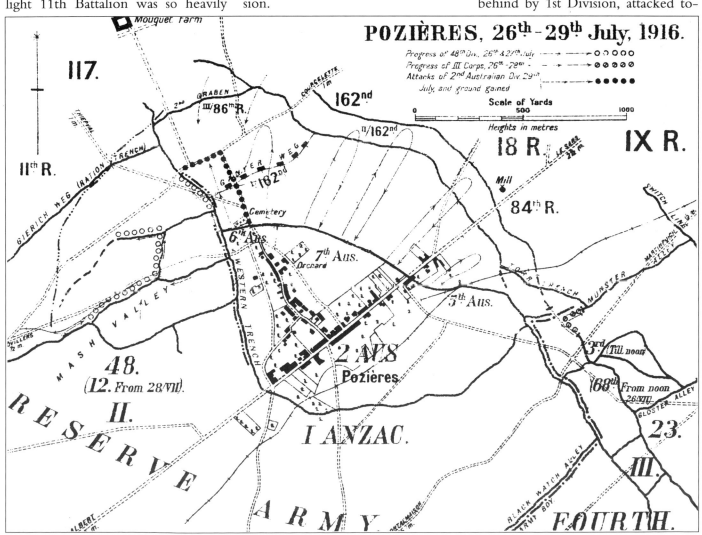

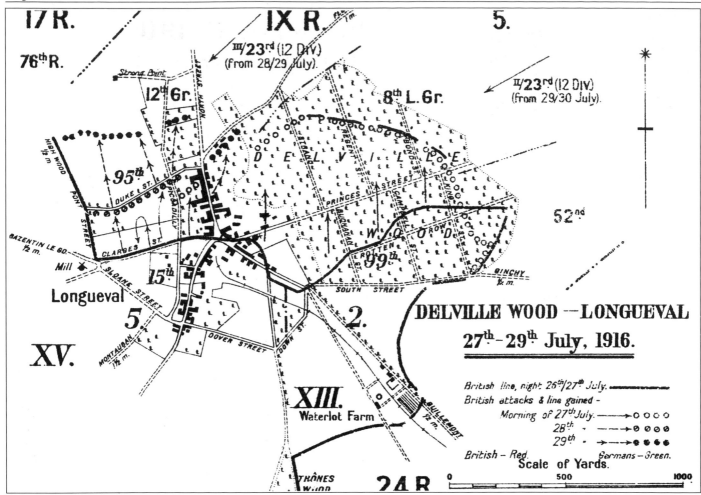

DELVILLE WOOD -- LONGUEVAL
27th - 29th July, 1916.

British line, night 26th/27th July.
British attacks & line gained -
  Morning of 27th July.
         28th   "
         29th   "
British - Red.   Germans - Green.
Scale of Yards.
0   500   1000

---

wards the Switch Line at 3 p.m., but were driven back. Another attempt was made with the help of the Australians and was more successful.

23rd Division relieved 1st Division. 68 Brigade (23rd Division) carried on with the fight that night, but with no positive success.

Thursday 27 July

Temperature 81°F; hazy, becoming clearer in the afternoon (8mm rain)

XIII CORPS
2nd Division

At 6.10 a.m. on the 27th a severe barrage was laid on Delville Wood. At 7.10 a.m. 1st KRRC and 23rd Royal Fusiliers (99 Brigade) advanced, following the lift in the barrage. By 9 a.m. they had reached their objective and held a line about 50 yards inside the Wood. 1st Royal Berks mopped up but did not push out to the eastern edge. Consolidation took place. The Germans began to shell Princes Street, the new support position.

XV CORPS
5th Division

15 Brigade were on the left of 99 Brigade. With 1st Norfolks in front and 1st Bedfords in support, the Norfolks advanced well forward in Delville Wood and the Bedfords carried on the advance, linking up with 99 Brigade. Longueval proved harder and the enemy held on to the northern portion of the village.

The line reached by 15 Brigade after part of 16th Royal Warwicks had been absorbed into the fight, ran south-west from the north-west portion of Delville Wood, leaving the orchards near the junction of Duke Street and Piccadilly in the hands of the enemy.

At 9.30 a.m. the Germans counter-attacked and, at length, got in behind Princes Street and forced the right of the line to fall back a little and face north-east. Sniping and bombing continued throughout the day. That night 17th Middlesex and 2nd South Staffords (6 Brigade) took over 99 Brigade front and 15 Brigade was relieved by 95 Brigade.

ANZAC

Bombing by 17th Battalion and the bombers of 18th Battalion around Munster Alley was inconclusive.

II CORPS
48th Division

The 1/8th Royal Warwicks (143 Brigade) bombed forward just short of the Ovillers–Courcelette track.

Friday 28 July

Temperature 77°F; overcast and hot

XIII CORPS
2nd Division

At 9.30 p.m. a counter-attack was driven back by 6 Brigade.

XV CORPS
5th Division

The line of Duke Street was taken without opposition by 95 Brigade.

Saturday 29 July

Temperature 81°F; overcast

XV CORPS
5th Division

At 3.30 p.m., after a 30-minute bombardment, 12th Gloucesters and 1st East Surreys attacked. On the left, the Gloucesters occupied a line 500 yards north of Duke Street. On the right, the East Surreys made a little headway.

51st Division

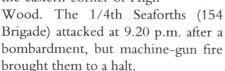

The Division attempted to storm the strongpoint at the eastern corner of High Wood. The 1/4th Seaforths (154 Brigade) attacked at 9.20 p.m. after a bombardment, but machine-gun fire brought them to a halt.

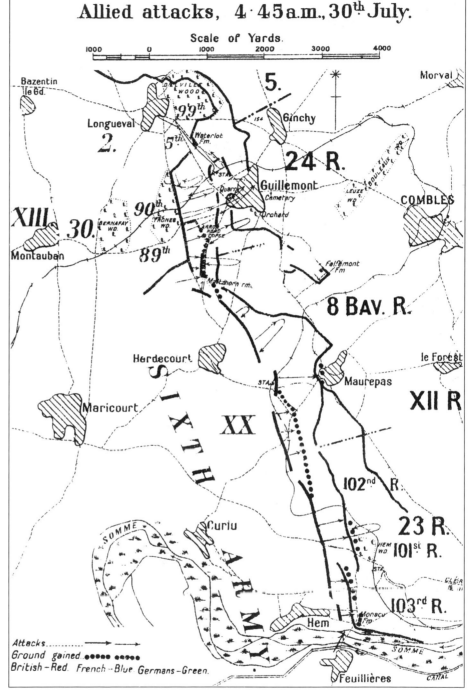

THE SOMME, 1916.
Allied attacks, 4·45 a.m., 30th July.

III CORPS
23rd Division

During the night of 28/29 July, the 10th Duke of Wellington's (69 Brigade) made an attack above ground and along Gloster Alley. By 5.30 a.m. they were only 25 yards from Switch Line.

ANZAC
2nd Australian Division

At 12.15 a.m. 28th Battalion (7 Brigade) on the right overran OG1. The wire stopped the attack on OG2 and the battalion were driven back to their starting-position. A similar fate befell 25th and 26th Battalions (7 Brigade). On the left, 23rd Battalion

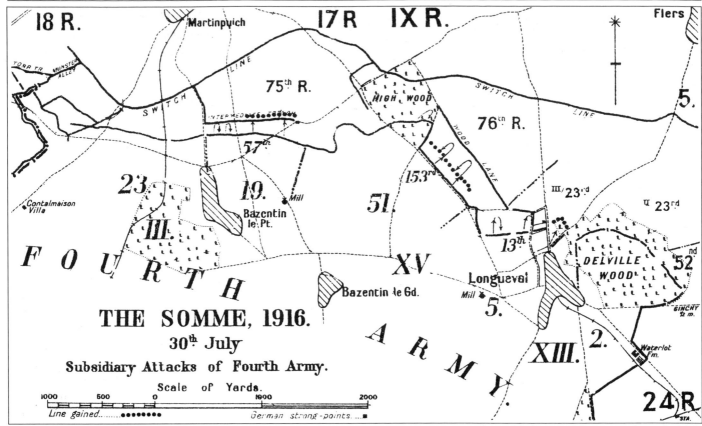

18 R.   Martinpuich   17 R.   IX R.   Flers

75th R.

HIGH WOOD

76th R.

57th

5.

23.   19.   Mill

III/23rd

II 23rd

Contalmaison Villa

III   Bazentin le Pt.

153rd

13th

51

XV   DELVILLE WOOD   52

F O U R T H

Bazentin le Gd.

Longueval

Mill

GINCHY 12 m.

5.

2.

Waterlot Fm.

THE SOMME, 1916.
30th July
Subsidiary Attacks of Fourth Army.

A R M Y.

XIII.

24 R.

Scale of Yards.

1000   500   0   1000   2000

Line gained........●●●●●●   German strong-points....■

(6 Brigade) overshot their objective and suffered under their own barrage. The failure of the right forced them to relinquish part of their gains and throw out a defensive flank to the cemetery. 5 Brigade attacked the line south-east of the Bapaume road but was stopped at the outset. Heavy losses were suffered before the attack was abandoned and 7 Brigade was put into reserve.

II CORPS
12th Division

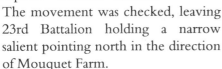

The 11th Middlesex (36 Brigade) made an effort to capture Western Trench. The movement was checked, leaving 23rd Battalion holding a narrow salient pointing north in the direction of Mouquet Farm.

Dressing the wounds of Australian soldiers in Beaucourt Château, July 1916. A Field Surgical Pannier (a medical tool box) can be seen by the leg of the man on the left. (Q.908)

Sunday 30 July

Temperature 82°F; clear and very hot

XV CORPS
5th Division

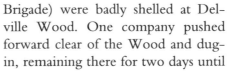

At 6.10 p.m. the advance on Longueval began. On the right, 2nd KOSB (13 Brigade) were badly shelled at Delville Wood. One company pushed forward clear of the Wood and dug-in, remaining there for two days until

it withdrew. The attack of 14th Royal Warwicks (13 Brigade) was checked by machine-gun fire and went to ground in shell-holes. They were supported during the day by 1st Royal West Kents, 1st Bedfords (15 Brigade) and 16th Royal Warwicks (16 Brigade).

51st Division

At 6.10 p.m. 1/5th Gordons and 1/6th Black Watch (both 153 Brigade) were to attack the southern point at

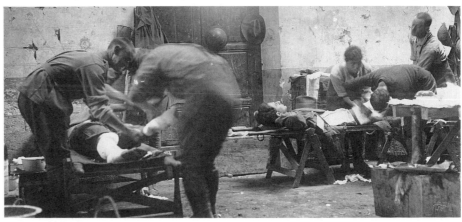

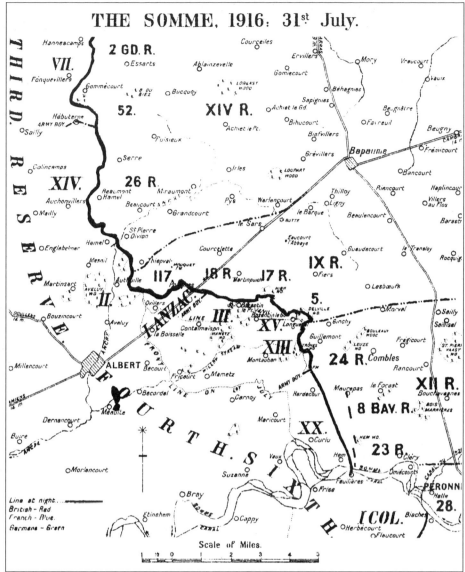

THE SOMME, 1916: 31st July.

Line at night........
British – Red
French – Blue
Germans – Green

Scale of Miles.

took the German front-line trenches and reached the Hardecourt–Guillemont road. They began to consolidate with the help of 17th King's. 19th King's on the left suffered heavy casualties but managed to secure a position in an orchard on the southeastern edge of Guillemont. Later in the day they believed themselves to be cut off and pulled back.

90 Brigade, on the left, advanced with 2nd Royal Scots Fusiliers on the right, astride the Trônes–Guillemont track, and met little resistance; consolidation was started within the village with a party of 18th Manchesters. A counter-attack from the cemetery was repulsed. The Fusiliers were cut off and eventually overrun.

The 18th Manchesters went forward with the Trônes Wood–Guillemont railway on their left. They took the front line but were held up by machine-gun fire from the station and Quarry, and this forced a withdrawal. A second attack by two companies each of 16th and 17th Manchesters also failed. Two companies of 16th Manchesters made up the left of the attack, but they were held up on uncut wire south of Guillemont station and were forced to retire.

the eastern corner of High Wood. The survivors dug in 200 yards in front of their start-line. The 1/7th Black Watch (153 Brigade) tried to go through the Wood but were beaten back.

III CORPS
19th Division
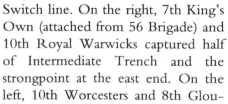
Under cover of a smoke-screen on High Wood, 57 Brigade attacked the Switch line. On the right, 7th King's Own (attached from 56 Brigade) and 10th Royal Warwicks captured half of Intermediate Trench and the strongpoint at the east end. On the left, 10th Worcesters and 8th Glou-

cesters attacked, but failed under machine-gun fire. Intermediate Trench was consolidated with the assistance of 5th South Wales Borderers (Pioneers) and a counter-attack was repulsed.

XIII CORPS
30th Division
The Division attacked at 4.45 a.m. through the 35th Division with 89 Brigade on the right and 90 Brigade on the left. 89 Brigade attacked from trenches south of Trônes Wood. A company of 2nd Bedfords, with a company of French 153rd Regiment, took Maltz Horn Farm. 20th King's

2nd Division
The 2nd Ox & Bucks Light Infantry and 24th Fusiliers (5 Brigade) advanced from Waterlot Farm towards Guillemont station but had to withdraw. That night 55th Division relieved 30th and 35th Divisions

Monday 31 July

Temperature 82°F; very hot and hazy in the morning

III CORPS
19th Division was relieved by 34th Division.

6in, 26cwt howitzers being drawn by
caterpillars along the main Albert–
Fricourt Road, 25 August 1916. (Q.4146)

AUGUST

Tuesday 1 August

Temperature 86°F; very hot

XV CORPS

17th Division relieved 5th Division in Longueval and Delville Wood.

III CORPS
34th Division

On the night of 1/2 August 16th Royal Scots (101 Brigade) tried to extend its hold on Intermediate Trench by bombing westward, but with no success.

Wednesday 2 August

Temperature 88°F

XV CORPS
51st Division

On the left of the Corps, the Division handed over its line as far as High Wood to III Corps. In High Wood saps were pushed out towards the Germans in advance of Switch Line and a trench was dug closer to Wood Lane, east of High Wood.

III CORPS
34th Division

At 11 p.m. a distance of 100 yards was gained by 16th Royal Scots.

Thursday 3 August

Temperature 84°F; hot, with clear sky

II CORPS
12th Division

At 11.15 p.m. 8th Royal Fusiliers (36 Brigade) attacked and captured the south-west section of Fourth Avenue. At the same time, 6th Buffs (37 Brigade) took a strongpoint at the lower end of the trench. Bombers of both Battalions then gained a footing in the centre of Ration Trench.

Friday 4 August

Temperature 79°F

XV CORPS
17th Division

52 Brigade attacked Orchard Trench with 12th Manchesters and 9th Northumberland Fusiliers. They were caught by a German bombardment of HE and gas shells, which halted the attack.

III CORPS
34th Division

At 2.30 a.m. two companies of 16th Royal Scots and two companies of 11th Suffolks reached Intermediate Trench from which they were to have made a frontal attack, but only one company of the Suffolks reached the trench and were soon beaten back. The same evening, 15th Royal Scots (101 Brigade) tried to bomb westwards but were unsuccessful.

23rd Division

The 13th Durham LI (68 Brigade) gained 60 yards by bombing up Munster Alley but failed in their frontal assault on Torr Trench in the night of 4/5th.

ANZAC
2nd Australian Division

At 9.15 p.m. south-east of the Bapaume road, 5 (NSW) Brigade attacked with 20th Battalion on the right and 18th on the left. OG1 was captured easily but OG2 did not fall until the third and fourth waves. Consolidation was intermittent. Lewis-gun posts were set up on the site of OG2. On the right, 20th Battalion blocked the entrance to Torr Trench after hearing that the attack by 68 Brigade had failed.

Between the Bapaume road and the track to Courcelette, 7 Brigade attacked with (from left to right) 27th (S. Australian), 25th (Queensland), 26th (Queen's and Tasmanian) and 22nd (6 Victoria Brigade) Battalions. After some confusion OG1 was captured fairly easily and carried on to OG2. On the right a line was formed just past OG2. The Mill near the road and OG2 were obliterated. On the left, 23rd Battalion (6 Brigade) was to have linked up with the OG lines but was held up by machine-gun fire from the north. (Not until 5 August was the gun captured and the flank secured.) During the night the Australians fought off a number of strong German counter-attacks.

II CORPS
12th Division

At 9.15 p.m. 7th Royal Sussex and 9th Royal Fusiliers attacked Ration Trench frontally with 8th Royal Fusiliers (all 36 Brigade) bombing up from the left. Fighting all night, they captured Ration Trench by morning. Further left, 6th Royal West Kents and 6th Queen's (37 Brigade) had captured the portion of Ration Trench in their sector by bombing.

Saturday 5 August

Temperature 68°F; clear

III CORPS
34th Division

The Division was counter-attacked and 50 yards of Intermediate Trench was re-taken.

Men of the Border Regiment resting in a front-line trench, Thiepval Wood, August 1916. Note the non-standard water-bottle. (Q.871)

ANZAC

At 4 a.m. 7 Brigade fought off a large counter-attack. The 27th and 28th Battalions pushed forward and dug-in on the OG2 position and around the windmill. On the right, 26 Brigade also fought off a counter-attack at 5 a.m. and spasmodic bombing attacks on the left were defeated with the help of 24th Battalion

Sunday 6 August

Temperature 75°F

III CORPS
23rd Division

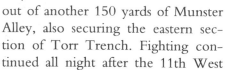

In the afternoon 8th Green Howards (69 Brigade) bombed the Germans out of another 150 yards of Munster Alley, also securing the eastern section of Torr Trench. Fighting continued all night after the 11th West Yorks had taken over the attack with the Australians on the left helping with Torr Trench. That night 112 Brigade relieved 101 Brigade. A bombing attack launched by 8th East Lancs was unsuccessful. 33rd Division relieved 51st Division.

ANZAC

After midnight 5 Brigade was relieved by 45th (NSW) Battalion (12 Brigade, 4th Australian Division), and 48th Battalion relieved 7 Brigade as far as the Elbow. The Germans launched a counter-attack from Courcelette which was repelled with small-arms fire.

II CORPS

FIGHTING FOR MOUQUET FARM (6 August–3 September)

12th Division

The right of the Division in Ration Trench had been subjected to repeated attacks. At 4 a.m. the Germans advanced from the north-east with flame-throwers and bombs, forcing back 9th Royal Fusiliers (36 Brigade). The Fusiliers extended in the open on either side of Ration Trench and kept them in check with rifles and Lewis-guns.

Monday 7 August

Temperature 73°F

XV CORPS

17th Division
relieved 2nd Division (99 Brigade) in Delville Wood.

Left: A 15in howitzer manned by Royal Marine Artillerymen in action at Engle-belmer Wood, 7 August 1916. (Q.4196) Below left: Men of the Wiltshire Regiment advancing to the attack, Thiepval, 7 August 1916. (Q.1142)

At 4.30 p.m. 51 Brigade attacked to establish a line of posts beyond Delville Wood. The 7th Border Regiment and 8th South Staffords were stopped by fire, but at midnight 10th Sherwood Foresters were able to establish posts in front of Longueval.

ANZAC

5th Australian Division

Soon after 4.15 a.m., when 14th Battalion had taken over the line from the Elbow onwards, and 15th Battalion were holding on the left flank, a German counter-attack broke through the posts of 14th and 48th Battalions in the vicinity of the Elbow. There was confused fighting but the Australians eventually routed the enemy, primarily thanks to Lieutenant Jaccker who emerged from a dugout in OG1 with a small party and attacked the Germans in rear. Meanwhile 45th Battalion had assisted 69 Brigade during the night in its progress up Munster Alley.

Tuesday 8 August

Temperature 77°F

XIII CORPS

ATTACK ON WATERLOT FARM–GUILLEMONT (8–9 August)

2nd Division

The 1st King's (6 Brigade) advanced eastwards, north of the railway, and three companies reached the station. The fourth found that the Germans had re-occupied their front line and therefore could

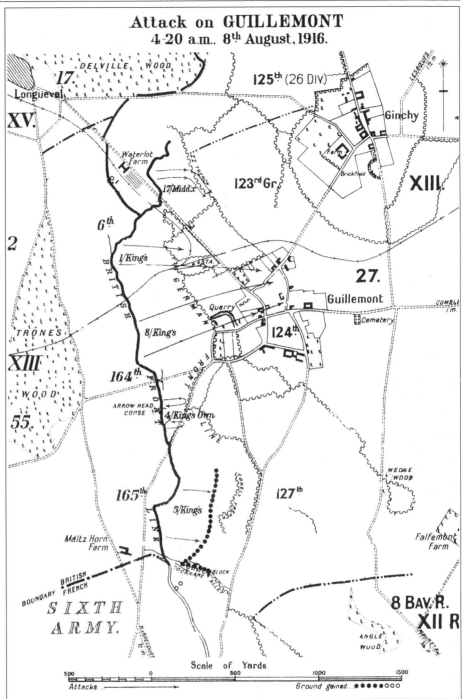

not support the attack. 17th Middlesex attacked from Waterlot Farm and entered ZZ Trench, but failed to join with 1st King's.

55th Division

At 4.20 a.m. 1/5th King's (165 Brigade) advanced a little way and bombers pushed forward along Cochrane Alley, to be blocked by a party of

sappers. They were later forced to retire back to their assembly trench.

The 1/4th King's Own (164 Brigade) were stopped by wire at the south-western corner of Guillemont and were eventually forced to retire, while 1/8th King's (Liverpool Irish) broke through and, passing north and south of the quarry, occupied Guillemont. The 1/4th Loyal North Lancs were to have held the old German

69

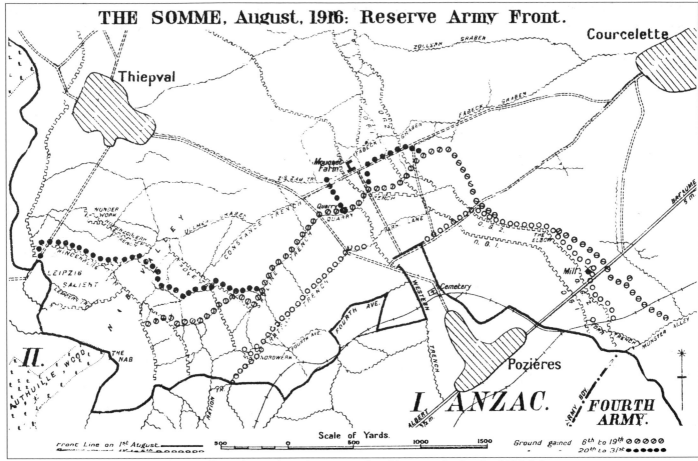

THE SOMME, August, 1916: Reserve Army Front.

Scale of Yards.

Front Line on 1st August. Ground gained 6th to 19th 20th to 31st

front line, but were bombed out of it, isolating 1/8th (who held out at the station until the evening of the 9th and then surrendered).

III CORPS
15th Division relieved 23rd Division.

ANZAC
4th Australian Division
At 9.20 p.m. 15th Battalion drove the Germans from Park Lane and entered the OG Trenches. On the right, 7th Suffolks (35 Brigade) failed in their attack up Western Trench to Ration Trench. The Australians were withdrawn from Park Lane west of Mouquet Farm Track.

II CORPS
12th Division
In Ration Trench 35 Brigade (which had relieved 36 Brigade) was attacked on both flanks. The attacks, delivered at 3 a.m. and 7.30 a.m., had little effect, but on the right 5th Royal Berks were forced to retire.

Wednesday 9 August

Temperature 84°F

XIII CORPS
55th Division
The same objectives were set as on the previous day, and at 4.20 a.m. the attack was launched. They had no better luck than on the 8th, however. 166 Brigade relieved 164 Brigade. At 4.20 a.m. 1/10th King's (Liverpool Scottish) twice attempted an attack but were forced back. On the left 1/5th Loyal North Lancs fared the same. The 1/7th King's attacked from the trench won by 165 Brigade, but they too were unsuccessful.

2nd Division
The Division attacked with 13th Essex (6 Brigade) south of the railway but were driven back. The 17th Middlesex attempted to bomb south from Waterlot Farm but they failed.

ANZAC
At midnight 16th Battalion attacked and captured the whole of Park Lane.

Thursday 10 August

Temperature 70°F; heavy rain and low cloud all day (4mm rain)

ANZAC
4 Australian Brigade took over 12th Division's front line as far as the Poziéres–Thiepval road.

Friday 11 August

Temperature 77°F; stormy, with mist in the morning

XV CORPS
33rd Division

In High Wood, sap heads were pushed out towards Switch Line and a forward trench was dug closer to Wood Lane, east of the Wood. In the Wood itself, two flame-throwers (each weighing 2 tons), a number of burning oil drums and a pipe-pusher (a machine for making saps) were brought up for future use. Patrols were carried out by both sides.

III CORPS
34th Division

At 2 a.m. 10th Loyal North Lancs made the next attempt, advancing up the trench and across the open, winning another 200 yards.

ANZAC
4th Australian Division

At 1 a.m. 13th and 16th Battalions pushed forward from Park Lane. In the OG line, 13th Battalion established a post south-east of Mouquet Farm and repelled a German bombing attack at dawn. On the left, 16th arrived at the lip of a depression, facing a quarry on the other side of the road. Both Battalions repelled counter-attacks with smallarms fire.

Saturday 12 August

Temperature 82°F; 1mm rain

XIII CORPS
55th Division

The bombardment started at 3.30 p.m. with zero hour at 5.15 p.m. Two companies of 1/9th King's (165 Brigade) and the battalion bombers reached their objective, the spur south of Guillemont, by going down Cochrane Alley, but were pulled back that night.

XV CORPS
15th Division

At 10.30 p.m. the Division attacked Switch Line after a 15-minute bombardment. On the right 12th Highland LI (46 Brigade) was checked by machine-gun fire. On the left 6/7th Royal Scots Fusiliers and 6th Camerons (45 Brigade) occupied and consolidated the trench. The Camerons were in touch with the Australians at the head of Munster Alley.

III CORPS
34th Division

The Germans bombed some saps held by 1st Queen's. The 11th Warwicks made an unsuccessful frontal attack on the remainder of Intermediate Trench that night.

ANZAC

Later that day, 50th Battalion relieved 16th Battalion. At 10.30 p.m. 50th Battalion pressed forward from Park Lane and Ration Trench. On the right 13th Battalion had little to do but support the 50th. On the left at Thiepval road, the objective was reached and touch was made with 12th Division, but the centre swung right-handed. Eventually the Australians occupied a line of posts 100 yards short of their objective on the left at Thiepval road.

II CORPS
12th Division

South-west of this point, 7th Norfolks and 9th Essex (35 Brigade) successfully assaulted Skyline Trench and, occupying it, sent out more patrols towards Nab Valley which were resisted strongly. The Battalions then established two strongpoints in Skyline Trench and withdrew all but the holding troops. The 7th East Surreys and 6th Royal West Kents (37 Brigade) carried out 'holding attacks' further to the west which resulted in heavy casualties.

49th Division

The 1/8th West Yorks (146 Brigade, 49th Division) assaulted a German barricade in the original German front line opposite the Nab and made some headway.

Sunday 13 August

Temperature 81°F; windy

III CORPS
34th Division was relieved by 1st Division.

4th Australian Division replaced 4 Brigade with 13 Brigade, putting 51st Battalion on the right in the OG trench, but retaining 13th Battalion in the line.

II CORPS
49th Division

After a heavy bombardment, a German counter-attack was launched at midnight, overrunning the two companies of 1/4th Ox and Bucks LI (145 Brigade) at the second attempt, except at a point near the Thiepval road where a party remained in touch with the Australians.

The enemy tried to continue their advance against Ration Trench, but were beaten back.

Monday 14 August

Temperature 77°F; showery (2mm rain)

ANZAC

The Anzacs suffered a heavy bombardment during the evening. On the right, 51st Battalion was forced back to its start-line by machine-gun fire. The 49th (Queensland) Battalion (13 Brigade) occupied ground well to the east of the OG lines. In the centre, 13th Battalion pressed forward and swerved to the right, establishing bombing posts in Fabeck Graben between OG1 and OG2. But it could not hold them and withdrew before dawn. On the left, 50th Battalion were smashed by the German barrage; although small groups tried to

A Lewis-gun section of 8th Devons resting after an attack near Fricourt, August 1916. The vehicles are Lewis-gun carts. The 8th Devons were in 20 Brigade, 7th Division. Note the figure in greatcoat, kilt and glengarrie. (Q.1395)

dig-in beyond the Quarry, they were forced back.

II CORPS
49th Division

At 5.15 a.m. 1/4th Royal Berks counter-attacked Skyline Trench from Ration Trench, but were beaten back. At 10 p.m. bombers from 1/1st Bucks (145 Brigade) worked along the communication trench from Ration Trench and, after some hard fighting, had managed to clear most of Skyline Trench by 5 a.m. on the 15th.

Tuesday 15 August

Temperature 75°F; hard rain at night

II CORPS
12th Division

The 1/6th Gloucesters (144 Brigade) were fighting for a trench at the

south-western end of Skyline Trench but were unsuccessful. The attack was resumed after dark by 145 Brigade, consisting of 1/5th Gloucesters assisted by 1/1st Bucks and 1/4th Gloucesters (144 Brigade), but with no lasting success.

By 3 p.m., because of casualties from the German bombardment, the Bucks had been limited to holding only the heads of the communication trenches in Skyline Trench. In the evening they pushed posts out to 100 yards in front of the trench, withdrawing to the trench when the bombardment died down.

XIV CORPS
3rd Division relieved 55th Division.

Wednesday 16 August

Temperature 75°F; 2mm rain

XIV CORPS had taken over from XIII Corps.

3rd Division

At 5.40 a.m. 2nd Suffolks (76 Brigade) cleared Cochrane Alley as far as the road and also the trench along the Hardecourt–Guillemont road. The 8th King's Own (76 Brigade) and 13th King's Own (9 Brigade) could not capture Lonely Trench because of a trench mortar barrage. The 4th Royal Fusiliers, advancing to meet 9th East Surreys (72 Brigade, 24th Division), also failed to reach their objective which was a strongpoint immediately south of Trônes Wood-Guillemont Track.

ANZAC

The Anzacs suffered throughout the night of the 16th from a series of spasmodic counter-attacks which were stopped by a protective barrage and rifle and machine-gun fire. 4th Australian Division was relieved by 1st Australian Division at 5 p.m.

III CORPS

34th Division was relieved by 1st Division.

Thursday 17 August

Temperature 72°F; showery, with bright intervals

XIV CORPS
3rd, 25th Divisions

Heavy howitzers bombarded Lonely Trench and, at 8 p.m. and 10 p.m., 10th Royal Welsh Fusiliers (76 Brigade, 25th Division) and 12th West Yorks (9 Brigade, 3rd Division) attempted unsuccessfully to take the Trench. At 4 a.m. six companies drawn from 12th West Yorks, 2nd Suffolks, 8th King's Own and 10th Royal Welsh Fusiliers also attacked,

but they, too, were unsuccessful. The 1/4th Ox and Bucks LI (145 Brigade), holding Skyline Trench, spotted a German counter-attack forming, but a pre-arranged barrage stopped it before it could develop.

III CORPS
15th Division

The 7th Camerons (44 Brigade) made a successful attack on Switch Line, but

were later to suffer under a German bombardment. The Germans started to bomb westward from the Elbow but they were cleared out by 8th Seaforths. Meanwhile 10/11th Highland LI (46 Brigade) on the right, extended the hold on Switch Line to a point 120 degrees east of the Elbow.

A Worcestershire in the trenches at Ovillers, August 1916. (Q.4100)

Friday 18 August

Temperature 70°F; overcast (1mm rain)

XIV CORPS
3rd Division

Zero hour was at 2.45 p.m. Two companies of 1st Gordons and two companies of 10th Royal Welsh Fusiliers (76 Brigade) attacked. The Highlanders reached the Guillemont–Hardecourt road, while the Fusiliers took the southern part of Lonely Trench, some reaching the road. The 1st Northumberland Fusiliers (9 Brigade) made little headway and had to withdraw, exposing the flank of the Welsh Fusiliers and forcing them to withdraw also.

The French made some progress in the Maurepas Ravine and were in touch.

The Northumberland Fusiliers made two unsuccessful attempts to take Lonely Trench and one bombing effort. Meanwhile 8th East Yorks (9 Brigade, on attachment from 8 Brigade) on their left, made no headway in their attack from Arrow Head Copse.

24th Division

South of Trônes Wood–Guillemont track, 12th Middlesex advanced well but were checked by machine-gun fire at the front line and efforts to gain a footing failed. North of the track, 7th Northamptons had the same result on their left where they lodged in the front line near the Quarry. They were later reinforced by a company of 9th Royal Sussex and consolidated their position. The 3rd Rifle Brigade (17 Brigade) took the station and part of Waterlot Farm road, part of their second objective.

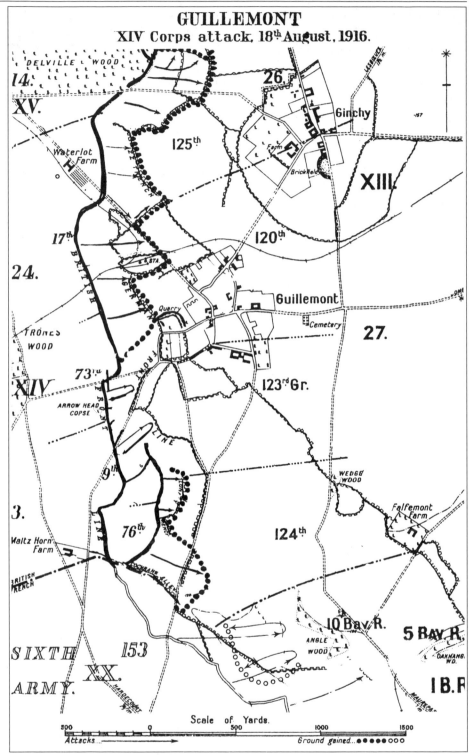

GUILLEMONT
XIV Corps attack, 18th August, 1916.

Scale of Yards.
Attacks ——→
Ground gained... ●●●●●○○○

Further north, 8th Buffs captured their only objective, ZZ Trench (north section), mainly with bombers. In the extreme north they made contact with 14th Division (XV Corps).

That night the French were driven back to the Wedge Wood position so that, on 19 August the British were able to consolidate the line beyond the Hardecourt–Guillemont road.

XV CORPS
14th Division

At 2.45 p.m., after a 36-hour bombardment on the right,

6th Somerset LI advanced and captured their objective. The southern section of Beer Trench was found nearly obliterated. On the left, 6th Duke of Cornwall's LI managed to clear Edge Trench but were bombed out by a German counter-attack from the north. The Somersets, however, held Hop Alley and barricaded Beer Trench. They consolidated during the night and repulsed two counter-attacks from the Germans in Pint Trench.

On the right, 7th KRRC (43 Brigade), on the left of 33rd Division's attack, captured Orchard Trench and dug a new line beyond. On the left, 7th Rifle Brigade advanced well but were enfiladed on their left and only a small section of Wood Lane was secured.

33rd Division

On the right, 4th King's did not achieve Wood Lane Trench and 1/4th Suffolks, although reaching the trench, were ousted by bombers and machine-gun fire from High Wood. The 2nd Argylls attacked in the Wood itself with the aid of thirty burning oil-drums and two flame-throwers (the former were not successful and the latter were buried by shellfire). They made repeated attempts to get forward, but all were unsuccessful. That night, 19 Brigade relieved 98 Brigade.

III CORPS
1st Division

Zero hour was at 2.45 p.m. Two companies of 1st Loyal North Lancs (2 Brigade) attacked. The right company went too soon and walked into the British barrage and was practically annihilated. On the left, the trench on the north-west edge of High Wood fell to 1st Northamptons who bombed forward from the section of trench taken the day before.

The 1st Black Watch (1 Brigade), advancing on Intermediate Trench at 4.15 a.m., were disorganized by shellfire. Small parties penetrated 70 yards beyond the trench, but were forced back.

At 2.45 p.m. 8th Royal Berks also made an attempt to take Intermediate Trench under cover of smoke which was let off along 15th Division's front. But the British shells were dropping short, and this stopped the

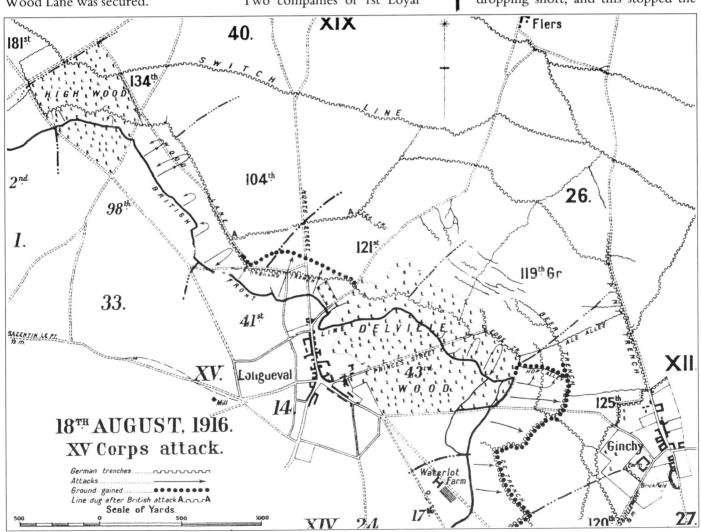

18ᵀᴴ AUGUST, 1916.
XV Corps attack.

German trenches ....
Attacks ....
Ground gained ....
Line dug after British attack A⌐⌐⌐A
Scale of Yards.

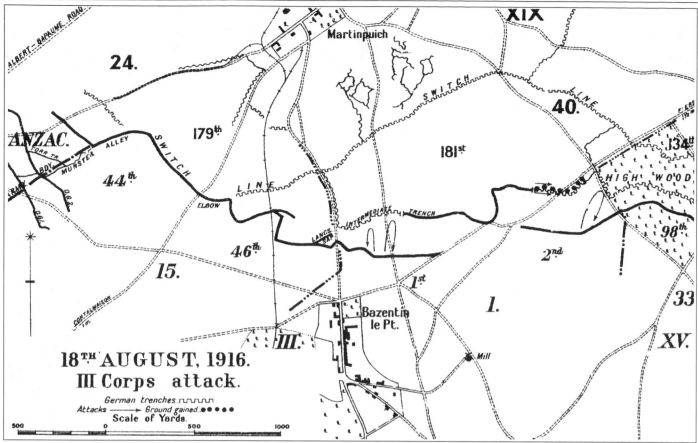

18TH AUGUST, 1916.
III Corps attack.

German trenches ....
Attacks ⟶ Ground gained ..●●●●
Scale of Yards.
500   0   500   1000

flank attack from Lancs Sap. The frontal attack was stopped by machine-gun and artillery fire.

ANZAC
1st Australian Division

2 Australian Brigade advanced at 9 p.m., south-east of the Bapaume road. The 8th Battalion attacked three times on the right but all failed. Beyond the light railway line 7th Battalion had no more success and, by dawn on the 19th, was back to its starting-trench.

North-west of the road, 6th Battalion was ordered to dig a trench to the Elbow from the strongpoint at which 7th Battalion was caught (junction of the Bapaume–Courcelette track). They now joined 7th Battalion on the road.

The 3rd Battalion (1 Australian Brigade) were ordered to attack the new trench in front of Fabeck Graben. The attack was made by bombers and troops east of the OG lines and had little success. The 4th Battalion established posts in Quarry Trench near the track leading to Mouquet Farm. On the left, a line was consolidated level with the Quarry.

II CORPS
48th Division

The 1/5th and 1/6th Royal Warwicks attacked at 5 p.m. with bombers of 1/7th Royal Warwicks (143 Brigade) on the left

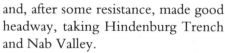

and, after some resistance, made good headway, taking Hindenburg Trench and Nab Valley.

On the right, around the slopes of Skyline Trench Spur, 1/4th Berks (145 Brigade) gave effective support and, at dawn on the 19th, took more ground. The line then consisted of the area due west from Skyline Trench to the original German front line to the east of the Nab.

Saturday 19 August

Temperature 70°F; overcast (2mm rain)

XV CORPS
14th Division

The 9th Rifle Brigade (42 Brigade) established posts along Beer Trench south-east of Cocoa Lane and pushed out a sap from the end of Princes Street.

33rd Division

The Division took over the left of 14th Division.

Right, top: Carnoy Valley. Note the megaphone in the hand of the man on the right. (Q.4066)
Right, bottom: Royal Australian Battery of 9.2in howitzers Mk VI in action at Fricourt, August 1916. (In fact the gun is a Mk I; it would appear that no Mk VI was produced.) (Q.4408)

III CORPS
1st Division

West of High Wood, patrols of 1st Northamptons (2 Brigade) entered an un-defended section of Switch Line in the afternoon. At night a battle station was dug (200 yards of the northern bulge in the trench). After dark, 2nd KRRC relieved 1st Loyal North Lancs and took up an outpost line right of the Northamptons. 1 Australian Brigade was relieved by 3 Australian Brigade. 144 Brigade replaced 145 Brigade in preparation for taking over the whole of 48th Division's line the next day.

II CORPS

25th Division relieved 49th Division.

Sunday 20 August

Temperature 72°F; overcast

XV CORPS
33rd Division

The 2nd Royal Welsh Fusiliers (19 Brigade) tried to clear the trench on the western edge of the Wood. The 1/9th Highland LI (100 Brigade) moved up Wood Lane for 60 yards without opposition.

III CORPS
1st Division

The 1st Northamptons (2 Brigade) repelled two enemy counter-attacks between 2 a.m. and 4 a.m., but retreated after a third at 8 a.m. Two companies of the Northamptons made two attempts to recapture Switch Line, the second with two companies of 2nd/Royal Sussex; both were unsuccessful. The 2nd KRRC were engaged all day but held their forward line.

II CORPS
48th Division

A bombing attack was made in the trench north-east of the Nab by 1/6th Gloucesters (144 Brigade) and continued until the following day, with no real result.

Monday 21 August

Temperature 72°F

XIV CORPS
35th Division

relieved 3rd Division. At 5 a.m. 35th Division made an unsuccessful attempt to seize the strongpoint opposite Arrow-head Copse. The French had occu-pied Angle Wood the previous night.

24th Division

In the morning, parties of 3rd Rifle Brigade and 8th Buffs occupied most of ZZ Trench leading to Guillemont. At 4.30 p.m. 35th Division discharged smoke to cover the flank of 24th Division. The 8th Queen's (72 Brigade) attacked the Quarry but were forced back in a bombing fight. One company each of 1st Royal Fusiliers and 3rd Rifle Brigade (17 Brigade) advanced south-east from the station but could not hold any gains because of losses received.

XV CORPS
14th Division

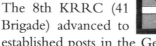

The 8th KRRC (41 Brigade) advanced to established posts in the German front line in Delville Wood. The advance was stopped by smallarms fire.

33rd Division

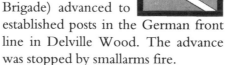

At midnight 1/9th Highland LI (100 Brig-ade) attacked the trench running from Wood Lane eastwards towards the Flers road, but was checked by machine-gun fire.

ANZAC
1st Australian Division

The Division attacked at 6 p.m. with 10th (S Australian) Battalion on the right thrusting into Fabeck Graben, but was forced by machine-gun fire to retire to a line south of Mouquet Farm-Courcelette Track. The 12th (S&W Aus and Tasm) Battalion met little opposition and got a party into Mouquet Farm, but they were forced to withdraw to the track. Bombers accounted for a strongpoint at the junction of Courcelette Track and OG1. Raiding parties of 11th Battalion started late and linked with the flank battalions.

II CORPS
48th Division

At 6 p.m., and from behind a barrage, 1/4th Gloucesters attacked the south-east face of the Leip-zig Salient from the Nab trenches. Little opposition was encountered and they joined 1/6th at the entrance to the Hindenburg Trench. On the left flank 1st Wiltshires (7 Brigade, 25th Division) increased their hold on the Leipzig Salient by taking Lem-burg Trench.

Early in the morning of the 22nd the Germans mounted four counter-attacks, but all were repulsed.

Tuesday 22 August

Temperature 72°F

XIV CORPS

24th Division was relieved by 20th Division.

Digging a communication trench through Delville Wood. (Q.4417)

35th Division took over Angle Wood from the French on the night of 22/23 August.

ANZAC
2nd Australian Division
6 Brigade took over the front. The centre was established on the Courcelette Track from OG1 to the south-east corner of Mouquet Farm.

II CORPS
48th Division
Early in the morning the Germans counter-attacked the forward posts of the 1/6th Gloucesters (144 Brigade), east of Hindenburg Trench, but were driven back by Stokes mortars. They tried again in the evening, but with no success. From 10 p.m. 1/4th Gloucesters received three counter-attacks, but threw them off with Lewis-gun fire.

Wednesday 23 August
Temperature 72°F

XIV CORPS
20th Division
At 9.15 p.m. a heavy German bombardment opened and, at 10.30 p.m., 11th KRRC (59 Brigade) were attacked south of the railway, but repulsed the attack with machine-gun fire. The barrage started again at 12.30 a.m. on the 24th.

ANZAC
2nd Australian Division relieved
1st Australian Division.

II CORPS
48th Division
In the afternoon two companies of the Bucks lost heavily in an attempt to advance along the eastern slope of Nab Valley.

Thursday 24 August
Temperature 78°F

XV CORPS
14th Division
The Division was set the task of clearing Delville Wood and attacked with 8th KRRC (41 Brigade) and 9th KRRC; 5th KSLI and 5th Ox and Bucks LI (42 Brigade) were on the right. The 8th KRRC were checked in front of Ale Alley. The other Battalions moved well through the Wood assisted by a creeping barrage. The 5th Ox and Bucks LI on the left—their flank rested on the Flers road—were in touch with 33rd Division.

33rd Division
The 2nd Worcesters, 16th KRRC and 1st Queen's (100 Brigade) from left to right, attacked the German front line

135th Siege Battery artificers attending to two of their 8in howitzers at La Houssoye, 25 August 1916. A stop-gap measure cobbled together from re-bored 6in guns spanning Mks 1 to 5 in undefined Marks. (Q.4147)

II CORPS
25th Division

While consolidating from the previous day's action under a German bombardment, it was observed that the German trenches were packed with troops. A barrage was called for and the impending counter-attack was prevented.

Saturday 26 August

Temperature 75°F; 7mm rain

XV CORPS
7th Division

22 Brigade relieved The Rifle Brigade of 14th Division.

III CORPS
1st Division

The Division continued its action on Intermediate Trench. The 1st South Wales Borderers (3 Brigade) bombed west as far as the Martinpuich road. (More progress was made next day with some help from the Munsters.)

ANZAC
2nd Australian Division

At 4.45 a.m. 5 Brigade on the right and 6 Brigade on the left facing Mouquet Farm, attacked. Bombers of 24th Battalion on the right were held up by machine-gun fire and bombs from Fabeck Graben, but on the left 21st Battalion and a company of 22nd Battalion, swept over Constance Trench and Courcelette Track to Zig Zag Trench. The absence of land-

---

between Wood Lane and the Flers road including Tea Trench. On the left, bombers of 1st Queen's pressed forward up Wood Lane and secured the trench junction.

III CORPS
1st Division

Another attempt was made to take Intermediate Trench, each end being attacked by a company of 2nd Royal Munster Fusiliers (3 Brigade). This was unsuccessful, being stopped by small-arms fire.

15th Division

At the same time, 6th Camerons (45 Brigade, 15th Division) made an unsuccessful bombing attempt to clear the trench along the Bazentin-le-Petit–Martinpuich road from the Switch Line.

The Switch Line was now in British hands as far east as the road.

II CORPS
25th Division

At 4.10 p.m. 1st Wiltshires and 3rd Worcesters (7 Brigade) captured the Hindenburg Trench under a smoke-screen. On the extreme left of the road to Thiepval, the Wiltshires' bombers were held up.

Friday 25 August

Temperature 81°F; overcast and cloudy (8mm rain)

XV CORPS
14th Division

Early in the day 9th Rifle Brigade (42 Brigade) cleared Edge Trench nearly as far as its junction with Ale Alley.

marks caused them to swerve right and, although taking a trench running to the Farm, they were forced to surrender. On the left a strongpoint at the junction of the Thiepval road and Mouquet Farm Track was won and lost. Nevertheless, a post was kept in the centre of Zig Zag Trench which repelled a counter-attack on it at 7.20 a.m. 6 Brigade was relieved that night by 4 Brigade (4th Australian Division).

II CORPS
25th Division

At 7 p.m. 8th Loyal North Lancs tried unsuccessfully to clear the western end of Hindenburg Trench.

Sunday 27 August

Temperature 73°F; 4mm rain

XV CORPS
14th Division

The 10th Durham LI (43 Brigade) drove the Germans out of Edge Trench and allowed a barricade to be placed in Ale Alley, leaving Delville Wood completely in British hands.

III CORPS

1st Division took over High Wood and the greater part of Wood Lane from 33rd Division.

ANZAC

The 14th (Victoria) Battalion (4th Australian Division) attempted to seize two strongpoints, one at the junction of the Thiepval road and Mouquet Farm Track and the other at Zig Zag Trench near the Farm. Both attempts were unsuccessful.

II CORPS
48th Division

The 1/8th Royal Warwicks (143 Brigade) assaulted part of Constance Trench on either side of Pole Trench at 7 p.m., but ran into their own barrage and so swerved to the flanks. Counter-attacks from Pole Trench and down Constance Trench

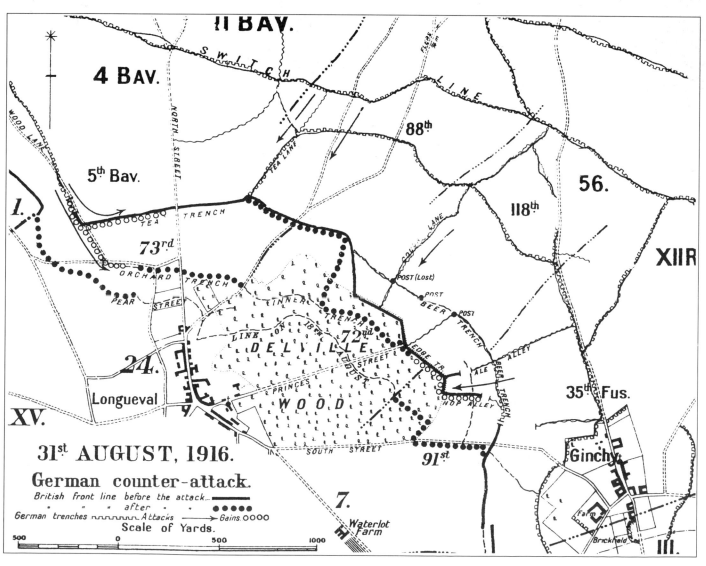

31st AUGUST, 1916.
German counter-attack.

British front line before the attack _____
"   "   "   after   "   •••••••
German trenches ⌐⌐⌐⌐⌐ Attacks ——→ Gains. 0000
Scale of Yards.

135th Siege Battery artificers attending to two of their 8in howitzers at La Houssoye, 25 August 1916. (Q.4148)

forced the Battalion to withdraw. Further west, 1/4th Royal Berks and 1/5th Gloucesters (145 Brigade) took the loop of the trenches south-west of Pole Trench.

Monday 28 August

Temperature 73°F; slight rain

XV CORPS
14th Division
In the evening, 10th Durham LI and 1st

Royal Welsh Fusiliers (2 Brigade) tried to clear Ale Alley as far east as Beer Trench, but were unsuccessful.

III CORPS
1st Division
On the night of 27/28th the Division had taken over the High Wood position and most of the line facing Wood Lane from 33rd Division.

15th Division took over the front of 3 Brigade (1st Division).

25th Division
At 4 p.m. 8th South Lancs (75 Brigade) made another

unsuccessful attempt on the left flank of the Hindenburg Trench, but they were defeated by machine-gun fire.

II CORPS
48th Division was relieved by 25th Division (III Corps).

Tuesday 29 August

Temperature 82°F; heavy rain

III CORPS
1st Division
The 1st Division made some progress up Wood Lane.

ANZAC
4th Australian Division
The 13th (NSW) and 16th (S&W Aus) Battalions (4 Brigade) made an unsuccessful attack on Fabeck Graben, Mouquet Farm and Zig Zag Trench. At 11 p.m. 13th Battalion on the right failed to gain a foot-hold, but the right of the 16th managed to enter the Fabeck Graben behind Mouquet Farm. A fierce fight ensued until the Australians withdrew.

Wednesday 30 August

Temperature 63°F; overcast and very wet (8mm rain)

III CORPS
15th Division
Posts established in the rear and on the flanks had cut off the Germans who were still holding on in Intermediate Trench. They surrendered in the afternoon.

Thursday 31 August

Temperature 70°F; fine

XV CORPS
24th Division relieved 14th and 33rd Divisions. A German counter-attack was launched against Delville Wood at 1 p.m., after a heavy bombardment. The 21st Manchesters (91 Brigade, 7th Division), holding the extreme right, were not involved.

24th Division
The 1st South Staffords (72 Brigade) were attacked by bombers from along Ale Alley and down towards Hop Alley. The first assault at 1 p.m. was repulsed and the second at 2 p.m. was likewise dealt with from the

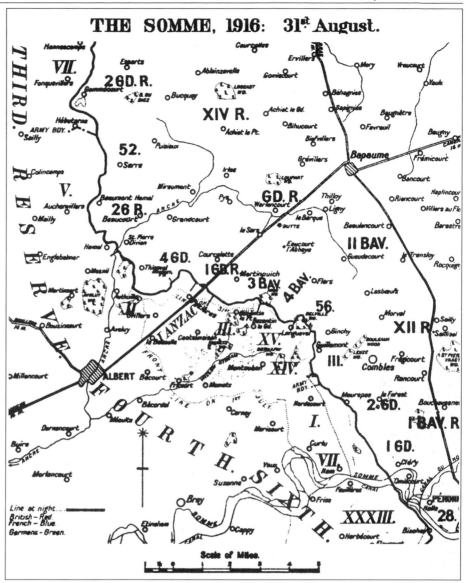

trench immediately east of the Wood. After an increase in bombardment, a third attack at 7 p.m. drove the South Staffords back into the Wood. A stand was made in Edge Trench, in touch with the right flank of 1st North Staffords. On the right, the Longueval–Ginchy road was held, and in the Wood a platoon of 2nd Queen's came up at night to reinforce the South Staffords.

The North Staffords had no frontal attacks to contend with and only relinquished a portion of Edge Trench. The 8th Royal West Kents pulled back to their right to Inner Trench because of the bombardment. An outpost in Cocoa Lane was lost. The 9th Royal Sussex (73 Brigade) held the Germans, who attacked at 1 p.m., with rifle and machine-gun fire. Further west, 13th Middlesex (73 Brigade) were advanced on by the Germans from the barricade in Wood Lane and were forced back along Tea Trench nearly as far as North Street. Another enemy detachment went into Orchard Trench, but was contained there by 2nd Leinsters (73 Brigade), brought up from support. Fire from 1st Division's right flank also helped to check the advance.

1st Canadian Division
1 Canadian Brigade took over the right sector of the ANZAC front.

The road leading to Guillemont, 10
September 1916. (Q.1163)

SEPTEMBER

Friday 1 September

Temperature 72°F

XV CORPS
24th Division

Just after dawn 2nd Leinsters (73 Brigade) tried bombing along Orchard Trench, but were thrown back. At 9.50 a.m. they made another attempt along Pear Street. In the afternoon 3rd Rifle Brigade (17 Brigade) were brought up and by 6.30 p.m. the Germans had been cleared out of Orchard Trench and Wood Lane was secured. At 3 p.m. 1st North Staffords, on the right of the Division, bombed forward along some 20 yards of Edge Trench.

7th Division

At 5 a.m. 91 Brigade on the east of Delville Wood had sent bombers of 2nd Queen's to bomb along the edge as far as Hop Alley, but they were stopped by machine-gun fire.

Saturday 2 September

Temperature 73°F; windy

XV CORPS
24th Division

At noon 2nd Queen's tried to bomb down Edge Trench and a little ground was gained among the shell craters. The preliminary bombardment started on the fronts of XIV and XV Corps at 8 a.m.

Sunday 3 September

Temperature 72°; 4mm rain

BATTLE OF GUILLEMONT
(3–6 September)

XIV CORPS
5th Division

13 Brigade was in an assembly trench at 8.50 a.m. The 2nd KOSB attacked the right on Point 48 and the left on Falfemont Farm. The French 127th Regiment in the Ravine were pinned down by machine-gun fire. The KOSB failed, with nearly 300 casualties.

At noon 12th Gloucesters on the right and 1st Duke of Cornwall's LI (95 Brigade) on the left, attacked south of Guillemont. The Gloucesters came under enfilade fire from Falfemont Farm and carried the German Front Line. At 12.50 p.m. the advance continued and captured the German second line from Wedge Wood to the south–east edge of Guillemont. Also at noon 13 Brigade made another attack using 14th and 15th Royal Warwicks. The 14th Warwicks managed to get a footing in the loop of the trench south of Wedge Wood. At 2.50 p.m. 95 Brigade advanced to the Wedge Wood–Ginchy road. The Gloucesters and Duke of Cornwall's LI then consolidated in touch with 20th Division. 13

Wrecked wagons at Guillemont railway station, September 1916. (Q.1170)

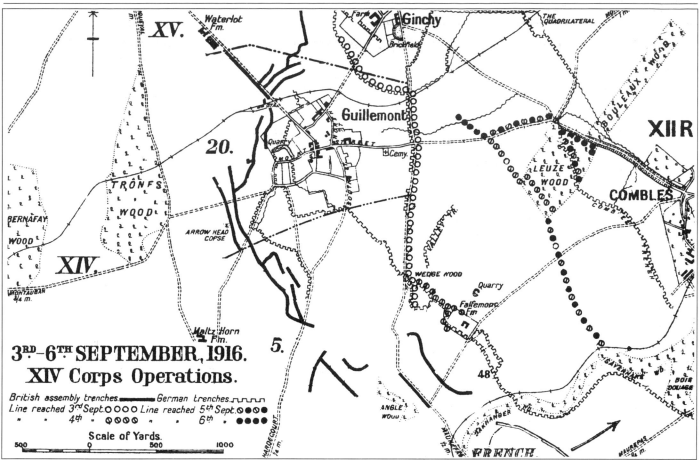

3ᴿᴰ-6ᵀᴴ SEPTEMBER, 1916.
XIV Corps Operations.

British assembly trenches ━━━ German trenches ⌐⌐⌐⌐
Line reached 3ʳᵈ Sept. ○○○○ Line reached 5ᵗʰ Sept. ●●●
   „   „   4ᵗʰ „ ◑◑◑◑   „   „   6ᵗʰ „ ●●●●

Scale of Yards.

Brigade was replaced by 15 Brigade and a further attack was made on the Falfemont Farm – Wood line. The Wedge Wood was taken by 1st Bedfords, but 1st Cheshires, supported by 16th Warwicks, failed because of machine-guns which the French had not cleared.

20th Division

59 Brigade, attacking the southern end of Guillemont, was reinforced by 6th Ox and Bucks LI (60 Brigade) and 7th Somerset LI (61 Brigade). 47 Brigade (16th Division) was brought up from the Corps Reserve for the attack.

On the extreme left, 10th KRRC (59 Brigade) moved forward before zero hour close to the British barrage and was able to surprise the Germans. The 6th Connaught Rangers (47 Brigade) did the same on the northern side of Mount Street.

Zero hour was at noon and the rest of 59 Brigade (11th and 10th Rifle Brigade and 10th KRRC) reached their objective, the Hardecourt road, in twenty minutes and moved off northward to Mount Street, leaving 10th KRRC to mop-up. The Connaughts on their left moved on without clearing the Quarry. On the left flank, 7th Leinsters (47 Brigade) cleared all before them.

The attack on the second objective was met with heavy artillery and machine-gun fire. By 1.15 p.m. the troops were consolidating ground near North Street and South Street. At 2.50 p.m. the assault continued on the line of the Wedge Wood–Ginchy road. By 3.30 p.m. the position had been taken and 59 Brigade ordered 7th Duke of Cornwall's LI into Guillemont to help with the consolidation. At 5.30 p.m. and 6.30 p.m. counter-attacks were repelled by Lewis-gun fire.

XV CORPS
7th Division

During the night of 2/3 September, 22 Brigade relieved 91 Brigade south of, and on, the Longueval–Ginchy road. At 11.55 a.m., after an hour's bombardment, bombers of 91 Brigade attacked up the south-eastern edge of Delville Wood towards Hop Alley. The 9th East Surreys (24th Division) tried to assault from the sap north of Ale Alley, but both attacks were unsuccessful. At noon, 20th Manchesters (22 Brigade) and 1st Royal Welsh Fusiliers advanced; the Manchesters entering the southern portion of the village. The Fusiliers were enfiladed by fire from Ale Alley and checked. An attempt to take Hop Alley and Beer Trench across the open, resulted in parties establishing a post in shell-holes forty yards south of Hop Alley, and the southern portion of Beer Trench was taken. The right

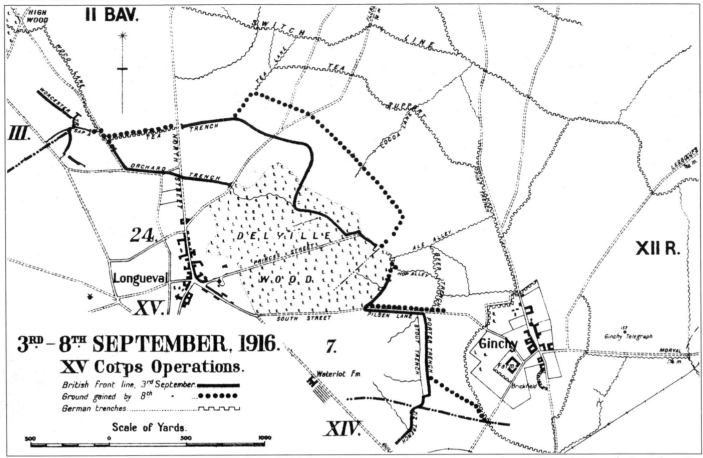

II BAV.

HIGH WOOD

III.

24.

Longueval

XV.

3RD – 8TH SEPTEMBER, 1916.
XV Corps Operations.

British front line, 3rd September. ————
Ground gained by 8th · •••••••
German trenches .... ⊓⊔⊓⊔

Scale of Yards.

500   0   500   1000

DELVILLE WOOD

PRINCES STREET

SOUTH STREET

PILSEN LANE

7.

Waterlot Fm.

XIV.

XII R.

Ginchy Telegraph

Ginchy Farm

Brickfield

MORVAL

company got into the northern part of Ginchy and were never heard of again. The 2nd Royal Warwicks were in support during this action.

The 20th Manchesters had reached the far side of Ginchy and begun to consolidate the east and south-eastern edges, but a counter-attack from the north of the village forced them back towards Porter Trench. Two companies of Warwicks were involved; one party held on near the sunken section of the road, mainly with Lewis-gun fire. A strong counter-attack took place in the afternoon. At 5 p.m. 2nd Royal Irish were ordered to re-occupy the village, starting at Pilsen Lane. Two attempts were made from Pilsen Lane to attack Hop Alley but these were unsuccessful and on the right flank they joined parties of Manchesters and Warwicks in Stout and Porter Trenches. That evening 20 Brigade relieved 22 Brigade and 21st Manchesters (detached

from 91 Brigade) were to take over in Delville Wood.

24th Division

At noon a company of 8th Buffs (17 Brigade) advanced southwards in a frontal attack from Worcester Trench, while a party of bombers worked forward from Sap A on the right. These were checked by a strongpoint at the junction of Wood Lane and Tea Trench. Another attempt was made at 4 p.m. with the same result.

During the night 7th Northants (on loan from 73 Brigade to 17 Brigade) occupied the near end of Tea Lane.

III CORPS
1st Division

At noon 1st Camerons attacked Wood Lane with a detachment of 8th Royal

Berks (1 Brigade) on their right. On the extreme right, next to the Buffs of 24th Division, no progress was made but on the left the attack was successful and they continued for another 100 yards and then consolidated. The 1st Black Watch (1 Brigade) attacked the German front line in High Wood with the aid of blazing oil drums and flame-throwers. A mine containing 3,000 pounds of ammonal was exploded 30 seconds before the attack under the strongpoint in the eastern corner of the Wood. The crater was seized by the right company of the Black Watch and consolidated with 23rd Field

Right, top: Hauling a 156th Siege Battery, RGA 8in Howitzer into position, Longueval, September 1916. This was a Mk 6 howitzer which fired a 200lb shell to a distance of 10,500 yards. (Q.1374)
Right, bottom: Australian troops in a sunken road near Contalmaison, September 1916. (Q.945)

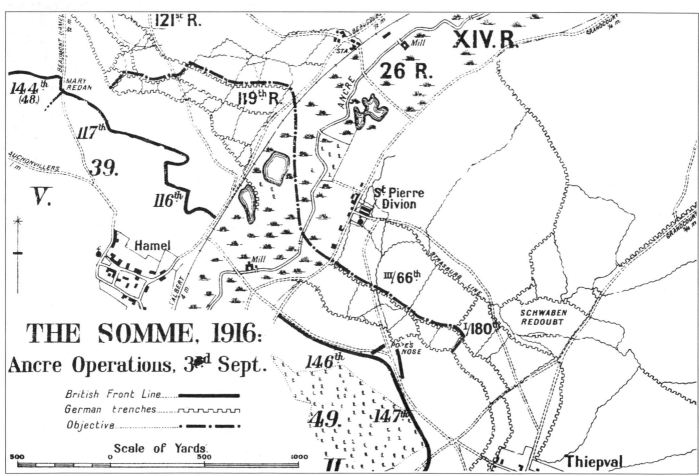

THE SOMME, 1916:
Ancre Operations, 3rd Sept.

British Front Line _____
German trenches _____
Objective _____

Scale of Yards.

Company, RE; some bombers of the Black Watch worked westwards, the remainder of the Black Watch were caught by machine-gun fire. At 3 p.m. a determined counter-attack from the Switch Line forced the British back to their start-line, including the men at the crater.

At 6 p.m. 2nd Welsh (3 Brigade) advanced to the centre of the Wood; the right company achieved their objective, the left was checked by fire. Further left, 1st Gloucesters (31 Brigade) attacked the south-western face of the Wood and eventually captured their objective. Two companies of

Left: A dead British soldier in a trench near Guillemont, September 1916. The breech cover of his Lee Enfield is still in place. (Q.3964)
Below: Men of 2nd Australian Division at lunch near Beaucourt Wood, September 1916. The officer on the left is wearing the gorget of a staff officer. (Q.922)

9th Black Watch (44 Brigade, 15th Division) entered the western corner of the Wood and repelled a counter-attack with Lewis-gun fire. Another counter-attack was repulsed at 8 p.m. and then all withdrew bar an isolated company of the Welsh, who hung on until 4 a.m.

ANZAC
4th Australian Division

The Division made another attempt to capture Fabeck Graben westward from Courcelette Track and Mouquet Farm. 13th Australian Brigade: 49th (Queensland), 52nd (SW Aus and Tasm) and 51st (WA) Battalions advanced at 5.10 a.m. On the right 49th Battalion captured Fabeck Graben. The centre attacked, and a heavy barrage and counter-attack drove back 52nd Battalion and enveloped a company of 51st Battalion who had taken Mouquet Farm;

eventually they were captured and the Farm was lost. 50th Battalion (Brigade Reserve) had now to safe-guard the left of 49th Division which still held 300 yards of Fabeck Graben.

In the afternoon 13th Canadians arrived and more came next day. The Germans were then forced back with bombs and a barricade was erected on the right. The left of Fabeck Graben was linked to the OG lines (now in Australian hands).

II CORPS
25th Division

The Division was to attack at 5.10 a.m. from Hindenburg Trench to the south of the Wonder Work: 75 Brigade deployed two companies of 3rd Worcesters (attached from 7 Brigade) in the centre, two companies of 2nd South Lancs on the right, and 1st

with 4/5th Black Watch (188 Brigade) in the Ancre Valley. At 5.10 a.m. the advance began after an intense barrage. In 116 Brigade both battalions had secured the front line, meeting little opposition. In the valley, the Black Watch could do little more than support the right of 11th Royal Sussex because of machine-gun fire. The 16th Rifle Brigade on the right of 177 Brigade lost direction and a few men entered the German trench. The position was tenuous and by nightfall all units had returned to the British lines. On the extreme left, 17th Sherwood Foresters were held up by machine-gun fire.

Monday 4 September

Temperature 66°F; showery all day (25mm rain)

XIV CORPS
20th Division

59 Brigade sent 1st East Surreys to occupy Valley Trench. Two companies of 1st Devons pushed through and reached the edge of Leuze Wood at 7.30 p.m. They waited for the British barrage to lift then entered the Wood and consolidated. On the right 7th Somerset LI established a post on the western corner of the Wood northwards to the Ginchy road. 59 Brigade was relieved by two battalions of 49 Brigade (16th Division).

5th Division

The 1st Norfolks (15 Brigade), in touch with the French on the right, left their trenches to attack Falfemont Farm at 3.05 p.m. but were checked

---

Wiltshires (7 Brigade) on the left. All managed to enter the German front line; however, they were unable to consolidate and were forced to withdraw.

49th Division

The Division attacked at 5.13 a.m. from its assembly trench along the Thiepval–Hamel road after a field gun barrage on the near face of the Schwaben Redoubt, and a bombardment of gas and ammonal bombs on Thiepval by Special Brigade, R.E. On the right, 1/4th and 1/5th Duke's (147 Brigade) took the German front line trench and support line. There was a loss of direction by 1/5th Duke's and they failed to take the salient called the Pope's Nose. A counter-attack by German bombers

was made from the Strasburg Line, under cover of machine-gun fire from Schwaben Redoubt.

On the left, 146 Brigade were enfiladed by fire from the Pope's Nose and failed to gain entry into the German front line trench. A few men of 1/8th West Yorks (next to the river) reached the support line, but began to drift back and by 7.30 a.m. the whole of 146 Brigade had returned to the British line. By 10 a.m. 147 Brigade were back, too.

V CORPS
39th Division

Beyond the river, on the right, were 11th Royal Sussex and 14th Hampshires (166 Brigade), and on the left 16th Rifle Brigade and 17th Sherwood Foresters (117 Brigade), by machine-gun fire from Combles Ravine. A few troops entered the farm but were bombed out. On the left a company of 1st Cheshires worked their way round under the shelter of the spur.

Meanwhile 1st Bedfords, starting from Wedge Wood, bombed south-eastwards along the German trench. By 4 p.m. the northern and western corners of Falfemont Farm had been taken. The Norfolks were reinforced by 16th Royal Warwicks and made another attempt to storm the Farm at 5.30 p.m., but again they were unsuccessful.

XV CORPS
7th Division

The 9th Devons (20 Brigade) attacked Ginchy at 8 a.m., but were forced to retire to Stout, Porter and ZZ Trenches soon after 9 a.m.

The 21st Manchesters in Delville Wood attacked eastwards with two companies at 2 p.m. The attack failed between Ale Alley and Hop Alley. Another company attack northwards from Pilsen Lane to Hop Alley also failed.

During the night part of 2nd Border Regt (20 Brigade) relieved the troops on the left flank of 20th Division, in the area of XV Corps.

55th Division

165 Brigade relieved 17 Brigade in the left sector of 24th Division's front.

Tuesday 5 September

Temperature 63°F; overcast all day

XIV CORPS
5th Division

By 3 a.m. the Norfolks had occupied Falfemont Farm. They then sent out

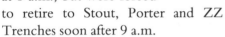

patrols towards Point 48. By 7.30 a.m. the whole objective was cleared.

At 8.30 a.m. two companies of 16th Royal Warwicks (15 Brigade) were sent to establish a line down the slope of the ravine, linking up with 95 Brigade in Leuze Wood. 15 Brigade called upon 7th Royal Irish Fusiliers (49 Brigade) to relieve the Warwicks and attack Combles Trench at 4 p.m. They were stopped by wire hidden in the standing corn, tall weeds and machine-gun fire, as was another attempt at 7.30 p.m.

On the other flank, the Devons (95 Brigade) advanced at 4 p.m. and occupied the German trench in Leuze Wood.

That night 56th Division began to relieve 5th Division.

Sorting the packs of dead and wounded for letters and personal effects to send home. Horse-drawn and Ford Model T ambulances in the background. South of Guillemont, September 1916. (Q.4245)

Men resting in a shell-hole at Waterlot Farm (a stronghold near Ginchy on the Guillemont Road seized on 15 July 1916), September 1916. (Q.4260)

20th Division

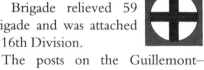

49 Brigade relieved 59 Brigade and was attached to 16th Division.

The posts on the Guillemont–Leuze Wood road were converted to a continuous trench. That evening 7th Royal Irish Fusiliers linked up with 5th Division at the north end of Leuze Wood. 48 Brigade relieved 60 Brigade.

XV CORPS
7th Division

At 5.30 p.m. 2nd Queen's (91 Brigade) attacked the eastern edge of Delville Wood after a 2-hour trench mortar bombardment, and cleared the edge as far as Hop Alley, consolidating with the support of 8th Devons from the right.

24th Division

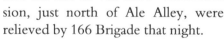

72 Brigade, on the right between the Flers road and the left of 7th Division, just north of Ale Alley, were relieved by 166 Brigade that night.

Wednesday 6 September

Temperature 70°F; overcast

XIV CORPS

By 3 a.m. the Kensingtons (168 Brigade, 56th Division) had relieved 7th Royal Irish Fusiliers (attached to 15 Brigade). The Kensingtons entered Leuze Wood that night, but were disorganized by a counter-attack and nothing came of it. During the night of 5/6 September 8th Royal Irish Fusiliers (49 Brigade) relieved the Devons on 95 Brigade's front.

In the morning they advanced across the Combles–Ginchy road, entering Bouleaux Wood on the right. That night 168 Brigade (56th Division) began to take over 5th Division. At 7.30 p.m., when the London Scottish were about to relieve the Royal Irish Fusiliers, a counter-attack was reported and the Fusiliers withdrew across the road. But the trench in Leuze Wood held, and by 10.30 p.m. the London Scottish had repulsed the Germans.

16th Division

Patrols sent out from the left of the Division suffered heavily from fire from the Quadrilateral. Fighting continued in Ginchy with the left of 48 Brigade under continuous shellfire. 49 and 48 Brigades were ordered to advance their inner flanks across the spur south-east of the railway.

XV CORPS
7th Division

The 2nd Gordons, with 9th Devons in support, attacked at 5.30 a.m. The Gordons could not take Ginchy because of machine-gun fire, but the Devons had captured and held Pilsen Lane to support their left flank. At 2 p.m. the Gordons attacked again with two companies of Devons coming in from the right in the direction of the Guillemont–Ginchy road. Parties got into the village but at 4.30 p.m. were subjected to a counter-attack and compelled to withdraw to the British front line.

55th Division

At 7p.m. 1/6th King's made bombing attacks along Wood Lane, but with little success. The 1/7th King's, however, made headway along Tea Trench.

Thursday 7 September

Temperature 70°F; fine, clear day

XV CORPS
55th Division

The 1/5th South Lancs and 1/10th King's, coming up from reserve, dug and occupied a new forward line.

7th Division

At 4 p.m. 2nd Queen's made an unsuccessful attack on the eastern corner of Delville Wood under a barrage of

rifle grenades. During the night the relief of 7th Division by 55th and 16th Divisions began. 164 Brigade relieved the left of 7th Division.

XIII CORPS
2nd Division

The 1/5th King's encountered no opposition in Wood Lane and occupied the eastern end well beyond the Tea Trench junction.

II CORPS

25th Division was relieved by 11th Division.

Friday 8 September

Temperature 70°F; warm, but overcast until early afternoon

The Germans counter-attacked Fabeck Graben and recaptured it after several attempts. Over the next few days, various counter-attacks were defeated.

XIV CORPS
56th Division

The Division relieved the right of 168 Brigade, The London Rifle Brigade occupying trenches south of Leuze Wood in touch with the French in Combles Ravine. 169 Brigade attempted to bomb down the Combles Trench from Leuze Wood, with some success. At 5.15 a.m./p.m., however, a counter-attack by bombers forced them to withdraw.

16th Division

The Division abandoned the forward trench dug by 8th Inniskilling Fusiliers and held the front with 47 and 48 Brigades.

XV CORPS
55th Division

At 1.20 a.m. a German counter-attack proved unsuccessful (being beaten back by Lewis-gun fire) on Wood Lane – Tea Trench. The 1/5th and 1/9th King's joined at Tea Trench and patrols were sent up North Street and the Flers road, meeting no hindrance.

III CORPS
1st Division

At 6 p.m. an attack on the western half of High Wood began. The 2nd Welsh (3 Brigade), right company, achieved their objective, but the left were held up. The 1st Gloucesters (3 Brigade) attacked the south-western face of the Wood and eventually achieved their objective. The 9th Black Watch (44 Brigade, 15th Division) came in on the left and took the German trench beyond the west corner of the Wood. Two counter-attacks were repulsed and a general withdrawal was ordered and completed by midnight; the Welsh coming back after 4 a.m.

Saturday 9 September

Temperature 75°F; 5mm rain

BATTLE OF GINCHY

XIV CORPS
56th Division

169 Brigade were to establish a defensive flank along the slopes of the Combles Ravine (the French had done the same on the opposite side). At 4.45 p.m. The London Rifle Brigade, reinforced by part of 1/2nd London, advanced from the south-eastern edge of Leuze Wood against Loop Trench,

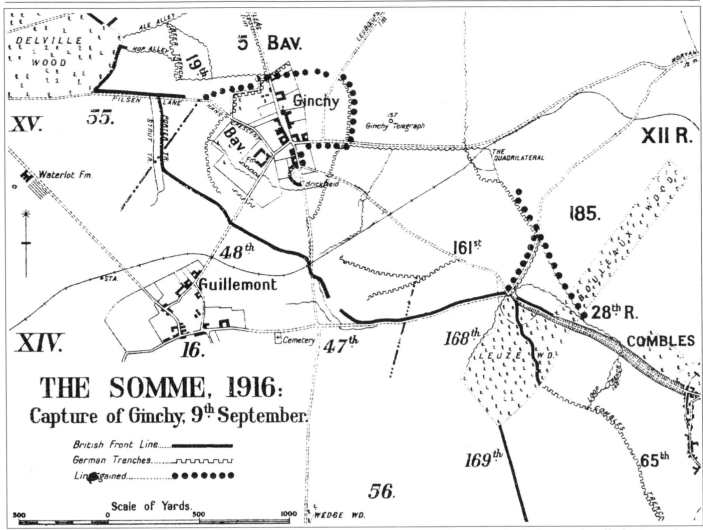

THE SOMME, 1916:
Capture of Ginchy, 9th September

British Front Line .... ▬▬▬▬
German Trenches .... ⌐⌐⌐⌐⌐⌐
Line gained .... ●●●●●●

Scale of Yards.
500   0   500   1000

but were forced back by machine-gun and artillery fire. The 1/16th (Queen's Westminster Rifles) were also sent up, and they arrived at 11 p.m. Meanwhile, by 6.15 p.m. the 1/9th London had captured the German main line in Bouleaux Wood and north-west as far as the Morval road.

168 Brigade was to move north-east, pivoting on their right to attack Leuze Wood–Quadrilateral Line. On the right, 1/4th London (Royal Fusiliers) took their objective. The 1/12th London (Rangers) were held up by machine-gun fire, and only the right company reached the first objective, Leuze Wood–Ginchy road. The Fusiliers, missing the barrage, captured the German trench south-east of the Quadrilateral.

16th Division

The Division also had trouble on the left. The right of the Rangers advanced on the Quadrilateral, lost direction and came up behind the centre of the Fusiliers. During the night the London Scottish were called to link up between the Quadrilateral and Ginchy.

On the right, 6th Royal Irish Regiment and 8th Royal Munster Fusiliers (47 Brigade), with a detachment of 6th Connaught Rangers in support, were held up by machine-gun fire at 4.47 p.m. 48 Brigade wheeled right, routed some Germans and pressed on.

Beyond the Guillemont road 7th Royal Irish Rifles and 7th Royal Irish Fusiliers (attached from 49 Brigade)

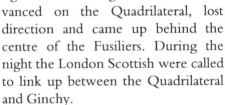

reached the road called Hans Crescent at 5 p.m. At 5.25 p.m. 8th Royal Dublin Fusiliers passed through the village, the Royal Irish Fusiliers (49 Brigade) coming in on the right. Meanwhile 9th Royal Dublin Fusiliers with men of 7th Royal Irish Rifles and 7th Royal Irish Fusiliers cleared the western part of Ginchy. The Germans made several attempts to recapture the village, all of which were unsuccessful.

Guards Division

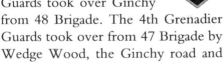

On the night of 9/10 September 1st Welsh Guards took over Ginchy from 48 Brigade. The 4th Grenadier Guards took over from 47 Brigade by Wedge Wood, the Ginchy road and Leuze Wood.

III CORPS
1st Division
The Division was to try to clear High Wood. The 2nd KRRC and 2nd Royal Sussex (2 Brigade) took Wood Lane. On the right The Rifles linked with 165 Brigade (55th Division, XV Corps). The 1/5th and 1/6th King's secured the lower end of Wood Lane by bombing forward from Orchard Trench. The Sussex on the left had to dig a defensive flank to connect with the line in High Wood where the attack failed.

In the Wood, 1st Northants (2 Brigade) and 3rd Royal Munster Fusiliers were to attack. The Northamptons occupied a new mine crater, blown 30 seconds before zero hour, but were bombed out of it 90 minutes later. The Munsters could make no headway, and neither could 10th Gloucesters (1 Brigade) advancing on the western face.

CANADIAN CORPS
1st Canadian Division
At 4.45 p.m. 2nd Canadian Battalion (1 Brigade) attacked the German front line trench astride the railway leading to Martinpuich. They took 500 yards and held through several counter-attacks, then linked with 15th Division (III Corps).

Sunday 10 September

Temperature 68°F; overcast (1mm rain)

XIV CORPS
56th Division
Various attempts to gain ground were made by 1/16th London attacking south-east from Leuze Wood at 7 a.m., but the machine-guns in Loop Trench and along the sunken Combles road halted them. At 3 p.m. one company of 1/2nd London advanced 100 yards

after a Stokes mortar bombardment, but was driven back. Likewise the attempt to bomb up to the Quadrilateral also failed. That night 169 Brigade was replaced by a composite brigade from 5th Division; 168 Brigade relieved 167 Brigade.

During the night the London Scottish were called to link up between the Quadrilateral and Ginchy, and advanced at 12.15 a.m. They lost their way, however, and scattered.

Guards Division
The Division took over from 16th Division and were forced to fight off a number of counter-attacks while attempting to re-take Ginchy.

XV CORPS
55th Division
164 Brigade was unable to secure Hop Alley and Ale Alley. A frontal attack from Pilsen Lane resulted in some troops entering Hop Alley but they were shelled and machine-gunned out of it.

Monday 11 September

Temperature 66°F; overcast (rain-trace)

XIV CORPS
Guards Division
3 Guards Brigade was relieved by 1st Grenadier and 2nd Scots Guards.

Tuesday 12 September

Temperature 72°F; fine but dull

XIV CORPS
Guards Division
At 6 a.m. 1st Grenadier Guards made ground towards Ginchy Telegraph*

astride the Morval road. The 1/8th Middlesex (167 Brigade) did likewise south-east of the Quadrilateral. 6th Division relieved the left of 56th Division and right of the Guards.

Wednesday 13 September

Temperature 72°F; overcast

XIV CORPS
6th Division relieved part of 56th Division from Leuze Wood to the outskirts of Ginchy. 71 Brigade attacked the Quadrilateral from the south-west, capturing the Leuze Wood–Ginchy road, but were then held up by machine-gun fire. At 6 p.m. another attempt was made, but was not successful. The 9th Suffolks and 2nd Sherwood Foresters lost 521 men in this action.

Guards Division
On the northern edge of Ginchy, 2nd Grenadier Guards (1 Guards Brigade) advanced and straightened the line. After dark, a company of 2nd Irish Guards (2 Guards Brigade) tried to take some machine-gun posts on the Ginchy–Morval road.

Thursday 14 September

Temperature 61°F; windy and cold

XIV CORPS
56th Division
The 1/2nd London dug assembly trenches south of Leuze Wood, parallel with Combles Trench.

*Ginchy Telegraph was the site of an old semaphore station, a relic of the Revolutionary Wars, on the highest point east of the village. It no longer existed, although it was shown on maps and mentioned in operational orders.

II CORPS

CAPTURE OF THE WONDER WORK

11th Division

Advancing from Hindenburg Trench at 6.30 p.m., two companies of 9th West Yorks and two companies of 8th Duke of Yorks carried the German front line and then the Wonder Work, and 250 yards of Hohenzollern Trench on the right and the trench on the left as far as the Thiepval road. Beyond the road a detachment of 6th Green Howards secured the left flank.

Friday 15 September

Temperature 59°F

BATTLE OF FLERS-COURCELETTE (15–22 September)

XIV CORPS

56th Division

169 Brigade advanced from the assembly trench south of Leuze Wood to secure Loop Trench and to keep in touch with the French on the railway track at the bottom of the ravine. A tank starting from the corner of Leuze Wood was in support. At 6.20 a.m. two companies of 1/2nd London occupied Loop Trench. The tank lent great assistance and Combles Trench was taken, but machine-gun fire stopped the attack on Loop Trench. In the afternoon bombing attacks were made up Loop Trench and down Combles Trench. Bombers from London Rifle Brigade were sent up. The tank was hit in the vicinity of the Loop, but kept its machine-guns firing for five hours, holding the Germans at bay. Under cover of

darkness Combles Trench was barricaded, but they were still 80 yards from the sunken road upon which, at 11 p.m., a last unsuccessful attack was made.

167 Brigade: Although two tanks were to assist in the attack, one lost a track. The other, at the western corner of Bouleaux Wood, moved to Middle Copse some twenty minutes before the attack. The 1/1st London attacked at 6.20 a.m. and were held up by the wire and machine-gun fire. They eventually reached the German line, penetrating as far as Middle Copse. In the meantime the tank had proceeded as far as Bouleaux Wood.

At 8.20 a.m. two companies of 1/7th Middlesex (167 Brigade) were sent to take Bouleaux Wood but were forced back to 1/1st Londons' position. A second effort was made and the survivors reinforced the Londoners in the captured line. At 1.40 p.m. 1/8th Middlesex took over the attack but were forced back to Leuze Wood. In the evening 1/1st London and 1/7th Middlesex pushed north and occupied Middle Copse.

6th Division

Three tanks were allotted but only one reached the start-line at the crossroads east of Guillemont. It moved along the railway line towards the Quadrilateral and, as it passed through 9th Norfolks, it opened fire on its own men until corrected. At 5.50 a.m. the tank moved off northwards and parallel with Straight Trench, only to return later.

At 6.20 a.m. 8th Bedfords (16 Brigade) moved north-east upon the Quadrilateral, but were stopped by machine-gun fire. Likewise 1st Buffs, who advanced at 6.35 a.m. from the head of the valley near the Leuze Wood–Ginchy road. On the right, bombers from 8th Bedfords were

held up in a trench south-west of the Quadrilateral. The 9th Norfolks and 1st Leicesters (71 Brigade) advanced against Straight Trench through the Suffolks and Foresters, but met uncut wire and machine-gun fire, forcing them to take shelter in shell-holes. The survivors took cover. At 8.20 a.m. 9th Suffolks and 1st Sherwood Foresters (71 Brigade) suffered the same fate.

Guards Division

Ten tanks were scheduled to take part. Five made the starting-places. On the right flank, one was unserviceable and one lost direction. On the left flank, the two that started late lost direction, a third ditched and a fourth returned low on petrol.

At 6.20 a.m., under a creeping barrage, 2nd Guards Brigade attacked the Triangle and Serpentine, and by 7.15 a.m. they had reached their objectives. 1 Guards Brigade also reached theirs at about the same time, suffering heavy machine-gun fire from the junction of Pint Trench and the sunken section of the Flers road. On the right 2 Guards Brigade were forced to form a defensive flank and bombers were sent to clear the Triangle, and this was successful. At about noon a mixed company of men pushed on to a point in front of the third objective, south of the sunken Lesboeufs–Ginchy road.

The 2nd Grenadier Guards (1 Guards Brigade) emerged from Ginchy at 7.30 a.m. in support. They came under fire from an unoccupied part of Serpentine Trench. They obtained a foot-hold and bombed outwards, joining the two Brigades there by capturing the first objective of the Division.

The 2nd and 3rd Coldstream Guards (1 Guards Brigade) pushed on to their second objective and by 11.15 a.m. some of it had been taken.

At 3.20 p.m. a battalion of 3 Guards Brigade was sent to each of the attacking Brigades. At 5 p.m. 4th Grenadier Guards moved up and one company reinforced the 2 Guards Brigade at the Triangle. At 5.30 p.m. 2nd Scots Guards were sent up in support.

XV CORPS
14th Division

Two companies of 6th KOYLI (43 Brigade) and three tanks were detailed to expel a pocket of Germans to the east of Delville Wood before zero hour. At 5.15 a.m. only one tank (D1) was operational but it started forward from Pilsen Lane, followed fifteen minutes later by KOYLI's bombers.

The tank was immobilized by a shell. The KOYLI came under machine-gun fire on the rear of their right flank. This was settled by bomb and bayonet.

At 6.20 a.m. one tank (D3) made for Cocoa Lane. (One was ditched in Delville Wood and another, D5, was late.) The 8th Rifle Brigade and 8th KRRC (41 Brigade) suffered losses from machine-gun fire from Pint Trench and Tea Support and at one stage ran into their own barrage, but went on to capture Switch Line at 7 a.m. (tank D3 was knocked out at Tea Support) and the position was consolidated.

At 6.30 a.m. the rear battalions of the Brigade advanced: the KRRC from Delville Wood and 7th Rifle

Ford Model T ambulances at 56th Divisional Field Ambulance Dressing Station near Guillemont, 15 September 1916. The vehicle furthest to the right bears the 56th (London) Divisional sign. (Q.1265)

Brigade over the open ground to the east of the Wood to the Switch Line. The KOYLI kept pace with the advance and aligned with the Guards, but 8th KRRC were not in touch, so formed a defensive flank. At 8 a.m. The Rifle Brigade occupied Gap Trench (the second objective) as did 7th KRRC.

At zero hour, 42 Brigade advanced from the rear slopes of Caterpillar Valley, 3,000 yards away. At 9 a.m. they passed over Gap Trench and, after coming under machine-gun fire

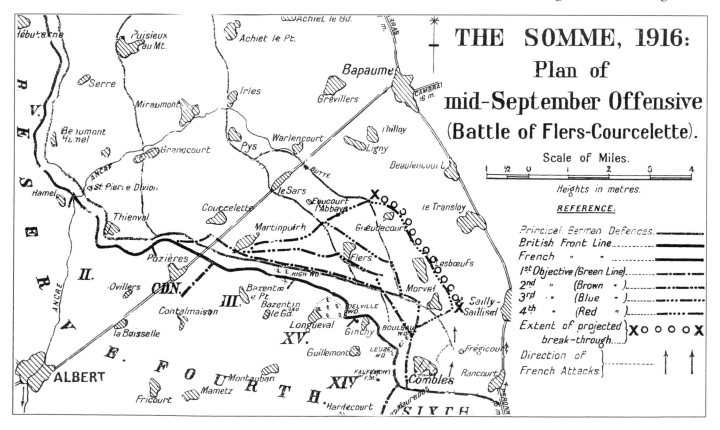

THE SOMME, 1916: Plan of mid-September Offensive (Battle of Flers-Courcelette).

Left: Battle of Flers–Courcelette. Men of 2nd Auckland Battalion (New Zealand) in a switch trench, near Flers, 15 September 1916. (Q.194)
Below left: Four Mk 1 tanks refuelling at Chimpanzee Valley near Trônes Wood, 15 September 1916. Tanks first went into action on this day. (Q.5576)

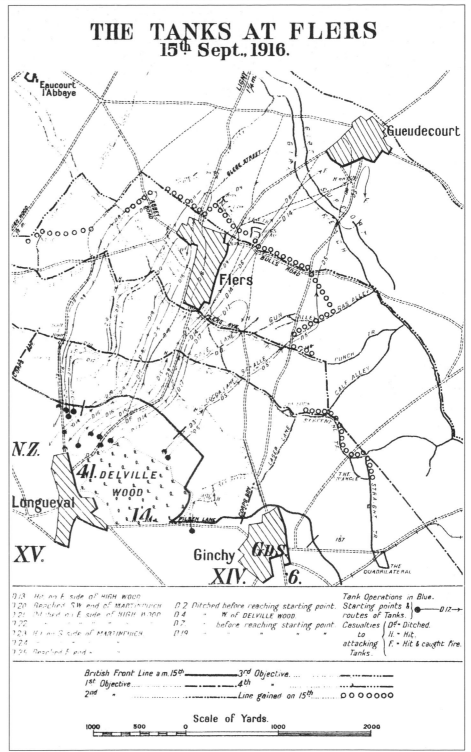

THE TANKS AT FLERS
15th Sept., 1916.

D.13 Hit on E side of HIGH WOOD
D.20 Reached S.W. end of MARTINPUICH
D.21 Ditched on E side of HIGH WOOD
D.22
D.23 Hit on S side of MARTINPUICH
D.24   "
D.25 Reached E end

D.2 Ditched before reaching starting point.
D.4   "   W of DELVILLE WOOD
D.7   "   before reaching starting point.
D.19   "   "   "   "

Tank Operations in Blue.
Starting points & routes of Tanks.
Casualties { Dd - Ditched.
to   H. - Hit.
attacking   F. - Hit & caught fire.
Tanks.

British Front Line a.m. 15th _____   3rd Objective ....
1st Objective ....   4th _____
2nd _____   Line gained on 15th .... o o o o o o o

Scale of Yards.
1000   500   0   1000   2000

as they approached Bulls Road (Flers–Lesboufs road), 9th Rifle Brigade were stopped just short of the road. Likewise 5th King's Shropshire LI on the left. The 9th KRRC and 5th Ox & Bucks LI passed through to the Ginchy–Gueudecourt road where they dug-in. At 11.20 a.m. 9th KRRC, on the right, failed to advance to Gird Trench, being stopped by machine-gun fire from the trench, so they improved a line of shell-holes running south-east to Gas Alley, linking up with the Guards Brigade. On the left they linked with 5th Ox & Bucks LI and 5th King's Shropshire LI on the Bulls Road. The tank (D5) that missed the start had caught up and did in fact reach Gueudecourt, but was eventually set on fire and destroyed. At 6.45 p.m. in the dusk, the Germans counter-attacked down the Guedecourt–Ginchy road and later from the north-east, but were repulsed. After dark 43 Brigade relieved 42 Brigade.

CAPTURE OF FLERS

41st Division

124 Brigade attacked on the right with the 10th Queen's and 21st KRRC in the lead; 32nd and 26th Royal Fusiliers were in support. They formed up in no man's land and advanced with the creeping barrage at 6.20 a.m. Tea Support fell with little resistance, likewise Switch Line at 7 a.m. At 7.50 a.m. Flers Trench was occupied. At 3.20 p.m. 200 men from the 10th Queen's and 21st KRRC, plus two companies of 23rd Middlesex (123 Brigade in reserve) reached the western end of Bulls Road where it linked with 122 Brigade on the left. The attempts on Gird Trench were unsuccessful.

122 Brigade attacked with 15th Hampshires and 18th KRRC, followed by 11th Royal West Kents and 12th East Surreys. They advanced at 6.20 a.m. under the barrage. By 6.40 a.m. Switch Line had been taken and they pressed on to Flers Trench. Of the tanks used in the attack, D15 was hit by a shell in front of Switch Line; D14 was ditched south of Flers and D18 was hit at Flers Trench but managed to withdraw later.

A dead German soldier in a trench at Flers, September 1916. His face has been obliterated by the Censor. (Q.1285)

The storming of Flers commenced with tank D16 entering the village at 8.20 a.m. with infantry from 122 Brigade following. Three other tanks (D6, D9, D17) worked along the eastern edge of the village, smashing strongpoints and houses containing machine-gun nests. All resistance had ceased by 10 a.m., with the Bavarians fleeing towards Guedecourt. There was some confusion but isolated groups reached the third objective. Between 11 a.m. and 1 p.m. there was little action. Two officers were sent round the village to collect stragglers and move on to the third objective which they consolidated with the isolated parties. Box & Cox and Hogs Head were also occupied. Of the four tanks, only D16 returned

without mishap: D6 reached the out-skirts of Guedecourt where it caught fire. D9 reached Box & Cox, but after working along Glebe Street was eventually put out of action. D17, having been hit twice by shells, was abandoned on the eastern side of Flers but was later recovered.

New Zealand Division

The 2nd (Otago) and 2nd (Auckland) Regiments (2 NZ Brigade) started thirty seconds before zero hour at 6.20 a.m. and got caught by the British barrage and machine-gun fire from High Wood, but pushed on to Switch Line which they captured. The 2nd (Otago) pursued the enemy down the further slope to the Switch Line. The 2nd (Auckland) took Coffee Lane and kept pace with the advance. By 6.50 a.m. they were digging-in sixty yards in front of Switch Line. The 4th Regiment

(New Zealand Rifles) passed through and waited for the barrage at 7.20 a.m. Thirty minutes later the second objective, Flag Lane, was taken.

The 2nd and 3rd Rifles leap-frogged and pressed on with the attack. At 8.20 a.m., on the right, 2nd Rifles took Flers Trench and Flers Support. They came under machine-gun fire from the north-western corner of Flers and Abbey Road, a 20-ft deep, sunken lane with many dugouts. By 11 a.m. they were digging-in, their right in 41st Division's area, north of Flers. The 3rd Rifles on their left were held up by wire before Flers Trench and had to wait for the tanks which started late. D10 was shelled and put out of action at Flat Trench, but at 10.30 a.m. D11 and D12 arrived and crushed the wire. The 3rd Rifles joined 2nd Rifles at the last objective. Two companies of 1st Rifles attacked Grove

Alley at 11.30 a.m. but were forced to withdraw at 2.30 p.m. Of the remaining tanks, D12 was ditched on the western side of the village. D8 reached Abbey Road but was blind, its viewing prisms having been shattered. D11 took up a position on the Ligny road near Box & Cox, waiting all night for further action.

III CORPS
47th Division

On the right, to the east of High Wood, 1/7th and 1/15th London (140 Brigade) advanced at 6.20 a.m., reaching the Switch line. On the reverse slope they dug-in and linked with the New Zealanders. At 6.20 a.m. four tanks started to advance: two reached the south of the Wood but were forced to turn east to more open ground; one losing direction and ditching in the British front line after opening fire on its own men. The other ditched in a shell-hole. The third succeeded in crossing the German front line in the Wood and enfiladed the support line until put out of action. The fourth, on the left, was ditched in no man's land.

The infantry assault in the Wood was stopped by machine-gun fire. While a confused struggle took place, a section of 1/8th London (140 Brigade) with 1/20th and 1/19th London (141 Brigade), advancing to attack the second objective at 7.20 a.m., crowded into the Wood and joined in the fight. On the extreme right, 1/8th London (140 Brigade), less two companies, had advanced and entered Flag Lane.

At 8.20 a.m. 1/6th London passed through to attack Cough Drop. A few men reached the Flers trenches but could not hold. Cough Drop held out, however, and efforts were made to link up with the New Zealanders, by digging eastwards. At 11.40 a.m., after 140th Trench Mortar Battery

had fired 750 Stokes mortar rounds into High Wood in fifteen minutes, the Germans started to surrender to bombing parties of Londoners working forward around the flanks. Several hundred prisoners were taken. The survivors of 141 Brigade were left holding the Wood at 1 p.m.

At approximately 3.30 p.m. 1/21st and 1/24th London (142 Brigade in reserve) were sent to attack the Starfish Line. The 1/21st plus one company of 1/24th went past the east of the Wood at 5.30 p.m. They were stopped just short of the Starfish Line.

At dusk three companies of 1/24th coming up on the western side of the Wood were also stopped. At nightfall the division had no organized front line, except at the extreme right where 1/6th London occupied Cough Drop in touch with the New Zealanders.

50th Division
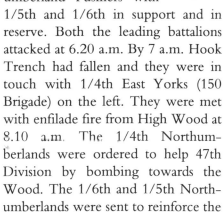
149 Brigade sent forward 1/4th and 1/7th Northumberland Fusiliers with 1/5th and 1/6th in support and in reserve. Both the leading battalions attacked at 6.20 a.m. By 7 a.m. Hook Trench had fallen and they were in touch with 1/4th East Yorks (150 Brigade) on the left. They were met with enfilade fire from High Wood at 8.10 a.m. The 1/4th Northumberlands were ordered to help 47th Division by bombing towards the Wood. The 1/6th and 1/5th Northumberlands were sent to reinforce the attack.

Soon after 10 a.m. 1/7th Northumberlands reached the sunken road south of The Bow. Fighting continued on the right, north-west of High Wood, where 1/6th Northumberlands provided a defensive flank. Later in the morning parts of the Starfish Line fell.

150 Brigade sent two tanks in advance of the infantry. One reached

Hook Trench which it enfiladed until blown up on being hit by two shells. The other crossed Hook Trench and went on to the third objective, accounting for three German machine-guns on the eastern outskirts of Martinpuich. It eventually returned to refuel.

The 1/4th East Yorks, 1/4th and 1/5th Green Howards in a line, with 1/5th Durham LI in support, attacked. The first objective fell by 7 a.m. At 10 a.m. parts of the third objective had fallen but 1/4th East Yorks had their flank in the air and had to retire to Martin Trench. At 9.05 a.m. 1/8th Durham LI (151 Brigade in reserve) were sent to 150 Brigade, as were 1/9th Durham LI to 149 Brigade.

By 3.30 p.m. shellfire had forced all the 4th Northumberlands Fusiliers back to Hook Trench. Of 1/7th Northumberlands, 100 men were in the sunken road south of The Bow. 150 Brigade was shelled out of Starfish Line but held on to Martin Trench and Martin Alley. At 5.45 p.m. 150 Brigade was ordered to attack Prue Trench, linking with 15th Division in Martinpuich.

At 9.40 p.m. 1/6th and 1/9th Durham LI (151 Brigade) attacked, but apart from small units, a machine-gun forced them back to dig in behind 1/7th Northumberlands. The 1/5th Border Regiment were late in assembling and attacked at 11 p.m. but they only made a little ground before digging-in.

CAPTURE OF MARTINPUICH
15th Division
On the right were 45 Brigade, with 11th Argylls and 13th Royal Scots in front and 6th Camerons in support; 8th York & Lancs (attached 23rd Division) and 6th and 7th Royal Scots were in reserve. The barrage

was effective and very little resistance was encountered. The 11th Argylls had to bomb Tangle South and encountered resistance in the sunken road (Longueval–Martinpuich).

46 Brigade had 10th Scottish Rifles, 7th and 8th KOSB and 10/

11th Highland LI leading, and 12th Highland LI, 9th York & Lancs (attached from 23rd Division) and 6th and 7th Royal Scots in support. They were also successful and their objective, Factory Lane, fell at 7 a.m. The 10/11th Highland LI linked with the

Canadians. The KOSB sent patrols along the west side of the village.

One tank made slow progress but helped clear the enemy from Bottom Trench to Tangle Trench and silenced some machine-guns in the village before returning for petrol. Later

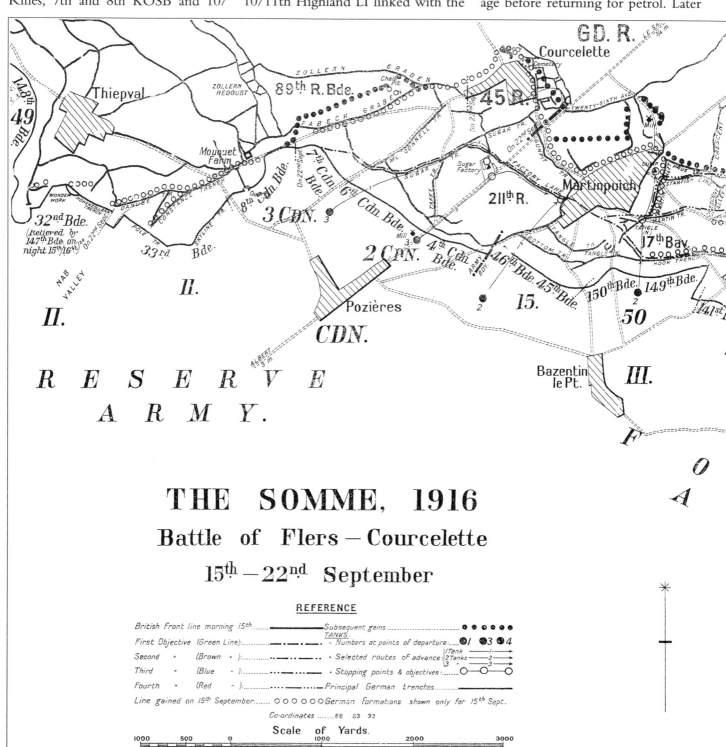

THE SOMME, 1916
Battle of Flers — Courcelette
15th — 22nd September

REFERENCE

it was used to carry up small-arms ammunition. The other tank was hit before it reached its departure point.

At 9.20 a.m. the artillery lifted from Martinpuich and both Brigades sent in strong patrols. Just after 10 a.m. 10th Scottish Rifles (46 Brigade) dug in along the objective. At 3 p.m. 6th Camerons (45 Brigade) drove the remaining Germans from the north-eastern end of the village. The ruins were occupied by 46 Brigade who set up posts facing Courcelette. That night 9th York & Lancs and 12th Highland LI took the front line where they were in touch with the Canadians in Gunpit Trench. On the right flank the Cameronians linked with 1/5th Green Howards at the junction of Martin Alley with Starfish Line.

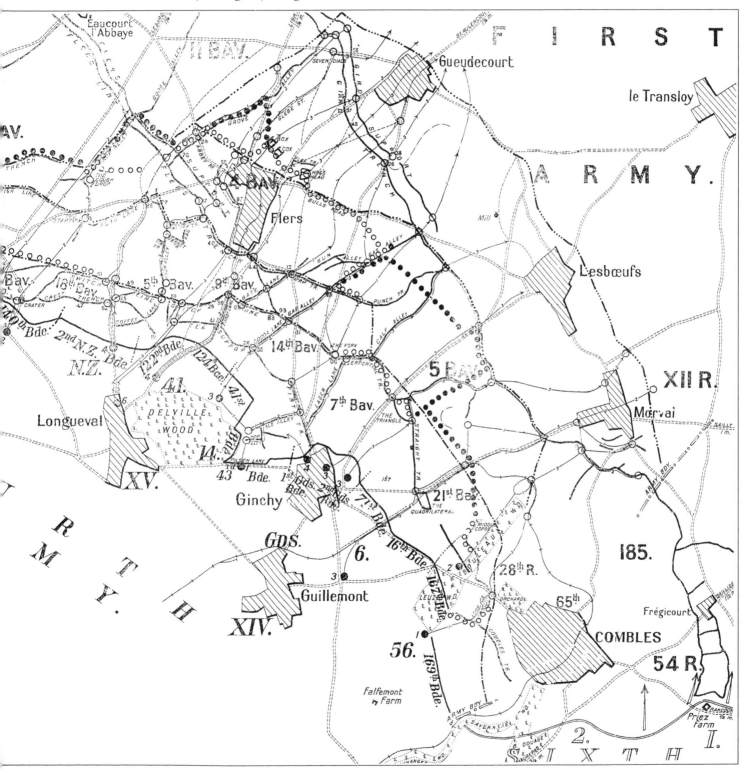

CANADIAN CORPS
2nd Canadian Division

On the right, 4 Brigade advanced with 18th (W Ontario), 20th (Central Ontario) and 21st (Central Ontario) Battalions. In 6 Brigade were 27th (City of Winnipeg) and 28th (North-West) Battalions with 31st (Alberta) Battalion in support.

Parties of German bombers advanced at 3.10 a.m. and 4.30 a.m. but were beaten off by 18th, 19th and 20th Battalions in time for the 6.20 a.m. attack. In less than fifteen minutes the front trenches had been cleared and, by 7 a.m., Factory Lane was reached by 4 Brigade. The 21st Battalion, with some of 20th Battalion, cleared the Sugar Factory under which there was a deep dugout. A little more slowly, 6 Brigade reached their objective by 7.30 a.m. The 28th Battalion on the left had to take a strongpoint on the Ovillers–Courcelette track but moved up McDonnell Trench. On the right, Lewis-gun posts were established in the sunken (Martinpuich–Courcelette) road beyond Gunpit Trench.

The tanks were outpaced. One in the right group ditched early before crossing the Canadian front line. Two went on to the Sugar Factory but found it taken and so returned. In the left group, one tank had trouble and the other two were ditched after the action in McDonnell Trench. At 9.20 a.m., after the barrage lifted, posts were established beyond Gunpit Trench and along the southern edge of Courcelette. A link with 15th Division (III Corps) was established. The Germans counter-attacked from the ruins of the village but were repelled by machine-gun fire.

5 Brigade: The 22nd (Canadien Français) and 25th (Nova Scotia

Royal Engineers fixing telephone wires in a tree near Fricourt, September 1916. The last man in the column is carrying a field telephone. (Q.4137)

Rifles) Battalions were brought up to attack Courcelette at 6.15 p.m. After the barrage lifted, the village was taken without much difficulty. The 26th Battalion (New Brunswick) mopped-up. The line reaching the cemetery and quarry on the eastern side of the village was taken by 7 p.m.

3rd Canadian Division

8 Brigade, consisting of 6th Canadian Mounted Rifles who were permanently dismounted and organized as four infantry battalions, held the entire front line of 3rd Canadian Division. 7 Brigade, shown as holding the right sector on the map, was in reserve at the opening of the battle.

The 5th Canadian Mounted Rifles secured the sector of the objective that would protect the left of the main attack, establishing a bombing block in the trench leading to Fabeck Graben. To the west, 1st Canadian Mounted Rifles were prevented by shellfire from entering the old German second position. Further west, a party under cover of a smoke barrage laid by 5th Battalion, Special Brigade, RE, raided Mouquet Farm.

At 6 p.m. 7 Brigade were brought up from reserve to start from Sugar Trench. Princess Patricia's Canadian LI, on the right, whilst suffering heavy casualties, cleared McDonnell Trench and took the eastern portion of Fabeck Graben, linking with 5 Brigade at the junction of Zollern Graben and Fabeck Graben. A gap of 100 yards remained in German hands. At 6.30 p.m. 4th Canadian Mounted Rifles (8 Brigade) joined in the advance and extended westwards the hold on Fabeck Graben, establishing a bombing block. By 8.15 p.m. 49th (Edmonton) Battalion was advancing. Two companies took and held the Chalk Pit but in the main they just reinforced the existing troops in Fabeck Graben as further advance was impossible.

Temperature 66°F; fine and sunny

XIV CORPS
56th Division

Except for some bombing encounters, 56th Division's task was to protect, in company with 6th Division, the right flank of the attack with artillery fire.

Guards Division

61 Brigade (attached from 20th Division) left Trônes Wood at midnight and assembled with 7th Duke of Cornwall's LI and 7th Shropshire LI in shell-holes some 200 yards in front of Serpentine Trench, held by 2 Guards Brigade. At 9.25 a.m. they advanced and captured the third objective of the previous day—a section of the Ginchy–Lesboeufs road. The 7th KOYLI were brought up to safeguard the right with Stokes mortars and machine-guns, with 12th King's reinforcing the left. German bombing attacks on the left flank continued until well into the afternoon.

On the left, 3 Guards Brigade had taken some time to reorganize after the action on the 15th, so that it was nearly 1.30 p.m. before they, without artillery support, advanced with 1st Grenadier and 1st Welsh Guards. Met by machine-gun fire, they continued until some 250 yards short of their objective and dug-in with their left in Punch Trench. At night, in pouring rain, 20th Division relieved the entire Guards Division with 60 and 59 Brigades.

XV CORPS

The Corps attacked all along the line at 9.25 a.m.

14th Division

On the Division's front the creeping barrage was weak and inaccurate. On the right, 6th Somerset LI came under fire from Gas Alley and made little progress. West of the Ginchy–Gueudecourt road, 10th Durham LI came under severe fire from the front and right flank and took cover in shell-holes. The 6th KOYLI and 6th Duke of Cornwall's LI attempted to reinforce but suffered the same fate. An order to renew the attack at 6.55 p.m. was carried out with no success.

41st Division

64 Brigade (attached from 21st Division) formed the 41st Division's attack. They experienced great difficulty in coming up to the front position in the darkness and rain so 15th Durham LI and 9th KOYLI in front and 10th KOYLI and 1st East Yorks in support, advanced some 1,300 yards behind the barrage and were also late in starting. They suffered considerably from machine-gun fire and shrapnel before passing even 41st Division's forward positions. A few troops got within 100 yards of Gird Trench but the attack could not be pushed home. A tank (D14) overtook the KOYLI and went on to Gueudecourt, but was hit by a shell and wrecked. 64 Brigade rallied on Bulls Road. An order for the renewal of the attack came too late in the evening to be acted upon.

New Zealand Division

1 New Zealand Brigade were brought up after repelling an enemy attempt to advance down the Ligny road at about 9 a.m. The 1st (Wellington) Battalion attacked at 9.25 a.m. (zero hour) and secured their sector of Grove Alley. Because of the failure of 64 Brigade, further advances were cancelled and the New Zea-landers' right flank was just short of the Ligny road. A trench was dug by 1st (Canterbury) Battalion back to Box & Cox to secure their position. Tank D11, which had stayed on the Ligny road all night, helped stop the attack at 9 a.m., but only managed 300 yards before a shell exploded beneath it and destroyed the gearbox.

III CORPS
47th Division

Thirty minutes before zero hour 1/23rd London (142 Brigade) left Crest Trench, its left directed to advance on Cough Drop, 1,300 yards away, and push on and take Prue Trench. Past Switch Line, machine-gun fire and shells scattered the attack and they were forced to occupy the Starfish. One company, however, reinforced the 1/6th London in Cough Drop.

50th Division

151 Brigade attacked Prue Trench, east of Crescent Alley. Some parties of 1/5th Border Regiment and 1/9th Durham LI reached the objective but were forced out. Not even Starfish Line was secured. West of Crescent Alley, 150 Brigade sent 1/5th Durham LI to attack Prue Trench but they were unsuccessful, having swerved too far to the left. Later in the day, attempts were made to bomb along Prue Trench from Martin Alley, but little ground was gained.

15th Division

The Division had to repel a counter-attack early in the morning and Martin-puich suffered heavy shelling all day. Posts were established closer to Twenty-Sixth Avenue, and the front, up to and including the Albert–Bapaume road, was taken over from the Canadians.

CANADIAN CORPS
3rd Canadian Division

The 1st Canadian Mounted Rifles (8 Brigade, CEF) acted before daylight and mounted a line of posts from the left boundary of Canadian Corps, along the Courcelette Track to Mouquet Farm. At 5 p.m. 3rd Canadian Division attacked with Royal Canadian Regiment and 31st Battalion (7 Brigade, CEF) northwards towards Zollern Graben and Zollern Redoubt from Fabeck Graben. They were stopped by machine-gun fire, and darkness fell before they could be reorganized.

During the night, 9 Brigade (CEF) relieved 7 Brigade (CEF). Meanwhile 49th (Edmonton) Battalion and Princess Patricia's Canadian LI of 7 Brigade had bombed inwards and closed the gap in Fabeck Graben. At 7.30 p.m. 2nd Canadian Mounted Rifles had bombed some of the dug-outs at Mouquet Farm.

II CORPS
11th Division

On the right of II Corps, 11th Division made progress between Mouquet Farm and Leipzig Salient south-west of Thiepval. Before dawn 6th Lincoln's bombers (33 Brigade) were in Constance Trench southwest of Mouquet Farm. That night they secured the entire trench up to the Thiepval–Pozières road. The 6th Border Regiment occupied the western half of Danube Trench. The Germans attempted to regain Constance Trench, but were stopped by 9th Sherwood Foresters.

49th Division

On the left 49th Division carried out several raids with varying success. Some progress was made by 1/7th Duke's (147 Brigade) towards Thiepval, up the old German front line.

Personnel (note the average age) of a 4.5in howitzer battery, Thiepval, September 1916. The shells have the 100–Type percussion fuze. (Q.1538)

Sunday 17 September

Temperature 63°F; 2mm rain

XIV CORPS
The Guards had been relieved by 20th Division.

20th Division

In the right-hand sector, south of the Ginchy–Lesboeufs road, 60 Brigade was attacked at 1.30 p.m., but eventually 12th KRRC and the 12th Rifle Brigade drove off the attack. In pouring rain at 6.30 p.m., 59 Brigade attacked to capture the third objective, but they were checked by machine-gun fire and no ground was taken.

XV CORPS
14th Division was relieved by 21st Division. 41st Division was relieved by 55th Division.

CANADIAN CORPS
At 5 p.m. 5 Brigade (2nd Canadian Division) advanced to clear the trenches east of Courcelette, but were beaten back.

Monday 18 September

Temperature 63°F; rain all day (13mm)

XIV CORPS
Heavy rain continued, turning the roads into deep slime.

56th Division
At 5.50 a.m. 1/16th London (Queen's Westminster Rifles) (169 Brigade) attempted to attack the sunken Combles road, but were checked. The London Rifle Brigade on the right made some progress by bombing. 167 Brigade, scheduled to attack the south-eastern face of Bouleaux Wood, could not even reach its assembly positions because of mud, etc., so the attack did not take place.

6th Division

At 5.50 a.m., after a barrage, 1st King's Shropshire LI (6 Brigade) attacked the Quadrilateral and Straight Trench. With their left on the railway, they took the Quadrilateral after a brief fight in which 14th Durham LI (18 Brigade) took a part. The Durhams cleared the dugouts in the sunken road beyond. The 2nd York & Lancs (16 Brigade), supported by Stokes mortar fire, had bombed in from the south-east and then assisted in carrying forward the right, linking with 56th Division at Middle Copse. Straight Trench at first defied a frontal attack by 1st West Yorks (18 Brigade), but the bombers

Battle of Flers-Courcelette. A dugout amidst shell-torn tree stumps at Martinpuich. (Q.4355)

fought their way to meet those of 14th Durhams, while a detachment passed over the trench near the left boundary of the Division and took the Germans in rear, capturing seven machine-guns and 140 prisoners. The right of 20th Division sent forward a fighting patrol. During the day the enemy seemed to be concentrating on higher ground near Morval, but were dispersed by artillery fire. 5th Division began to relieve 6th Division before dark.

XV CORPS
41st Division

The Division had been relieved by 55th Division at 3.30 a.m. Fighting was confined to the bombers of 1st (Otago) Battalion (1 NZ Brigade), forcing the enemy back up Flers

Support, almost to the junction with Goose Alley.

III CORPS
47th Division

The right of the Corps sent parties of 140 Brigade to bomb up Flers Trench and Drop Alley, towards the junction of these trenches. At the same time detachments of 1/23rd and 1/24th London Regiment (142 Brigade) attacked the Starfish Line, but could only reinforce the detachment already there. German bombers drove the Londoners east towards the Starfish, but were driven back at night.

50th Division

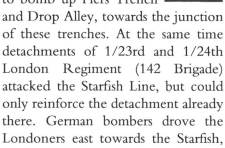

At 4.30 p.m. 150 Brigade (1/5th Durham LI assisted by bombers of 1/4th and 1/5th Green Howards) bombed east along Starfish Line and Prue Trench and almost reached Crescent Alley. The 1/8th Durhams (151 Brigade),

however, failed to bomb up this trench from the south. 15th Division consolidated its forward post, including the Mill.

23rd Division

The Division began to relieve 15th Division on the night of the 18th. It also took over Starfish Line and Prue Trench, west of Crescent Alley, from 150 Brigade (50th Division).

Tuesday 19 September

Temperature 55°F; wet and windy (3mm rain)

XV, III CORPS

At dusk, at the junction of XV and III Corps, 2nd Auckland (2 NZ Brigade) bombed up Flers Support towards its junction with Goose Alley, whilst 1/5th London (140 Brigade) advanced up Drop Alley to get into Flers Trench. The New Zealanders made progress, but the Londoners were forced back to the Cough Drop.

FOURTH ARMY

The Fourth Army carried on local skirmishes and III Corps eventually secured the remainder of their objective without opposition. On the right of XIV Corps, 56th Division dug an assembly trench north-east of Middle Copse and sapped forwards, south of the Copse, towards Boul-eaux Wood.

CANADIAN CORPS
1st Canadian Division

That night the Germans counter-attacked the north-eastern corner of Courcelette, attacking 4th Battalion (CEF), and a 2-hour struggle ensued

Canadian troops just out of the line after the Battle of Courcelette, September 1916. The truck is an Autocar UF21, 30cwt. (CO.827)

until finally the Germans were pushed back.

Wednesday 20 September

Temperature 61°F; showery all day (1mm rain)

XV CORPS

In the early morning of the 20th, 1st Division relieved 47th Division.

New Zealand Division

At 8.30 p.m. an attack was made by 1st Black Watch (1 Brigade, 1st Division) and 2nd (Canterbury) (2 NZ Brigade). There was no bombardment and 2nd (Canterbury) drove the Germans back to beyond Goose Alley. A company of Black Watch advanced up Drop Alley to link with the New Zealanders. A German counter-attack was repulsed from Drop Alley as far as its junction

with Flers Trench which was then occupied by The Black Watch.

3rd Canadian Division

At 4 a.m. the same Battalion repulsed a further attempt with Lewis-guns and bombs. At 5 a.m. 58th Battalion (9 Brigade, 3rd Canadian Division) started to bomb west along Zollern Graben, and a company of 43rd (Cameron Highlanders of Canada) captured a considerable length of it by frontal attack. This was lost later in the morning, however, and only a foothold remained. After dark 1st Canadian Division occupied part of the trench on the eastern side of Courcelette.

V CORPS

North of the Ancre, V Corps also raided. By the morning of the 20th, 39th Division had taken over the whole Corps front from the Ancre to Hebuterne, thus releasing 2nd Division.

Thursday 21 September

Temperature 59°F; cloudy and showery

III CORPS

At night patrols of 1st, 50th and 23rd Divisions found the enemy had pulled out of Starfish and Prue Trenches which were gradually occupied.

XIV CORPS

By morning the Guards Division had relieved 20th Division. At night 6th Division took over from 1 Guards Brigade. The Guards took over ground from XV Corps including Gas Alley. Bombing attacks down this trench towards Gird Trench by 1st Lincolns (62 Brigade, 21st Division) on the 20th, and by 4th Grenadier Guards (3rd Guards Brigade) on the 22nd, made little progress.

Friday 22 September

Temperature 64°F; sunny

III CORPS

Starfish and Prue Trench were consolidated. Patrols reported that no Germans were south-west of Eaucourt l'Abbaye.

23rd Division

The Division reported that Twenty-Sixth Avenue, a communication trench running back from Courcelette to the Le Sars defence, appeared to be empty.

Left, top: Canadians testing a Vickers machine-gun, September 1916. The Vickers was the standard medium machine-gun for British and Empire troops. (CO.771)
Left, bottom: Canadian official photographer with artillery observers watching an engagement on the Western Front, September 1916. (CO.820)

CANADIAN CORPS
1st Canadian Division

The Division occupied some trenches on the eastern side of Courcelette. West of the village, the Canadian front ran along Fabeck Graben and Mouquet Farm track.

Saturday 23 September

Temperature 66°F; fine and warm

The preliminary bombardment opened at 7 a.m. on Morval and Lesboeufs.

Sunday 24 September

Temperature 72°F; fine, warm day after misty start

XIV CORPS
56th Division

At 5.50 a.m. the Division tried to bomb down Combles Trench in an attempt to join with the French 73rd Regiment. The 1/9th London (169 Brigade) made some progress but were soon pushed back.

6th Division

At 6 a.m. a German counter-attack was repulsed by Lewis-gun fire of 1st Buffs (16 Brigade).

III CORPS
23rd Division

On the left of the Corps 68 Brigade attacked Twenty-Sixth Avenue east of the Bapaume road, but was repulsed by machine-gun fire.

At 8.30 p.m. on the other flank of the Corps, 1st Black Watch (1 Brigade, 1st Division) tried to bomb up the Flers trenches, but without success.

II CORPS

An abortive attempt was made on Mouquet Farm by a company of 6th York & Lancs (32 Brigade, 11th Division) that evening.

Monday 25 September

Temperature 73°F; fine, clear day

BATTLE OF MORVAL (25–28 September)

XIV CORPS

At 12.35 p.m. the creeping barrage fell and the Corps attacked, steadily reaching their objectives with little cost.

56th Division

The Division attacked only from 168 Brigade's trench, seven minutes after zero hour, so as to come into line with 5th Division. The 1/4th London cleared the north end of Bouleaux Wood, with London Scottish carrying the first trench which ran from the Wood to the light railway track. They then came under fire from the railway embankment. This was rushed by some of the East Surreys (5th Division) and the London Scottish helped mop-up. By 1.30 p.m. it was over and 80 prisoners and four machine-guns had been taken. The London Scottish went on to take an unknown trench with a good view over the Combles–Morval valley at 1.35 p.m. The advance continued with 5th, 6th and Guards Divisions. On the right of 5th Division, the East Surreys stayed where they were. The Devons and 1st Bedfords (15 Brigade) captured their sector of the sunken road in ten minutes.

5th Division

The 1st East Surrey (95 Brigade) suffered from machine-gun fire from the embankment north of Combles railway track. On their left a strongpoint at the Ginchy–Morval road held out until 1st Devons (95 Brigade), having swerved left to avoid uncut wire, worked down the trench from the north. The 1st Norfolks took their objective in one rush. The left of the battalion linked with 6th Division and received assistance from Stokes mortar fire of 16 Brigade and bombers of 1st Buffs.

On the other flank of 6th Division, the right of 2nd Grenadier Guards (1 Guards Brigade) was held up by uncut wire. They cut the wire by hand, then rushed and took the trench. 95 Brigade ordered 12th Gloucesters and 2nd KOSB to take the southern part of Morval. They managed it in less than an hour. The 1st Cheshires (15 Brigade) took the northern part soon after 3 p.m.

6th Division

CAPTURE OF LESBOEUFS

The Buffs (16 Brigade), 2nd Durham LI and 11th Essex (18 Brigade) were also successful in their attack on the road. The 2nd York & Lancs, supported by 1st King's Shropshire LI (16 Brigade) took the east of Morval–Lesboeufs road. On their left, 1st West Yorks (18 Brigade) went on to clear the southern part of Lesboeufs. They were in touch with 2nd Grenadier and 1st Irish Guards who took the remainder of the village. The two Coldstream battalions of 1 Guards Brigade were coming up in reserve.

5th, 6th Divisions

The two divisions occupied spurs projecting east and north-east of Morval. At 6 p.m. 16th Royal Warwicks (15 Brigade) went forward 200 yards in front of the eastern edge of the village and, later, 2nd York & Lancs (16 Brigade) established posts north-west from Morval Mill to Lesboeufs.

Guards Division

The 1st Irish Guards (1 Guards Brigade) and 2nd Scots Guards (3 Guards Brigade) met with little opposition, but 4th Grenadiers on the left were held up a little and were late. The 2nd Grenadiers and 1st Irish Guards bombed many dugouts in the sunken road. The Scots Guards (3 Guards Brigade) kept pace with them, but 4th Grenadiers were forced to hold the left flank because of XV Corps's failure to secure Gird Trench.

XV CORPS

21st Division on the right.

The 10th KOYLI and 1st East Yorks (64 Brigade) attacked Gird Trench, but were held up on the wire and remained in no man's land until nightfall. The 1st Lincolns (attached from 62 Brigade) were stopped by shellfire in the British front line. One company of 1st Lincolns on the right, joined 4th Grenadiers and attacked the junction of Gas Alley with Gird Trench. The attack was not successful, but touch with XIV Corps was maintained.

The 9th and 8th Leicesters (110 Brigade) took Goat Trench, but machine-gun fire from the right pre-

Battle of Morval. Waves of infantry going forward and passing one of the four Mk 1 tanks detailed to work with Fourth Army, but which became ditched soon after zero hour at midday. Near Ginchy, 25 September 1916. (Q.4513)

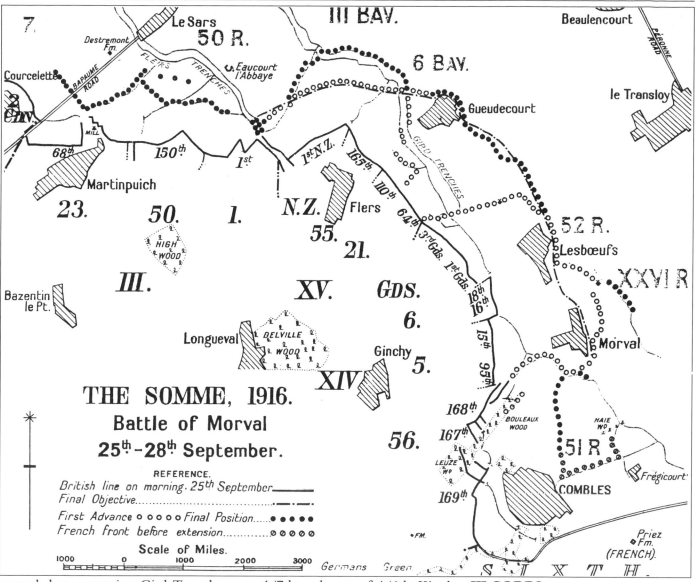

THE SOMME, 1916.
Battle of Morval
25th–28th September.

REFERENCE.
British line on morning. 25th September _____
Final Objective .... _ . _ . _
First Advance o o o o o Final Position ...... ● ● ● ●
French front before extension .... ⊗ ⊗ ⊗ ⊗ ⊗

Scale of Miles.
1000   0   1000   2000   3000

vented them capturing Gird Trench. The 9th Leicesters formed a defensive flank along Watling Street (a sunken portion of the Ginchy–Guedecourt road) and, on the left, a party of 8th Leicesters held a footing in Gird Trench, linking in the afternoon with 55th Division.

55th Division

The Division attacked with 165 Brigade, and 1/7th, 1/6th and 1/9th King's took Gird Trench soon after 1 p.m. The 1/6th King's blocked Gird Trench north of the road; 1/9th King's cleared Grove Alley. At 2.40

p.m.1/7th and part of 1/6th King's gained a foot-hold in a sunken road between Gird Trench and Gueude-court. Later in the day they linked up with the New Zealanders on the left and 110 Brigade on the right in Gird Trench.

New Zealand Division

The Division was to form a defensive flank astride Goose Alley running back to Gird Trench. The 1st (Canterbury), 1st (Auckland) and 1st (Otago) achieved this with little difficulty. They were in touch with 1st Division (III Corps) in Flers Support and later with 55th Division beyond Factory Corner.

III CORPS

1st Division

The 1st Black Watch (1 Brigade) bombed along Flers Trench, capturing 300 yards of it, which was later taken over by the New Zealanders. 150 Brigade (50th Division) held the posts they had established the previous night. On the night of the 25th, another was established beyond the turn of Crescent Alley. On the left 23rd Division was to attack the western end of Twenty-Sixth Avenue with the aid of two tanks, starting from Gunpit Road (west of Martinpuich). One tank ditched and, as the other crossed the crest, it brought down a

German barrage on the attacking troops, 10th Northumberlands (68 Brigade), which stopped the action.

A bombing attempt from the trench west of Martinpuich Mill also failed.

Tuesday 26 September

Temperature 75°F; fine day

XIV CORPS
CAPTURE OF COMBLES
56th Division

At 10.40 p.m. the London Scottish (168 Brigade) sent a detachment along the light railway and by dawn on the 26th were within 500 yards of Combles. While 1/4th London sent patrols through the north of Bouleaux Wood, without hindrance, 1/1st London (167 Brigade) did likewise through the southern half. (At 2.10 a.m. that morning a shower of red rockets, followed by a green one, had been fired from the German trench, signalling the retirement of the rearguard.)

The 1/1st London patrols entered the Orchard (one entering Combles) and met up with the French. The London Rifle Brigade (169 Brigade) advanced down Combles Trench and at 4.15 a.m. linked with the French at the light railway. The 1/1st London now occupied the village by the Ginchy road. At 7 a.m. the London Scottish met up with the French north-east of Combles.

The Division moved troops forward to dig-in, facing east between Combles and Morval, with the right in touch with the French. 168 Brigade was to stay in touch with the French by attacking Mutton Trench. This proved to be impossible as the two supporting tanks became ditched and the attack was called off.

The Division had made little progress down Mutton Trench but managed to seize a portion of Thunder Trench. That night it was relieved by 20th and 6th Divisions.

5th Division

At 10 p.m. the Division captured a German officer who stated that Combles was to be evacuated during the night.

XV CORPS
CAPTURE OF GIRD TRENCH AND GUEUDECOURT
21st Division

At 6.30 a.m. a tank came up Pilgrims Way to assist the capture of Gird Trench, firing as it went. Behind it, bombers of 7th Leicesters (110 Brigade attached from 37th Division), with two companies in support, drove the Germans towards the Guards Division along Gird Trench which was occupied by 15th Durham LI (64 Brigade). The tank moved towards the south-east of Gueudecourt before withdrawing. Infantry patrols moved into the village and a squadron of the Cavalry Corps was sent to reconnoitre the high ground to the north of the village with XV Corps Cavalry Regiment, the South Irish Horse. At noon 19th Lancers (1st Indian Cavalry Division) moved from Mametz towards Gueudecourt, via Flers. At 2.15 p.m., after coming under fire, they dismounted and

A Royal Fusilier wearing a German helmet, after the capture of Thiepval on 26 September 1916. The helmet plate indicates a Württemberg Regiment. (Q.1331)

entered Gueudecourt from the south-west. At the same time, a troop of South Irish Horse entered the north-west corner. Meanwhile 110 Brigade moved slowly forward, 6th Leicesters entering the village at 4.30 p.m. At 6 p.m. the cavalry pulled out and the Leicesters started to dig-in on the far edge of the village. The 64 Brigade advance continued with 10th and 15th Durham LI and part of 9th KOYLI.

The final position was a little short of the Gueudecourt – Le Transloy road. The 12th Northumberland Fusiliers (62 Brigade) came up to take over and advanced to the road itself. The right was resting on the junction with the Lesboeufs road in touch with the Guards and, at 10 p.m., the left was relieved by 10th Green Howards.

III CORPS

At 11 p.m. 1st and 50th Divisions attacked a new German trench, known as Flers Switch. On the right 1st Division was stopped by machine-gun fire; 50th Division took the western end and bombed up Crescent Alley as far as Spence Trench. The bombers of 1st Division had little success in Flers Trench.

CANADIAN CORPS
2nd Canadian Division

At 12.35 p.m. the Division advanced under a shrapnel barrage and with two tanks in support. The Germans immediately put down a counter barrage. On the right one tank had become ditched. The other, being hit by a shell, exploded in no man's land. The 28th Battalion (6 Brigade) came under heavy shellfire and could not leave its trenches. The 29th Battalion (6 Brigade) had captured the German front line within ten minutes, but 31st Battalion (6 Brigade), machine-gunned from the front and left flank,

failed to reach the German line except with one platoon and a Lewis-gun section on the extreme right of 29th Battalion. At 10.50 p.m. 31st Battalion (6 Brigade), with a company of 27th (City of Winnipeg) Battalion succeeded in taking the objective as far as the east Miraumont road, about 100 yards east of the junction with Courcelette Trench. Two counter-attacks were beaten back during the night.

1st Canadian Division

The Division, attacking with 14th (Royal Montreal) Battalion (3 Brigade) and 15th (48th Highlanders) Battalion (3 Brigade), crossed the 400 yards to Sudbury Trench and occupied it. At 1 p.m. the advance continued. By 2.40 p.m. 14th Battalion had occupied the eastern half of Kenora Trench which, from the top of the spur, ran back to Regina Trench. The Highlanders on the left had failed to keep up and German bombers began to attack the flanks of 14th Battalion, but were repulsed. Later 14th Battalion were reinforced by a company of 16th Battalion (Canadian Scottish).

The 15th Battalion, who formed up in no man's land, met with more resistance, but by mid afternoon they had achieved their second objective, which was just off the sky line (just short of the crest) and did not co-incide with a trench. Later, the left flank linked up with 2 Brigade. In the evening 16th Battalion sent up a company to reinforce.

Leading with 5th (Western Cavalry) Battalion (2 Brigade) and 8th (90th Rifles) Battalion (2 Brigade), each with a company of 10th Battalion, they attacked. The 8th Battalion were enfiladed by machine-gun fire from the left, but Zollern Trench was taken except on the left flank where 10th Battalion was required to help. At 1 p.m. they pushed on to Hessian

Trench which 10th Battalion captured without difficulty. On the right 5th Battalion were in touch with 3 Brigade, but on the left 11th Division had not appeared. The 10th Battalion were forced to bomb along Zollern Trench and barricade it. The left of Hessian Trench was under machine-gun fire and 8th Battalion were only able to hold the right section. At 4 p.m. a defensive flank was dug from Hessian Trench to Zollern Trench, mainly by 7th Battalion (1st British Columbia) who took over the left flank at 10.30 p.m.

BATTLE OF THIEPVAL RIDGE

II CORPS
CAPTURE OF MOUQUET FARM
11th Division

On the right of the Canadians, the Division attacked, 34 Brigade leading with 8th Northumberland and 9th Lancashire Fusiliers. A bombing party of Lancs seized the known exits of Mouquet Farm thirty seconds before zero hour. Both Battalions reached the first objective, the German support trench. The 5th Dorsets in support suffered severe casualties from the German barrage which fell on the British front-line trench as they were moving up.

The Northumberland Fusiliers met with strong resistance, especially around the deep dugouts of the Zollern Redoubt. Momentum was lost and moppers-up were killed almost to a man. The only remaining officer collected some 50 survivors and dug-in on the right facing Zollern Trench. A few other survivors were in shell-holes to the west of the old German second position.

The Lancashire Fusiliers had their right flank almost annihilated by fire from Zollern Redoubt, and met stiff opposition in Midway Line, a trench that connected Mouquet Farm with the Schwaben Redoubt. Only one officer and a few men reached Zollern Trench but were isolated. The 5th Dorsets pushed on to reinforce the Fusiliers.

At Mouquet Farm the fighting was confused. The 11th Manchesters relieved the Lancashire Fusiliers. The two tanks that were due to assist in the attack became ditched before reaching the farm, but the crew of one dismounted its machine-guns and helped in the fight. The 5th Dorsets also sent men up, as did 6th East Yorks (Pioneers). At 5.30 p.m. smoke bombs finally cleared the cellars of the survivors of the garrison, 55 men and one officer.

33 Brigade: The Brigade attacked from the end of Nab Valley with 9th Sherwood Foresters and 6th Border

Regiment taking Joseph Trench at 12.45 p.m. and moving on to Schwaben Trench which ran from Mouquet Farm to Thiepval. The Borderers then started to consolidate. By 1.30 p.m. the Foresters had captured Zollern Trench. By 4 p.m. all of Hessian Trench, except 250 yards on the right flank, had been occupied. They were in touch with 53 Brigade (18th Division) on the left in Zollern Trench. The 7th South Staffords were left to mop-up, clearing Midway Line also. They sent up four platoons in support to Hessian Trench where they helped repel a bombing attack from the right.

18th Division

The Division attacked on its right with 53 Brigade. The 8th Suffolks and 10th Essex led the advance from Nab

Valley. The 8th Norfolks supplied troops to mop-up. The assault troops left their assembly trenches before the barrage had lifted, avoiding the German barrage which immediately fell on the British front line (6th Royal Berks in reserve, waited before occupying the front line, for the same reason). The attack reached its first objective within twelve minutes. In the Suffolks' case it was Schwaben Trench. The Essex on the left took the Pozières–St Pierre Divion sunken road.

Two tanks hidden further down Nab Valley were due to help in the advance: one ditched before it came into action and the other soon after in Schwaben Trench.

Both battalions pressed on and had taken Zollern Trench by 1.15 p.m., meeting little resistance. Further advance proved much harder and after only 250 yards the Suffolks were

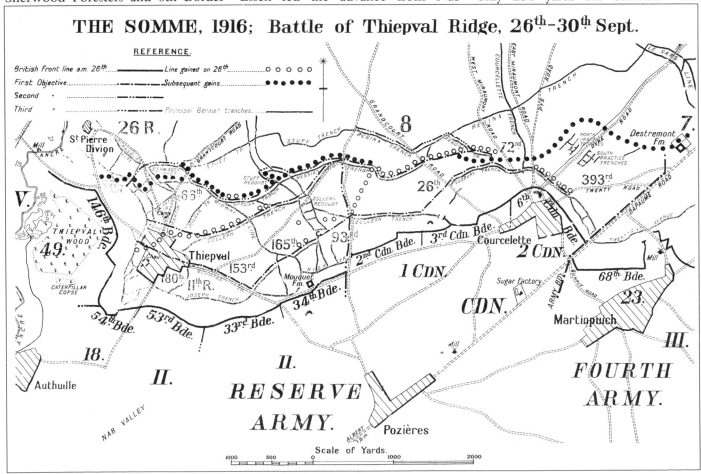

THE SOMME, 1916; Battle of Thiepval Ridge, 26th–30th Sept.

REFERENCE.

British front line a.m. 26th ———— Line gained on 26th ∘ ∘ ∘ ∘ ∘

First Objective ———— Subsequent gains ● ● ● ● ●

Second ″ ————

Third ″ ———— Principal German trenches ————

Scale of Yards.

British troops observing from a trench, near Thiepval, September 1916. The pouch on the back of the man on the right contains his gas helmet. (Q.1069)

forced into shell-holes. At dusk they fell back to Zollern Trench. The Essex could do no better, coming under fire from Bulgar Trench and Martin Trench. In the evening attempts were made to clear the position with bombs. The 8th Norfolks had been collected in Schwaben Trench.

54 Brigade: On a narrow front the Brigade attacked Thiepval with 12th Middlesex going through the village, and a company of 11th Royal Fusiliers working along the German front system. The Royal Fusiliers also supplied a company to mop-up the cellars for the Middlesex. The 6th Northants were in close support and

7th Bedfords were in reserve. Two tanks started from Caterpillar Copse, south of Thiepval Wood. As with 53 Brigade, they left their trenches before zero hour.

The Fusiliers had a hard fight in the trenches and dugouts. The Middlesex met little opposition until machine-gun fire from the ruins of the Château held them up at the edge of Thiepval until a tank came up and ended all opposition. The right continued well but the left was slower. The tank was soon ditched in the village.

The Fusiliers lost pace with the barrage and the mopping-up company was used to fill the gap on the Middlesex front, which had drifted to the right. By 2.30 p.m. the entire village, bar the extreme north-west corner, had fallen. The 6th Northants

started to move up and reinforce both the Middlesex and Fusiliers.

Wednesday 27 September

Temperature 72°F; overcast with some showers

XV CORPS
55th Division
At 2.15 p.m. 1/8th King's (164 Brigade) successfully attacked Gird Trench and Goose Alley.

New Zealand Division
1 New Zealand Brigade with 1st (Canterbury) on the right linked up with the King's on the Ligny road. In the centre, 1st (Auckland) were also

successful. On the left, 1st (Otago) lost three companies after reaching the slope beyond the Factory Corner–Eaucourt l'Abbaye road. The remaining company on the left bombed up Goose Alley and established posts. The Germans, however, still held the junctions of Goose Alley and Gird Trench.

III CORPS
1st Division
The Division secured most of Flers Switch by frontal attack, and was relieved that night by 47th Division.

50th Division

The Division sent out patrols, and posts were established between Crescent Alley and Twenty-Sixth Avenue, 200 yards from the Flers Trenches. After a bombardment 23rd Division occupied Twenty-Sixth Avenue south-west of Spence Trench and linked, on the left, with the Canadians at the Bapaume road.

CANADIAN CORPS
After suffering a constant heavy bombardment all night and morning 28th (North-West) Battalion, on the right of 6 Brigade, found that the

Panoramic view of the battlefield at Thiepval, September 1916. A tank can be seen in the Wood. (Q.1073)

Germans were pulling out and sent out patrols. At 6 p.m. 29th (Vancouver) Battalion found the same was happening on their front and also sent out patrols. While maintaining touch with III Corps on the right, 28th Battalion joined with 29th Battalion which had occupied the North and South Practice Trenches. The 31st (Alberta) Battalion were now able to occupy the previous day's objective. Later that evening they were reinforced by 27th (City of Winnipeg) Battalion.

1st Canadian Division
From 3 a.m. the Division had trouble holding Kenora Trench with 14th (Royal Montreal) Regiment. They lost touch with 15th (48th Highlanders) on their left and were forced back. Later that morning, reinforced by two platoons of 16th Battalion (Canadian Scottish), Kenora Trench was re-occupied. At about 6 p.m. a bombing attack was only just repulsed. Later that evening the Canadians withdrew to the support trench. It was not until 2 a.m. that a counter-attack was launched, with 75 men, but this too was unsuccessful.

II CORPS
11th Division
On 34 Brigade's front the Germans evacuated Zollern Redoubt and 8th Northumberland Fusiliers assem-

bled here from 6.30 a.m. on. Later they were withdrawn.

West of the redoubt 9th Lancashire Fusiliers and part of the 5th Dorsets occupied Zollern Trench as far as Midway Line, and 11th Manchesters east of the redoubt were in touch with the Canadians, also along Zollern Trench. The Manchesters were to have continued at 10 a.m. but were stopped by enemy machine-gun fire from Stuff Redoubt and Hessian Trench.

It was decided that 32 Brigade (in reserve) would continue the attack with 9th West Yorks and 6th Green Howards. This was postponed, but the West Yorks pressed on at the original time, 3 p.m., and gained a footing in the southern edge of Stuff Redoubt. One hour later the Green Howards attacked and captured Hessian Trench west of the Redoubt. At 9 p.m. 11th Manchesters bombed forward from Zollern Redoubt leading north-west to the left of the Canadian Corps.

At 6 a.m. a company of the 6th Border Regiment and another later were sent up to reinforce Zollern and Hessian Trenches. Before noon bombers of the 7th South Staffords had moved east and linked with 34 Brigade. At 3 p.m. the Borderers sent one company to take the remaining section of Hessian Trench.

Later the right linked with the Green Howards in 32 Brigade.

18th Division

53 Brigade were consolidating Zollern Trench. In the morning the 10th Essex, under a Stokes mortar barrage, gained some 50 yards of Bulgar Trench. 54 Brigade arranged for 7th Bedfords to take over the front from the Middlesex, Royal Fusiliers and Northants, and this had been completed by 7 a.m. The Bedfords, supported by 1/5th West Yorks (146 Brigade), were to attack and clear the village. The relief went so well that the Bedfords were ready to go at 5.45 a.m.

By 11 a.m. Thiepval had been cleared and the Bedfords were consolidating beyond the edge of the village, in touch on the right with 53 Brigade.

During the night 74 Brigade (25th Division) relieved 146 Brigade.

Thursday 28 September

Temperature 73°F; fine, with some heavy showers

XIV CORPS

On the night of 27/28th, the Corps started to hand over its right front to the French. This involved 56th, 20th and 6th Divisions and was completed without any problems.

XV CORPS

A proposed attack was cancelled until Gird Trench had been was taken because it overlooked the objective, Goose Alley; 41st Division relieved 55th Division.

III CORPS

The Corps consolidated. The left of 23rd Division pushed forward with the Canadians. One company of 70 Brigade advanced against Destremont Farm but were driven back by machine-gun fire and bombs.

CANADIAN CORPS

At dawn a cavalry patrol rode out to the right of 28th Battalion, at once coming under machine-gun fire from Destremont Farm. At 7 a.m. 19th Battalion (Central Ontario) eventually established a line facing northeast beyond the Practice Trenches. The 26th Battalion (New Brunswick) advanced astride Courcelette Trench at 7 a.m., after passing through 31st Battalion, but met strong machine-gun fire from Regina Trench. Another two attempts were made at 3 p.m. and 8.30 p.m., but with no more success. The 26th Battalion then relieved 31st Battalion on the line of the first objective.

During the night 4 Brigade relieved 6, 5 and 3 Brigades; 8 Brigade took over from 2 Brigade.

II CORPS
11th Division

32 Brigade took over the right sector of 11th Division and was to capture Stuff Redoubt, using 8th Duke's, which had put two companies in Zollern Trench to take Hessian Trench, and the troops in Stuff Redoubt to complete the capture of the Redoubt.

At 6 p.m., zero hour, the Duke's were not ready and the hour passed. A bombing attempt was made in the Redoubt but ground taken could not be held; 33 Brigade patrolled close to Stuff Trench.

18th Division

The Division was to attack Schwaben Redoubt; 53 Brigade had the Suffolks on the right astride Zollern Trench to take Midway Line, while 7th Queen's (attached from 55 Brigade) were to assault the Redoubt. The moppers-up were 8th Norfolks. Two companies of 7th Bedfords (54 Brigade) were to assault between the Redoubt and the front line.

At 1 p.m. the attack began. Bulgar Trench fell but Midway Line offered more fight. By 2.30 p.m. the Suffolks were approaching the eastern end of Schwaben Redoubt and were in

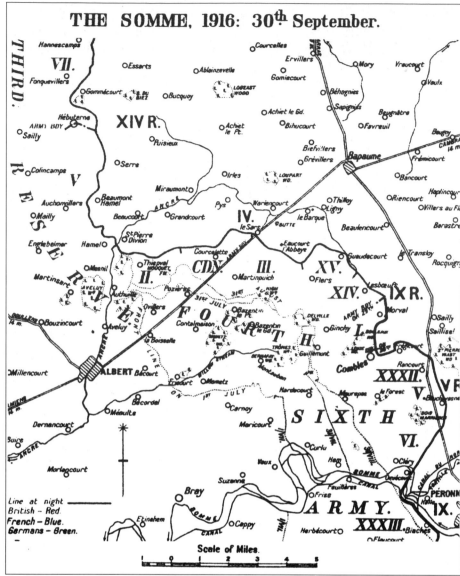

THE SOMME, 1916: 30th September.

Line at night _____
British – Red.
French – Blue.
Germans – Green.

Scale of Miles.

touch with 11th Division. The Queen's, after losing their bearings, arrived at the south-western corner and south face, together with parties of the Bedfords and 1/5th West Yorks.

By 5 p.m. the south face of the Redoubt was in the possession of the Queen's and the latter's right linked with the Suffolks in Midway Line; the left linked with a mix of troops from 54 Brigade. The Bedfords and West Yorks had cleared the western face of the Redoubt, and also a trench facing north-west on the slope beyond, by 8 p.m. Patrols sent out by 11th Lancashire Fusiliers (74 Brigade) secured foot-holds in the enemy front

line, linking up with the left of 54 Brigade.

There were occasional bombing encounters during the night, and 7th Royal West Kents (55 Brigade) relieved the front of 54 Brigade.

Friday 29 September

Temperature 61°F; very wet and windy (17mm rain)

XIV CORPS
6th Division, Guards Division
The Divisions occupied some trenches beyond Lesboeufs, unopposed.

III CORPS
23rd Division
At 5.30 a.m. a company of 8th York & Lancs (70 Brigade) stormed Destremont Farm. Later that day they linked with the Canadians on their left. The 1/18th London (141 Brigade, 47th Division) began to bomb up Flers Trench in the evening.

CANADIAN CORPS
3rd Canadian Division
At noon 8 Brigade attacked with 2nd Canadian Mounted Rifles in combination with 11th Division, and got a footing in Hessian Trench. During the afternoon after heavy shelling, two counter-attacks by the Germans recaptured some ground, only to be retaken by Canadian bombers.

II CORPS
11th Division
32 Brigade attempted to clear Stuff Redoubt & Hessian Trench to the east of it. Three companies of 6th York & Lancs attacked Hessian Trench, capturing most of it and linking with the Canadians. The attack on Stuff Redoubt was unsuccessful.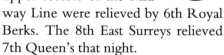

18th Division
The 8th Suffolks on the right of 53 Brigade in the upper sectors of the Midway Line were relieved by 6th Royal Berks. The 8th East Surreys relieved 7th Queen's that night.

At 6.30 a.m. 7th Royal West Kents (55 Brigade) began to take over the entire line of 54 Brigade from the western face of Schwaben Redoubt to the German front line. By 7.30 a.m. a fierce bombing fight had developed on the western face which lasted all day. The West Kents replied at 10 p.m., but could not hold any

Cooks preparing dinner, Carnoy Valley, September 1916. The large pots were known as 'dixies'. The men appear to be of the Royal Artillery. (Q.4114)

gains. They were later called on to relieve 74 Brigade who were in the German front system. This was completed by 3 a.m. on the 30th.

Saturday 30 September

Temperature 63°F; overcast at times

XIV CORPS
47th Division

The 1/18th London (141 Brigade, 47th Division) forced the Germans back beyond Flers Switch. The 2nd Rifles (NZ Rifle Brigade, attached to 2 NZ Brigade) kept level in Flers Support.

23rd Division

The 8th York and Lancs (70 Brigade) stormed Destremont Farm, gaining touch with the Canadians on their left later in the day.

II CORPS
11th Division
At 4 p.m. the attack was renewed by three groups of bombers. The 6th York & Lancs (32 Brigade) moved along Hessian Trench from the east. The 7th South Staffords (33 Brigade) advanced up Zollern trench and along the old German support line; the mixed Yorkshire units were on the south of Stuff Redoubt. The fight lasted all day and by nightfall all the objectives had been taken except the northern half of the Redoubt. Bombers of 2nd Canadian Mounted

Rifles helped 11th Division to capture Hessian Trench, but exhaustion took its toll; 25th Division relieved 11th Division that night.

18th Division

The Division was engaged heavily. At dawn a counter-attack drove the East Surreys from the southern face of the Schwaben Redoubt which was retaken in hand-to-hand fighting. The West Kents were forced back along the western face which the Germans retained. At 4 p.m. the East Surreys attacked the northern face of the Redoubt successfully, but two platoons of 7th Buffs, supported by the West Kents, made no impression on the western face. The Germans counter-attacked at 9 p.m., forcing the East Surreys back to the entrance of Stuff Trench, where they held on.

Shells bursting in the ruins of
Courcelette, October 1916. (CO.860)

OCTOBER

Sunday 1 October

Temperature 63°F; sunny day

BATTLE OF TRANSLOY RIDGE (1–18 October)

XV CORPS

12th Division relieved 21st Division. The bombardment started at 7 a.m., increasing in ferocity until zero hour at 3.15 p.m. Special Brigade, RE had installed 36 oil projectors in Gird Trench. Thirty of these fired, enveloping the German line opposite the New Zealand troops in red flame and heavy black smoke.

New Zealand Division

The 2nd Canterbury (2 NZ Brigade) captured the Gird Trench lines at their junction with Goose Alley and also the east section of Circus Trench. The 2nd Otago (2 NZ Brigade) took their objective, a German strongpoint known as The Circus. They reached the Le Barque road, were reinforced by 2nd Wellingtons and formed a line near Abbey Road with 1/19th London (47th Division).

III CORPS
CAPTURE OF EAUCOURT L'ABBAYE

47th Division

The Division attacked with 141 Brigade and two tanks. The 1/19th London on the right were forced to wait in shell-holes 50 yards from the German positions because of machine-gun fire, until the tanks came up moving from right to left along Flers Line. After this they moved up with little trouble and linked with the New Zealanders on the Le Barque road. The 1/20th London in the centre also waited for the tanks, then swept through Eaucourt l'Abbaye linking with 1/19th London. Both tanks were ditched in the Flers Line west of the village.

The 1/17th London on the left were held up by uncut wire and machine-gun fire and so, when the Germans counter-attacked south-east down the trenches, the tanks were abandoned.

50th Division

For the attack 151 Brigade consisted of 1/6th Durham LI (a composite Battalion made up of 1/5th Border Regiment and 1/8th Durham LI) and 1/5th Northumberland Fusiliers (attached from 49 Brigade). The

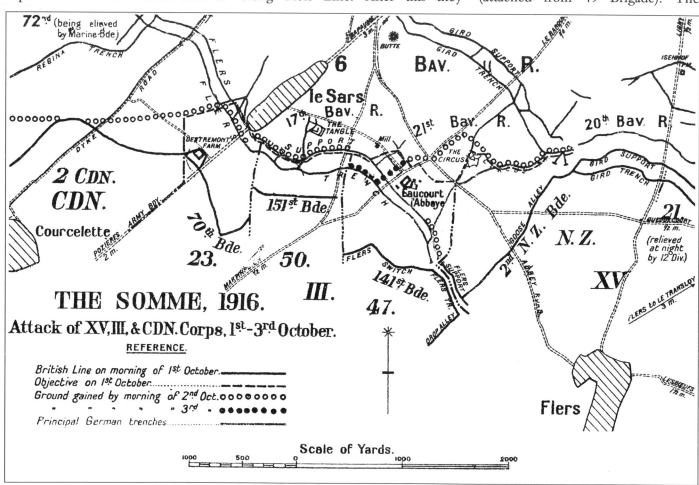

THE SOMME, 1916.
Attack of XV, III, & CDN. Corps, 1st–3rd October.
REFERENCE.

British Line on morning of 1st October.
Objective on 1st October.
Ground gained by morning of 2nd Oct.
    "   "   "   3rd
Principal German trenches

Scale of Yards.

Battle of the Transloy Ridges. Hauling a 60pdr gun (the largest gun that a horse team could manage) into position at Bazentin-le-Petit, October 1916. (Q.4365)

1/6th Durhams, suffering in the wake of 1/17th London's lack of success, had their right flank exposed and only gained a footing in Flers Trench. Their commanding officer was wounded and so 1/9th Durhams, who were in support, came up and rallied the front troops and by 9.30 p.m. elements of both Battalions had secured Flers Trench. In the centre and on the left the composite Battalion and 1/5th Northumberlands captured the Flers Lines with little difficulty.

23rd Division

On the Corps left 70 Brigade, made up of 11th Sherwood Foresters and 8th KOYLI, formed up in no man's land and successfully took Flers Trench and most of Flers Support, where 8th KOYLI linked with the Canadians and 11th Sherwood Foresters joined with 151 Brigade. The 9th York & Lancs, sent up to reinforce the attack, pushed out patrols which tried to enter Le Sars, but were checked by fire from houses.

CANADIAN CORPS
2nd Canadian Division

At 3.15 p.m. the Canadians attacked the part of Regina Trench in their sector: 4 Brigade (2nd Canadian Division) advanced east of Miraumont road, with 20th (Central Ontario) and 18th (W Ontario) Battalions. They managed to dig a trench 400 yards in front of the Brigade position to straighten the line and join with 23rd Division who attacked at the same time. To the west of the Miraumont road 5 Brigade's engagement was a different story: 22nd (Canadien Français) Battalion on the right, suffered from the enemy barrage on its rear wave and machine-gun fire on the front and few managed to reach the front line. The 25th Battalion (Nova Scotia Rifles), in the centre, took Kenora Trench and dug in.

On the left, 24th Battalion (Victoria Rifles) were initially successful, but when 5th Canadian Mounted Rifles (3rd Canadian Division) on its left flank were driven back by a counter-attack, the Germans began to bomb down Regina Trench and fierce fighting ensued. That night 5 Brigade held most of Kenora Trench, and advanced posts in the sunken west Miraumont road and Courcelette Trench were established. All was handed over to 6 Brigade before morning.

3rd Canadian Division

The 5th and 4th Canadian Mounted Rifles (8 Brigade, 3rd Canadian Division) attacked at zero hour, but were held up by the German barrage, machine-gun fire and uncut wire.

They eventually reached Regina Trench, where a bombing fight ensued, and stayed in position until 2 a.m. when they fell back. Because of bad weather the attack was postponed until 8 October.

BATTLE OF ANCRE HEIGHTS (1 October–11 November)

II CORPS

In the morning 25th Division relieved 11th Division on the right and spent its time in consolidation, before attacking Stuff Redoubt.

18th Division

55 Brigade continued the fight for the Schwaben Redoubt.

Monday 2 October

Temperature 57°F; wet and misty (3mm rain)

III CORPS
CAPTURE OF EAUCOURT L'ABBAYE
47th Division

To redress the failure of 1/17 London, the Division went forward with 1/23rd London (attached from 142 Brigade) at 6.45 a.m. to renew the attack on Eaucourt l'Abbaye, but were unsuccessful mainly because of machine-gun fire.

50th Division

The 1/6th and 1/9th Durhams had taken Flers Support before dawn, barricading their right flank because of 47th Division's lack of success.

II CORPS
18th Division

At 5.15 a.m. the Germans launched a counter-attack between the eastern end of the Schwaben Redoubt and the old German front line, where small gains were made.

Tuesday 3 October

Temperature 70°F; wet and misty

III CORPS
CAPTURE OF EAUCOURT L'ABBAYE
47th Division

At noon patrols of 1/18th London, who had relieved 1/17th, reported that there were few Germans in the Flers Trenches covering Eaucourt l'Abbaye. The Battalion moved forward and occupied a position north-west of the buildings, linking with 1/20th London. On the left they linked with 68 Brigade (23rd Division) which had relieved 151 Brigade (50th Division).

23rd Division

69 Brigade, which had relieved 70 Brigade in front of Le Sars, made an attempt to bomb up Flers Support beyond the Bapaume road during the night.

Wednesday 4 October

Temperature 66°F; overcast, wet morning, fine afternoon (4mm rain)

XV CORPS
41st Division relieved New Zealand Division.

III CORPS

47th Division completed its occupation of Flers Trench.

23rd Division

At 6 p.m. the Division made an unsuccessful attack on Flers Support, north of the Bapaume road. They tried various small local attacks over the next few days, but met with no success.

II CORPS
18th Division

The action on Schwaben Redoubt continued with no gains to either side.

Thursday 5 October

Temperature 66°F; overcast, windy and showery (6mm rain)

II CORPS
47th Division

After dark, the Division pushed its line forward to include the ruined mill north-west of Eaucourt l'Abbaye.

18th Division

At 10 a.m. 8th Norfolks (attached from 53 Brigade) tried to bomb Schwaben Redoubt from two converging directions, but became bogged down in the mud.

Friday 6 October

Temperature 70°F; sunny day with rain at night (2mm rain)

XV CORPS

On the night of 5/6th 41st Division relieved New Zealand Division; 39th Division relieved 18th Division.

III CORPS
23rd Division

One company of 11th Northumberland Fusiliers (68 Brigade) occupied The Tangle—a complex of trenches on the east side of Le Sars—but were later withdrawn because of heavy fire.

Saturday 7 October

Temperature 66°F; fine day, windy and wet at night

XIV CORPS
56th Division

The Division attacked next to the French and on the right at 1.45 p.m. with the London Scottish, 1/4th London and 1/12th London (168 Brigade), and 1/1st London, 1/7th Middlesex

(167 Brigade). The London Scottish had difficulty keeping in touch with the French who were advancing east rather than north, but they captured a group of gun pits and the southern end of Hazy Trench. At 1.47 p.m. 1/4th London advanced but were held up by machine-gun fire. At 1.49 p.m. 1/12th failed in their attack on Dewdrop Trench. Likewise 1/1st London on Spectrum Trench, except on the left where bombers linked with 1/7th Middlesex and took the southern section of the continuation of Rainbow Trench. The London Scottish and 1/4th London repulsed a counter-attack, but after nightfall were forced to withdraw.

20th Division

The Division easily took Rainbow Trench with 6th Ox & Bucks LI and 12th Rifle Brigade (60 Brigade).

Two Highlanders at the entrance to their shelter during a rest period. They are wearing winter leather jackets. North of Mametz Wood, October 1916. Note the strange shape of the shovel. (Q.4445)

They went on to take Misty Trench where they linked with 1/7th Middlesex on the right; and on the left 61 Brigade. The 7th KOYLI and 12th King's occupied Rainbow Trench and went on to occupy the south-eastern end of Cloudy Trench. The new line was from Cloudy Trench westwards towards the Beaulencourt road and was called Shine Trench. At 5 p.m. an unsuccessful counter-attack was launched by the Germans.

XV CORPS
12th Division

Just before zero hour the Germans put down a machine-gun barrage on

131

the British front-line trench held by the Division, hampering the attack. Although 8th and 9th Royal Fusiliers (36 Brigade) and 6th Buffs (37 Brigade) entered their objectives, Rainbow and Bayonet Trenches, they were forced out.

41st Division

The Division also encountered machine-gun fire. The 32nd and 26th Royal Fusiliers (124 Brigade) were forced to dig-in halfway to their objective, Bayonet Trench. That night they were reinforced by 21st KRRC and 10th Queen's. The entire establishment of the Brigade mustered less than a Battalion. On the left 122 Brigade reinforced 15th Hampshires and 11th Royal West Kents with 18th KRRC and 12th East Surreys.

At Gird Trench a discharge of burning oil was used to no avail and bombers of the Royal West Kents made little progress up either trench. Further west 122 Brigade had made contact with 140 Brigade.

III CORPS

ATTACKS ON THE BUTTE DE WARLENCOURT (7 October–5 November)

47th Division

The front was being held by 140 Brigade; 142 Brigade was resting. Their first objective was to take Snag Trench. The 1/8th London led the attack but were stopped by machine-gun fire. The 1/15th London, with 1/7th London in support, met a similar fate. All that was achieved were some posts near the Le Barque road in touch with 41st Division.

23rd Division

CAPTURE OF LE SARS

At zero hour 68 Brigade was on the right. The 12th Durham LI, with a tank in support, successfully entered The Tangle. The tank played a helpful part, but after turning left at the sunken Eaucourt l'Abbaye–Le Sars road it was hit by a shell. The 12th Durham LI were held up by machine-gun fire enfilading the road at Le Sars. Meanwhile 9th Green Howards (69 Brigade) moved into the south-west of Le Sars. At 2.30 p.m. 13th Durham LI linked with the Green Howards at the crossroads, and the village was eventually cleared. The 12th Durhams had dug in on the sunken road in front of The Tangle.

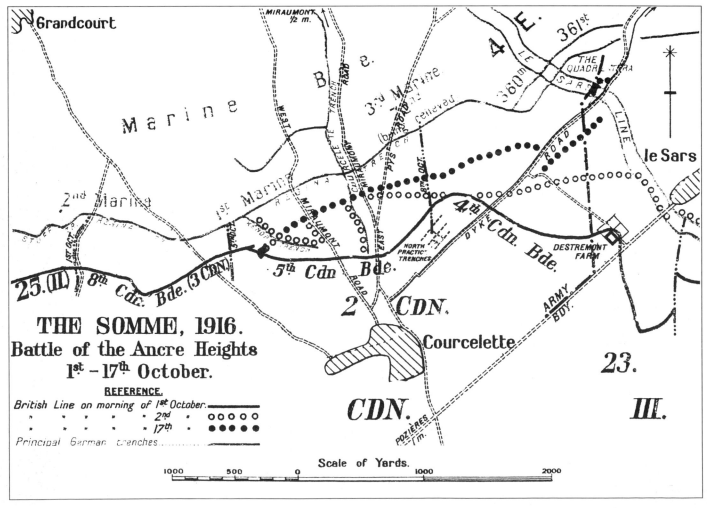

THE SOMME, 1916.
Battle of the Ancre Heights
1st – 17th October.

REFERENCE.
British Line on morning of 1st October. —————
" " " " 2nd " ooooo
" " " " 17th " ●●●●●
Principal German trenches ....

Scale of Yards.

The 11th West Yorks (69 Brigade) attacked Flers Support twenty minutes after zero hour, but were unsuccessful; this was remedied later when 10th Duke's went up in support.

That night 69 Brigade held Flers Trench and Flers Support.

II CORPS
18th Division was relieved by 39th Division.

That night the enemy attacked the Schwaben Redoubt with flame-throwers. They were repulsed by 16th and 17th Sherwood Foresters (117 Brigade).

The ruins of Mouquet Farm, October 1916. (Q.1423)

Sunday 8 October

Temperature 64°F; rain clearing to fine day

XIV CORPS
56th Division
On the right the Division attacked Hazy Trench at 3.30 p.m. with the London Rifle Brigade (169 Brigade). The 1/9th London (169 Brigade) and 1/3rd London (167 Brigade) attacked Dewdrop and Spectrum Trenches, but by nightfall they had all withdrawn back to their starting-place.

The Germans pushed forward to re-take Rainy Trench which had been left unoccupied by the British.

III CORPS
47th Division

That night the Division unsuccessfully attacked Snag Trench with the 1/21st and 1/22nd London (142 Brigade), although 1/22nd London did manage to establish posts on the Eaucourt l'Abbaye–Warlencourt road, linking with 23rd Division.

23rd Division
The Division attacked again at 4.50 a.m. Two companies of 8th York & Lancs (70 Brigade) cleared the Flers system, establishing a post dominating the Quarry on the Pys road—750 yards north-west of Le Sars, near the Quadrilateral—which had been abandoned by the Germans.

1st Canadian Division

At 4.50 a.m. in cold rain, the attack was launched. On the right, 4th and 3rd (Toronto) Battalions (1 Brigade) advanced, taking the front-line trench of the Le Sars line from Dyke Road to some 400 yards beyond the Quadrilateral.

At 1.20 p.m. a counter-attack was launched and heavy fighting ensued. At dusk the Canadians withdrew to their assault trenches. After dark 4th Battalion dug a forward trench on the right to within 50 yards of the Le Sars line, linking with 23rd Division (III Corps).

In 3 Brigade's initial assault were 16th (Canadian Scottish) and 13th (Royal Highlander) Battalions. The 16th entered Regina Trench but were forced to evacuate when 3rd Battalion withdrew. The 13th were stopped by wire and were forced to withdraw that night.

3rd Canadian Division

The Division fared no better: most of 58th Battalion (9 Brigade) entered Regina Trench but the rest were held up by the wire and were soon overwhelmed. The 43rd (Cameron Highlander) Battalion (9 Brigade) was also forced out.

On their right 7 Brigade had the Royal Canadian Regiment which made some advances but were forced to give up all their gains. On the extreme left of the attack, 49th (Edmonton) Battalion were held up by new wire and machine-gun fire on their way to Kenora Trench and were forced back.

Between 8 and 11 of October reliefs were started: 56th and 20th Divisions were relieved by 4th and 6th Division (XIV Corps), while 30th Division took over from 41st Division (XV Corps); 9th and 15th Division relieved 47th and 23rd Division (III Corps).

Monday 9 October

Temperature 64°F; fine

II CORPS
39th Division

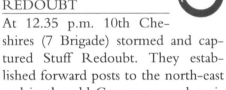

At 4.30 a.m. 16th Sherwood Foresters made a surprise attack in the dark on Schwaben Redoubt's northern face. The right company entered the trench but were forced out again.

25th Division
CAPTURE OF STUFF REDOUBT

At 12.35 p.m. 10th Cheshires (7 Brigade) stormed and captured Stuff Redoubt. They established forward posts to the north-east and in the old German second position, and repulsed two counter-attacks in the evening.

Tuesday 10 October

Temperature 68°F; sunny

CANADIAN CORPS

On the night of the 10th, 4th Canadian Division began to replace the 3rd in preparation for the complete relief of the Canadian Corps.

Wednesday 11 October

Temperature 61°F; dull, with a little rain

II CORPS
25th Division

The Division continued to hold its position in Stuff Redoubt against counter-attacks. On the 11th and 12th the enemy counter-attacked but were

A typical sunken road on the Somme battlefield. (Q.53146)

driven back by 8th Loyal North Lancs (7 Brigade, 25th Division).

Thursday 12 October

Temperature 61°F; dull but dry

XIV CORPS
4th Division

At 2.05 p.m., zero hour, 10 Brigade were on the right. The 1st Royal Warwicks advanced nearly 500 yards and dug-in south of Hazy Trench, in touch with the French on the left, and repelled an enemy counter-attack in the evening. The new trench was called Antelope Trench. On their left, however, 1st Royal Irish Fusiliers could do no better on Rainy and Dewdrop Trenches north-east of Lesboeufs.

An attempt was made by 12 Brigade to carry Spectrum Trench and some of 2nd Duke of Wellington's forced their way in to the trench and linked with 2nd Lancashire Fusiliers. A joint attack by both Battalions on Zenith Trench failed.

6th Division

North of the Le Transloy road, 2nd York & Lancs (16 Brigade) attacked Zenith Trench unsuccessfully. The 9th Suffolks (71 Brigade), next on the left in Misty Trench and part of Cloudy Trench, did not advance. The 1st West Yorks (18 Brigade) failed in their effort on Mild Trench and the remaining part of Cloudy Trench.

On the extreme left, 14th Durham LI stormed and occupied Rainbow Trench, moving on to clear the

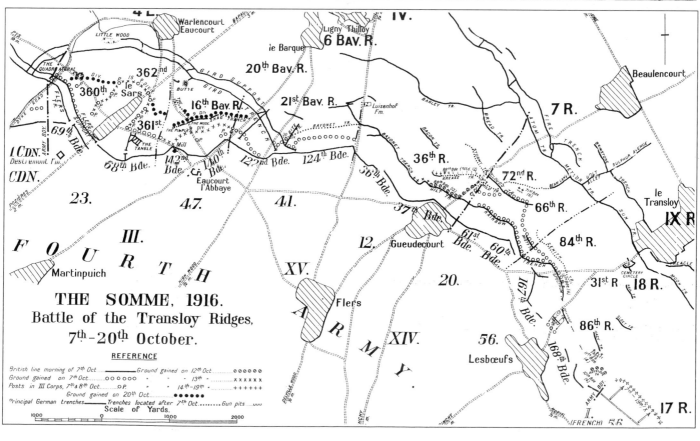

THE SOMME, 1916.
Battle of the Transloy Ridges,
7th-20th October.

REFERENCE

British line morning of 7th Oct. —————— Ground gained on 12th Oct. ⊙⊙⊙⊙⊙⊙
Ground gained on 7th Oct. ⊙⊙⊙⊙⊙⊙ " 13th " ✕✕✕✕✕✕
Posts in III Corps, 7th & 8th Oct. O.P. " 14th-19th " +++++
Ground gained on 20th Oct. ●●●●●●
Principal German trenches ——— Trenches located after 7th Oct. .... Gun pits ○○○

Scale of Yards.
1000   0   1000   2000

Captured German 5.9 field gun at Courcelette, October 1916. The officer is wearing a staff arm-band and gorget tab. (CO.846)

sunken Beaulencourt road mainly with bombs, and linking with the West Yorks on the right.

XV CORPS
12th Division

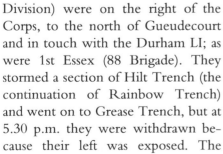

The Newfoundland Regiment (88 Brigade, 29th Division attached to 12th Division) were on the right of the Corps, to the north of Gueudecourt and in touch with the Durham LI; as were 1st Essex (88 Brigade). They stormed a section of Hilt Trench (the continuation of Rainbow Trench) and went on to Grease Trench, but at 5.30 p.m. they were withdrawn because their left was exposed. The

Newfoundlanders, however, hung on to Hilt Trench, bombing along it and erecting a barricade. The 7th Suffolks and 7th Norfolks (35 Brigade) encountered uncut wire in front of Bayonet Trench and, after sheltering in shell-holes, were obliged to fall back after dark.

30th Division

On the left of XV Corps, the Division attacked with 2nd Royal Scots Fusiliers who only made 150 yards and were forced to withdraw because of machine-gun fire. The 17th Manchesters had a similar experience, small groups making Bayonet Trench but later being forced out. The 2nd Bedfords (89 Brigade) were set to bomb up Gird Trench but only managed to take a small section of

Bite Trench. On their left 17th King's failed because of enfilading machine-gun fire from the north-west.

III CORPS
9th Division

The Division attacked under cover of smoke laid by 4th Special Company, RE on Little Wood and the Butte. The 7th Seaforth (26 Brigade) in attack, came under severe machine-gun fire, as did 10th Argylls who came up in support. Some 200 yards of ground was taken and they dug-in that night next to the South African Brigade. The 2nd Regiment (2 SA Brigade) followed the 4th but were stopped by machine-gun fire. Confused by smoke drifting from the Butte, they entrenched themselves halfway to Snag Trench. Some parties were still out front, but were withdrawn next morning.

II CORPS

The Germans made three counterattacks including two with flamethrowers, but all were repulsed.

Friday 13 October

Temperature 61°F; dull

No movements of any great consequence.

Saturday 14 October

Temperature 61°F; overcast

XIV CORPS

At 6.30 p.m. 2nd Seaforths (10 Brigade, 4th Division) entered Rainy Trench and the gun pits south of Dewdrop Trench in a surprise attack, but were forced out by a counter-attack. At the same time, 2nd Royal Dublin Fusiliers (10 Brigade) failed to take Hazy Trench. A bombing attack down Spectrum Trench towards Dewdrop by 1st King's Own (12 Brigade) that evening was also a failure. On the left of the Corps, 11th/Essex (18 Brigade, 6th Division) crossed Mild Trench and tried to bomb up Beaulencourt road, only to be forced back.

III CORPS

After dark the South Africans (3rd Battalion) seized The Pimple and 80 yards of Snag Trench.

II CORPS
25th Division

At 2.45 p.m. 8th Loyal North Lancs (7 Brigade) attacked and secured The

Mound—a position north-west of the Redoubt giving observation over Grandcourt.

39th Division
CAPTURE OF THE SCHWABEN REDOUBT

At 2.45 p.m. 4/5th Black Watch and 1/1st Cambridge (118 Brigade) assisted by 17th KRRC (117 Brigade) attacked the Schwaben Redoubt and, although the fighting lasted until 11 p.m., the Germans were driven entirely from the Redoubt. Meanwhile 1/6th Cheshires (118 Brigade) advanced the line on the left.

Sunday 15 October

Temperature 57°F; rain in morning, clearing later (3mm rain)

XIV CORPS

Before dawn 2nd Sherwood Foresters (71 Brigade, 6th Division) captured the gun pits in front of their position, Cloudy Trench.

II CORPS
39th Division

A total of three counter-attacks were launched against the Schwaben, two with flame-throwers, but all were repulsed.

Monday 16 October

Temperature 54°F; white frost, but bright and sunny

II CORPS
39th Division

The entire line north of the river Ancre was handed over to 63rd Division by 116 Brigade which began

taking over the Schwaben Redoubt from 118 Brigade.

Tuesday 17 October

Temperature 55°F; frost, but fine day, turning to rain at night (3mm rain)

II CORPS
39th Division

The Division was under heavy shelling all day in the Schwaben Redoubt.

Wednesday 18 October

Temperature 57°F; rain in morning, clearing later (4mm rain)

XIV CORPS
4th Division

At 3.40 a.m., zero hour, 11 Brigade were to attack Frosty, Hazy, Rainy and Dewdrop Trenches. The 1st Rifle Brigade reached the gun pits in front of Hazy Trench but had to pull back; 1st East Lancs were held up in front of Dewdrop Trench by machine-gun fire; 1st King's Own (12 Brigade) in Spectrum Trench, however, bombed down towards Dewdrop Trench, gaining 70 yards.

6th Division

The 9th Norfolks (71 Brigade) attacked and took the north-western portion of Mild Trench, defending it against a counter-attack at nightfall.

XV CORPS
12th Division

The Division assaulted Grease Trench on its right with 2nd Hampshires and 4th Worcesters (88 Brigade), and the south-eastern end of Bayonet Trench with 9th Essex (35 Brigade). The Hampshires captured Grease Trench and gave support to 9th Norfolks (6th Division) beyond the Gueudecourt–Beaulencourt road, and the Worcesters were just as successful; they blocked Hilt Trench to protect their flank. The 9th Essex made little progress: their left company entered Bayonet Trench at a point where there was no wire, but they were bombed out from the flanks.

30th Division

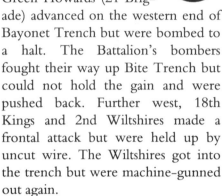

On the right 89 Brigade made no attack. The 2nd Green Howards (21 Brigade) advanced on the western end of Bayonet Trench but were bombed to a halt. The Battalion's bombers fought their way up Bite Trench but could not hold the gain and were pushed back. Further west, 18th Kings and 2nd Wiltshires made a frontal attack but were held up by uncut wire. The Wiltshires got into the trench but were machine-gunned out again.

Two tanks that were to have assisted the attack, broke down at Flers. At 8 a.m., however, after the fighting had died down, one of them managed to cross the British front line and sit astride Gird Trench for twenty minutes, clearing it. But the infantry were so exhausted and in such disorder that it was impossible to take advantage of this. The second tank could not reach the front line because of the mud.

III CORPS
9th Division

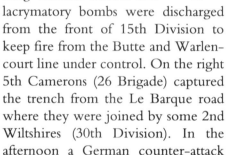

The Division made another attempt upon Snag Trench. Smoke and lacrymatory bombs were discharged from the front of 15th Division to keep fire from the Butte and Warlencourt line under control. On the right 5th Camerons (26 Brigade) captured the trench from the Le Barque road where they were joined by some 2nd Wiltshires (30th Division). In the afternoon a German counter-attack

gained a footing back in the trench but they were pushed out after dark.

On the left, 1st South African Regiment had two companies taking Snag Trench and pushing on beyond it, but machine-gun fire from the Butte took a heavy toll, leaving a small group in Snag Trench. On the left of the Camerons at daybreak, they started to bomb along the trench to The Pimple and at 5.45 p.m. they attacked from both flanks. The Germans now held only 100 yards of the trench on either side of the Nose.

Thursday 19 October

Temperature 57°F; heavy rain (4mm rain)

XIV CORPS
4th Division

After dark, one platoon of 1st Somerset LI (11 Brigade) found Frosty Trench empty,

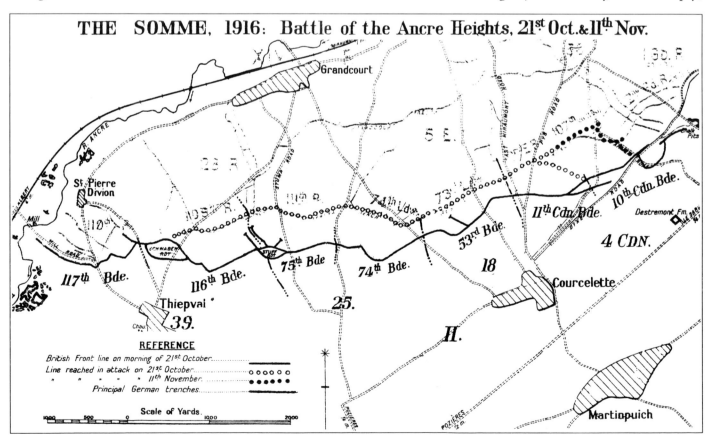

THE SOMME, 1916: Battle of the Ancre Heights, 21st Oct. & 11th Nov.

REFERENCE

British Front line on morning of 21st October..............
Line reached in attack on 21st October.............. o o o o o o
" " " " 11th November. .... ● ● ● ● ● ●
Principal German trenches..............

Scale of Yards

occupied it and fought off a counter-attack.

III CORPS
9th Division

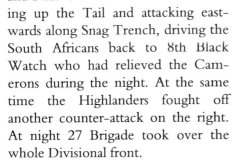

At dawn a counter-attack was launched by bombers and a flame-thrower moving up the Tail and attacking eastwards along Snag Trench, driving the South Africans back to 8th Black Watch who had relieved the Camerons during the night. At the same time the Highlanders fought off another counter-attack on the right. At night 27 Brigade took over the whole Divisional front.

Friday 20 October

Temperature 48°F; fine but very cold

XIV CORPS
8th Division relieved 6th Division.

III CORPS
9th Division

At 4 p.m. 6th KOSB (27 Brigade) attacked and took the Nose; losing it and finally retaking it later. That night they were established in Snag Trench and a company of 11th Royal Scots held 250 yards of the Tail.

Saturday 21 October

Temperature 45°F; fine but very cold

II CORPS
39th Division
CAPTURE OF STUFF TRENCH

At 5 a.m. the Germans counter-attacked the Schwaben Redoubt and entered it in two places. The 17th KRRC (117 Brigade) and part of 14th Hampshires (116 Brigade) drove them out with bombs.

Mail arriving at a Field Post Office, October 1916. (CO.955)

The Division led with 116 Brigade which on the right consisted of 13th Royal Sussex (who met with some initial resistance), 11th Royal Sussex in the centre and a company of 14th Hampshires on the left. All took their objectives, including Stuff Trench, with little resistance. A subsidiary attack on Pope's Nose was delivered by 117 Brigade, with a company each of 17th Sherwood Foresters and 16th Rifle Brigade, and gained some ground.

4th Canadian Division

Zero hour was at 12.06 p.m. The Canadians, attacking on the left with 87th (Canadian Grenadier Guards), 102nd Battalion (11 Brigade) and an overhead machine-gun barrage, took their objective, Regina Trench, with little opposition. East of the Pys road,

139

a defensive flank was formed with outposts well forward of Regina Trench. The 102nd Battalion on the left was in touch with 10th Essex (53 Brigade, 18th Division). The Canadians received at least three counter-attacks in the afternoon but repelled them. All units consolidated throughout the next day.

18th Division

The 10th Essex (53 Brigade, 18 Division) made gains similar to those of the Canadians. The 8th Norfolks (53 Brigade) likewise took their goal although, near the Courcelette–Grandcourt road, a bombing fight lasted some time. With the help of 11th Lancashire Fusiliers on the right of 25th Division, however, the resistance was overcome.

25th Division

The Division used two brigades: 74 Brigade on the right consisted of 11th Lancashire Fusiliers, 9th Loyal North Lancs and 13th Cheshires who attacked in extended line and suffered few casualties; 75 Brigade consisted of 8th Border Regiment, with one company of 11th Cheshires attached, and 2nd and 8th South Lancs. All had a similar experience, reaching as far as the dugouts in Stump Road; only to be stopped by the British standing barrage. The Borderers, who received casualties from staying too close to the British barrage, were then held up by bombing a large dugout. Bombers of 8th South Lancs cleared the dugouts in Stump Road but were stopped by the British standing barrage.

Sunday 22 October

Temperature not known; fine and bright, but bitterly cold

II CORPS

That night 19th Division relieved 25th Division and took over the right

Tank in action, October 1916. (CO.985)

sector 39th Division; 18th Division extended its left to the Pozières–Miraumont road.

Monday 23 October

Temperature 55°F; dull and misty morning (3mm rain)

XIV CORPS
4th Division

Zero hour was changed from 11.30 a.m. to 2.30 p.m. because of heavy mist. On the right the Division advanced with 1st Hampshires (11 Brigade) and 2nd Royal Dublin Fusiliers (attached from 10 Brigade). Both the Hampshires and the French on their left were stopped almost immediately by fire from Boritska Trench.

When 1st Rifle Brigade came up to reinforce, they established posts north-west of their objective. After dark they linked with the Royal Dublin Fusiliers at the gun pits and Strongpoint.

The 1st Royal Warwicks (attached from 10 Brigade) in support, got mixed up with the Fusiliers and they combined. 12 Brigade were stopped by machine-gun fire from Dewdrop Trench. Some men of 2nd Essex achieved the Trench but were forced out.

The 1st King's Own entered Spectrum Trench north of Dewdrop. Bombers from 2nd Duke of Wellington's gave assistance but only Spectrum Trench was captured in the end.

8th Division

On the right were 23 Brigade; 2nd Scottish Rifles and 2nd Middlesex took Zenith Trench. The Scottish Rifles pushed on to Orion Trench some 200 yards further on, but were forced back.

25 Brigade failed in their attempt on the northern part of Zenith Trench, 2nd Lincolns being stopped by rapid fire. The only gain was a line of posts 130 yards south-east towards the strongpoint held by 2nd Rifle Brigade.

24 Brigade, leading with 2nd East Lancs took most of Mild Trench and consolidated the flanks where they repulsed bombing attacks.

A night of rain stopped 25 Brigade's attempt to take Zenith Trench at 3.50 a.m. The 2nd Royal Berks and 1st Royal Irish Rifles lost the creeping barrage and were stopped by machine-gun fire after 70 yards. That night 33rd Division relieved 4th Division.

Tuesday 24 October

Temperature 63°F; overcast at times

CANADIAN CORPS

The Canadians took over from the left of Fourth Army, up to the chalk pits on the Le Sars–Pys road.

Wednesday 25 October

Temperature 52°F; rain in morning (2mm rain)

CANADIAN CORPS
4th Canadian Division

The 44th Battalion (10 Canadian Brigade) attempted to extend the Canadian occupation of Regina Trench, up to Farmer Road. They

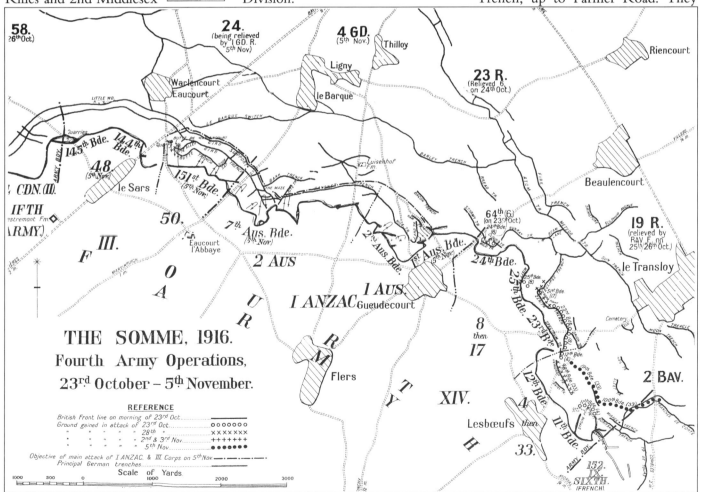

THE SOMME, 1916.
Fourth Army Operations,
23rd October – 5th November.

REFERENCE

British Front line on morning of 23rd Oct.
Ground gained in attack of 23rd Oct. ooooooo
"   "   "   "   28th xxxxxxx
"   "   "   "   2nd & 3rd Nov. +++++++
"   "   "   "   5th Nov. ●●●●●●●
Objective of main attack of I ANZAC. & III Corps on 5th Nov. —·—·—·—
Principal German trenches

Scale of Yards
1000 500 0 1000 2000 3000

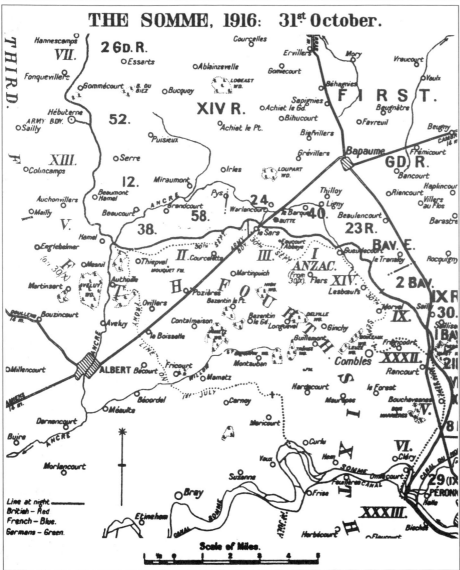

THE SOMME, 1916: 31st October.

were unsuccessful, however, because of a heavy barrage and machine-gun fire from the right flank.

Thursday 26 October

Temperature 55°F; showery (1mm rain)

II CORPS
19th Division

At 5 a.m. the Germans attacked Stuff Redoubt east of the old German second position. They were fought off by 7th East Lancs (56 Brigade) and an artillery barrage.

Friday 27 October

Temperature 55°F; showery (1mm rain)

No movements of any great consequence.

Saturday 28 October

Temperature 55°F; very wet and cold (8mm rain)

XIV CORPS
33rd Division

Attacking at 6 a.m., the Division succeeded in

capturing Rainy and Dewdrop Trenches with 1st Middlesex and 4th King's (98 Brigade). By 9.30 a.m., however, the Middlesex had been bombed out of Dewdrop, as were the King's.

NORTH OF THE ANCRE

A gas attack was made by Special Brigade, RE consisting of 1,126 lacrymatory bombs which were fired from 4in Stokes mortars into Beaumont Hamel. That night 135 40-pound phosgene bombs were also fired into Beaumont Hamel and Y Ravine. Up to 7 November the entire area was constantly raided and patrolled.

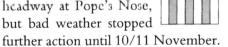

Sunday 29 October

Temperature 53°F; very wet (7mm rain)

XIV CORPS
33rd Division

At dawn (5.45 a.m.) 19 Brigade, consisting of 1st Camerons and 5/6th Scottish Rifles, tried to gain more of Boritska Trench but were stopped by machine-gun fire from fortified shellholes.

17th Division
17th Division relieved 8th Division.

II CORPS
39th Division
The Division made more headway at Pope's Nose, but bad weather stopped further action until 10/11 November.

Monday 30 October

Temperature 61°F; wet, dull and cold (7mm rain)

ANZAC
The Anzacs replaced XV Corps in the centre of Fourth Army, 1st Australian Division taking over from 29th Division and 5th Australian Division taking over from 30th Division.

Tuesday 31 October

Temperature 63°F

XIII CORPS
A patrol entered the German front line south-east of Hebuterne and found it unoccupied.

Paying the price. (Q.2477)

NOVEMBER

Wednesday 1 November

Temperature 59°F; 2mm rain

XV CORPS
33rd Division

At 5.45 a.m. 1st Cameronians and 5/6th Scottish Rifles (19 Brigade) attacked. Some of the Scottish Rifles entered Boritska Trench but were forced out. At 3.30 p.m. 100 Brigade— 1/9th Highland LI and 2nd Worcesters— tried in concert with the French to take Boritska Trench but failed to hold it because of machine-gun fire from Le Transloy cemetery, the mud and exhaustion.

Thursday 2 November

Temperature 57°F; 3mm rain

XV CORPS
17th Division

A surprise attack at 5.30 p.m. by a party of 7th Border Regiment (51 Brigade) took the remainder of Zenith Trench. After repelling a counter-attack, a bombing block was set up 150 yards along Eclipse Trench.

Friday 3 November

Temperature 59°F; 1mm rain

XV CORPS
17th Division

The 7th Lincolns (51 Brigade) repulsed another counter-attack on Zenith Trench from the north and over open ground. In the evening,

General view of Leuze Wood, November 1916. (Q.1623)

146

with bombers of 7th Green Howards, a pocket of Germans left in Zenith Trench was cleared. At 4 p.m. 1st Queen's (100 Brigade, 33rd Division) tried to take Boritska Trench but were unsuccessful.

Saturday 4 November

Temperature 54°F; wet and cloudy (2mm rain)

XV CORPS
33rd Division

98 Brigade failed to gain the ridge east of Dewdrop trench before being relieved.

Sunday 5 November

Temperature 59°F; clear

Zero hour was set for 11.10 a.m.

XV CORPS
33rd Division

The Division attacked with the 2nd Worcesters (100 Brigade) and took Boritska and Mirage Trenches. They linked with 16th KRRC (100 Brigade) which had taken Hazy Trench. The 2nd Royal West Kents (19 Brigade), next on the left, pushed forward up the Lesboeufs–Le Transloy road, but gained

little ground because of the failure of fighting patrols of 7th East Yorks and 7th Green Howards (50 Brigade) on their right.

ANZAC
1st Australian Division
At 12.30 a.m., in pouring rain, the left of Anzac Corps attacked the salient north of Guedecourt. The 3rd Battalion (1 Brigade) sent bombers forward in the German front line with some success, but all to no avail because 1st Battalion failed in two frontal attacks and a bombing attack on Hilt Trench and had to withdraw. 7 Brigade attacked with 27th Battalion on the right, a composite battalion in the centre (consisting of 25th

Battalion and one company each from 26th and 27th Battalions), and 28th Battalion on the left. The 27th Battalion entered Bayonet Trench at several points only to withdraw at dusk. Some of the composite battalion entered the Maze and managed to hold. The 28th Battalion failed twice and was forced to retire.

BATTLE OF THE ANCRE HEIGHTS

III CORPS
50th Division
The Division attacked with 1/8th Durham LI (151 Brigade) on the right.

The men had to pull one another out of the mud before they could start. They almost reached the German front line but were stopped by machine-gun fire and gradually fell back during the day. The 1/6th Durhams suffered a similar fate except on the left where they linked with 1/9th Durhams in the line. The 1/9th went through two lines of German trenches, reached the Butte and established a post on the Bapaume road—some entering the Warlencourt line. But these advanced posts were forced back and at 10 p.m. the enemy were still holding the quarry and 500 yards of the German front line. By midnight the Durhams had been forced back to their own lines.

Monday 6 November

Temperature 57°F; cloudy

XV CORPS
33rd Division
100 Brigade was re-
lieved by 24 Brigade
(8th Division).

Tuesday 7 November

Temperature 55°F; 12mm rain

XIII CORPS
In a raid south-east of Hebuterne, men of 30th Division killed 30 Germans.

Wednesday 8 November

Temperature 57°F; 2mm rain

XV CORPS
33rd Division was relieved by 8th Division.

Thursday 9 November

Temperature 54°F; frosty, bright and clear

Mud prevented any movement.

Friday 10 November

Temperature 50°F

Mud prevented any movement.

Saturday 11 November

Temperature 55°F; frosty and misty, with low cloud

II CORPS
At 5 a.m. No 2 Special Company, RE fired 180 lacrymatory bombs into Beaumont Hamel using 4in mortars. At 3.30 p.m. 47 gas drums were fired into the village and 39 into Y Ravine.

The Canadians attacked the eastern section of Regina Trench at midnight with 46th (South Saskatchewan) and 47th (British Columbia) Battalions (10 Brigade) and a company of 102nd Battalion (11 Brigade). Positions were established in the trenches leading north-east into the Le Sars–Pys line, and later several counter-attacks were dealt with.

Sunday 12 November

Temperature 50°F; overcast

II, IV CORPS
Troops moved up for the attack on the 13th.

Monday 13 November

Temperature 54°F

BATTLE OF THE ANCRE (13–18 November)

II CORPS
19th Division
On the right of the attack 7th East Lancs and 7th Loyal North Lancs (56 Brigade, 19th Division) assembled in no man's land in advance of Stuff Trench, with eight guns of 56th Machine-gun Company. This was accomplished under cover of a heavy mist. They were successful in this approach and by 8.15 a.m. had established a line along their object-ive, including a sunken road called Lucky Way leading to Grandcourt. Two companies of 81st Field Com-pany, RE and two companies of 5th South Wales Borderers (Pioneers) moved up to help with consolidation. One company of 7th King's Own reinforced the right of the Loyals. Further on the right, 6th Wiltshires (58 Brigade) failed to take Stump Road, the right boundary of the Division. No counter-attacks were attempted by the enemy.

39th Division
The Division attacked on the right with 118 Brigade. They formed up in no man's land on tape guides laid by 234th Field Company, RE, un-noticed by the Germans. The 1/1st Hertfords, facing north, had the Hansa Line as their objective and had reached it by 7.30 a.m. The 1/1st Cambridgeshires attacked north-west, reaching Mill Trench with little difficulty and, by 10 a.m., the station crossing and Beaucourt Mill (the point where they would later meet 63rd Division) were secured. The 1/6th Cheshires and 4/5th Black Watch were handicapped by fog and lost direction in the maze of trenches.

At 6.15 a.m. 16th Sherwood For-esters (117 Brigade), attacking from Mill Road up the Ancre Valley near the river on the left of the Corps, sur-prised the enemy. Two companies were to clear the dugouts in the banks of the river, and one along the top of the bank. They met a party of Black Watch who joined in the final assault on St Pierre Divion which fell to a mixed force of Foresters, Highlanders and Cheshires at 7.40 a.m.

Of the three tanks that were scheduled to start from Thiepval and aid the assault, one was lost to the mud before reaching Thiepval and another had mechanical trouble. The third reached the German front line at 7 a.m., but shortly after fell into a dugout and was attacked. It sent a pigeon for help but the Foresters and Black Watch arrived at 9 a.m. and drove off the attackers.

117 Brigade reinforced 116 Brigade with 17th Sherwood Foresters. At 11.30 a.m. 11th Hampshires (attached from 116 Brigade), who were waiting in the dugouts of the Schwaben Redoubt, advanced down the Ancre Valley, only to be withdrawn that afternoon. The Hertfords were digging-in 50 yards beyond the Hansa Line with 7th Loyal North Lancs (56 Brigade) on their right. The Cambridgeshires and Cheshires worked on Mill Trench as far back as St Pierre

12th (Labour) Battalion, Black Watch (Army troops) broadening a road at Fricourt, November 1916. 48th (South Midland) Divisional Heaquarters at top of step. (Q.4548)

Divion, which was organized for defence. All units then consolidated.

A section of 4th Motor Machine-gun Battalion with some guns on side-cars drove down to the Ancre via Mill Road and then man-handled forward. 118 Brigade was responsible for the defence of the ground gained and set the Hertfords to construct a redoubt at the junction of Mill Trench and Hansa Line. The Cambridgeshires dug a support line facing north across the base of the Hertfords' position. The Cheshires were made responsible for St Pierre Divion and the strongpoints in the river valley; also the posts at the Mill east of Beaucourt Station. The Black Watch, who were muddled up with the Cheshires, were ordered to reform and occupy the right of the Hansa Line. At 6.45 p.m. two small counter-attacks on the Hertfords' position were fought off.

At 8.32 a.m., by which time all the objectives had been taken, 227th Field Company, RE and part of 13th

Gloucesters (Pioneers) were to repair the Hamel–St Pierre Divion road and, by 4 p.m., a mud track was laid to the village.

V CORPS
63rd Division

The Division was on the right of the Corps, next to the river. 189 Brigade had Hood and Hawke Battalions in front and Drake and Nelson in rear. In support were 1st Honourable Artillery Company and 7th Royal Fusiliers of 190 Brigade. On the left were 188 Brigade with Howe Battalion and 1st Royal Marines in front. Anson Battalion and 2nd Royal Marines were in the second line. The 4th Bedfords and 10th Royal Dublin Fusiliers (190 Brigade) were in support.

At zero hour they all moved forward on the right. Hood and Drake Battalions met with heavy machine-gun fire but took the German front

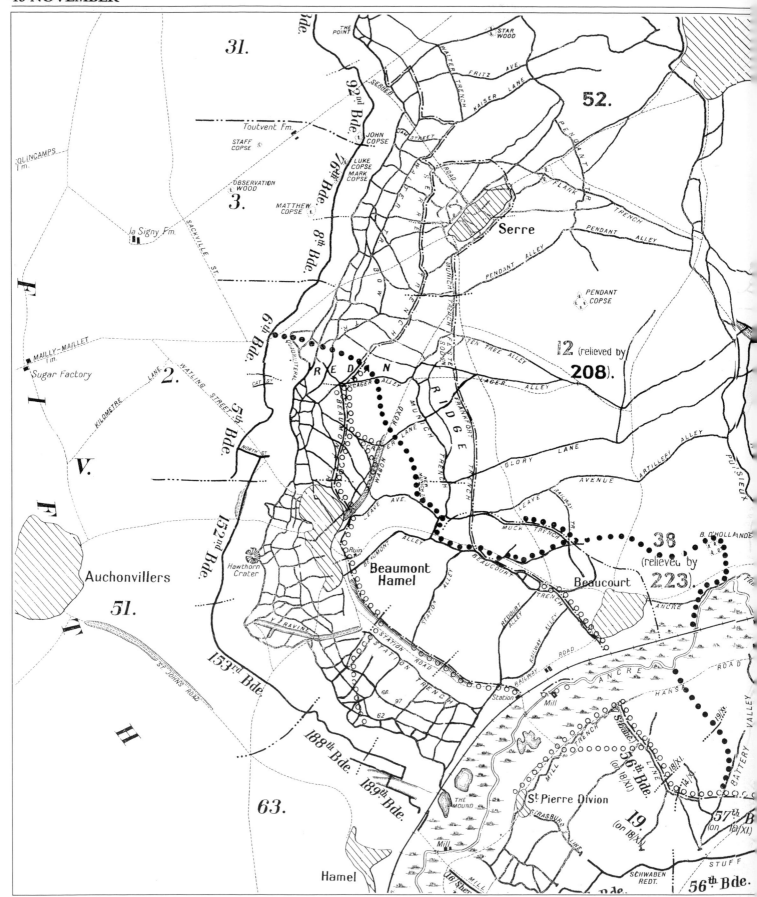

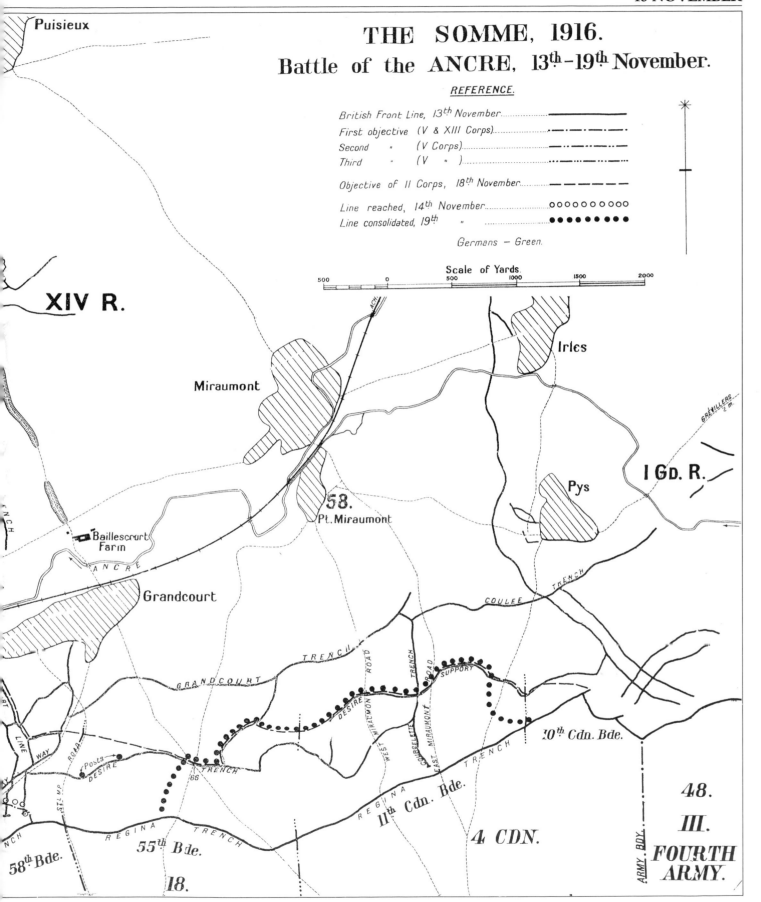

THE SOMME, 1916.
Battle of the ANCRE, 13th-19th November.

REFERENCE.

British Front Line, 13th November...........
First objective (V & XIII Corps)...........
Second " (V Corps)...........
Third " (V ")...........

Objective of II Corps, 18th November...........
Line reached, 14th November........... ooooooooo
Line consolidated, 19th " .... •••••••••

Germans — Green.

Scale of Yards.

Puisieux

XIV R.

Miraumont

Irles

I Gd. R.

Pys

58.
Pt. Miraumont

Baillescourt Farm

Grandcourt

COULEE TRENCH

GRANDCOURT TRENCH

DESIRE TRENCH

WEST MIRAUMONT ROAD

COURCELETTE TRENCH SUPPORT

EAST MIRAUMONT ROAD

10th Cdn. Bde.

REGINA TRENCH

11th Cdn. Bde.

Posts
DESIRE

REGINA TRENCH

58th Bde.

55th Bde.

18.

4 CDN.

48.

III.

FOURTH ARMY.

ARMY BDY.

Clearing mud from a trench near Trônes Wood, November 1916. Note the leather jerkins lined with khaki cloth which were very popular. (Q.1621)

the river at the Mill and received supplies of bombs.

Throughout the day many bombing attacks were made against the strongpoint on the spur with some small successes.

That night the situation was that 188 Brigade had linked up with 51st Division on their left in the German support trench, thereby outflanking the Germans left in their front line.

The 13th KRRC (from 111 Brigade brought up that night with 190 Brigade) were sent up to reinforce the Beaucourt attack and had extended the position to the left as far as Redoubt Alley by 9.30 p.m.. The other units of the Brigade (13th Royal Fusiliers and 13th Rifle Brigade) reached the old first objective at midnight while 10th Royal Fusiliers, in support, were moving up from Hamel to the original British front line.

lines. The troops were rallied and they went forward at the appointed time to take Beaucourt Station and Station Road. Some 400 prisoners were taken from dugouts along the road. One company of 1st HAC were to seize The Mound and clear the dugouts in the railway embankment on the extreme right of the attack. So by 6.45 a.m. the right of the attack had secured its first objective.

On the left of Hood and Drake Battalions, Hawke Battalion, followed by Nelson Battalion, suffered from heavy machine-gun fire as did 188 Brigade. A small force of stray men from Howe, Anson and Nelson Battalions (some 100 in all) did manage to reach the first objective. On the left of the Division, 1st Royal Marines only managed to advance in

isolated groups and a few linked with 51st Division.

By 6.30 a.m. it was clear that in places the front line had not been captured as far as the 'strongpoint' in the support lines; 188 Brigade organized bombing attacks, and 190 Brigade was then ordered to advance. By 7.40 a.m. 1st HAC on the right were digging-in along the German reserve line. The 7th Royal Fusiliers were held up in the front line as were the Bedfords and Royal Dublin Fusiliers farther north along the line. Some parties of these Battalions, however, joined in the struggle on the Beaumont Hamel spur.

At 7.45 a.m. 300 men of Hood Battalion, 120 of Drake and some HAC men advanced to the edge of Beaucourt, meeting with little resistance, but they were forced to withdraw a little and dig-in because of artillery fire. In the afternoon they gained touch with 1/1st Cambridgeshires (39th Division, II Corps) across

51st Division
CAPTURE OF BEAUMONT HAMEL

The Division attacked on the right with 1/7th Green Howards and 1/6th Black Watch in the front line, 1/5th Gordons in support, and 1/7th Black Watch providing carrying parties (all 153 Brigade). 152 Brigade was similarly deployed, with 1/5th Seaforth and 1/8th Argylls in front, and 1/6th Seaforths in support, but 1/6th Gordons were kept in reserve. 154 Brigade was in Divisional Reserve in Forceville, nearly four miles away.

Six minutes before zero hour the leading Battalion moved out to clear the British wire and the attack was started by the blowing of a mine in Hawthorn Crater. The 1/7th Gordons, with two companies in front, met with little opposition and passed by the east end of Y Ravine. They reached their first objective by 6.45 a.m., having picked up a small party of Marines (63rd Division) on the way, and continued up the hill northwards before falling back to Station Road. The left of the Battalion had more trouble, from machine-guns and snipers. The extreme left, together with 1/6th Black Watch, were held up by fire from Y Ravine. The 1/5th Gordons were put in to help at 7 a.m. Some of 1/6th Black Watch skirted the ravine to the north and pressed on. Early in the afternoon 1/4th Gordons (154 Brigade) advanced to assault the south end of Beaumont Hamel which was taken by a mixed force of 1/4th, 1/5th Gordons and 1/6th Black Watch.

By this time 152 Brigade had four Battalions in the village. The 1/5th

Machine-gun officers outside a captured German dugout beneath the ruined church at Beaumont Hamel, November 1916. Both men are wearing trench waders. Two Marks of Lee Enfield can be seen: on the right is an SMLE Mk III and in the centre a Mk I. (Q.1555)

Seaforths and 1/8th Argylls met with stiff resistance from the front system. The Seaforths south of Hawthorn Crater had trouble finding the gaps in the wire. The Argylls from the north of the Auchonvillers – Beaumont Hamel road met with machine-gun fire before the front-line trench was carried. The 1/6th Seaforths came in on the right in support of 1/5th. Bombing parties of 1/6th Gordons were sent to help take the German reserve line, and the advance continued to Beaumont Hamel. Two tanks were sent up from Auchonvillers. One ditched between the German front and support lines and the other on the northern edge of the village.

Consolidation continued with the assistance of 1/8th Royal Scots (Pioneers). Some reorganization was carried out also. The front was held by the 1/4th Gordons (154 Brigade), 1/6th Black Watch (153 Brigade), two companies of 1/6th Gordons and 1/8th Argylls (both 152 Brigade) who

were in touch on the left with 2nd Division. The 1/7th Gordons (153 Brigade) and 1/5th and 1/6th Seaforths (152 Brigade) were withdrawn to the reserve line of the German front position where they were reinforced by two companies of 1/7th Seaforths (154 Brigade) at 9 p.m. The 1/5th Gordons (153 Brigade), not knowing how far 63rd Division had advanced, formed a defensive flank to connect with the left of that Division.

2nd Division

The Division attacked Redan Ridge with 5 Brigade on the right; 2nd Highland LI and 24th Royal Fusiliers in front, and 17th Royal Fusiliers and 2nd Ox & Bucks LI in the second line. On the left, 6 Brigade led with 13th Essex and 2nd South Staffords, with 1st King's and 17th Middlesex in the rear. 99 Brigade was in the Divisional Reserve.

5 Brigade formed up in the open and stayed close to the barrage, taking the front line easily though not without suffering losses. The 2nd HLI and 24th Royal Fusiliers pressed on through to Beaumont Trench, arriving there on time. On the left, 24th Royal Fusiliers, assisted by 2nd Ox & Bucks LI, blocked the trench running north and repelled spasmodic bombing attacks because 6 Brigade was having difficulties.

The Quadrilateral was the main problem, the wire being mostly intact, and because of fog and mud progress was slow. Some of the Essex and King's on the right pressed on to the first objective with 5 Brigade.

They then formed a block at the junction of Beaumont Trench with Lager Alley. The South Staffords and Middlesex swerved north-east, confused by the presence of 3rd Division on their left who had lost their way. Sections of all four Battalions forced their way into the enemy front-line trench but were pinned down by machine-gun fire.

At 7.30 a.m. only 5 Brigade was ready to attack their second objective. There were only 120 men from 17th Royal Fusiliers and 2nd Ox & Bucks

Battle of the Ancre. The Mill at Beaucourt-sur-Ancre. Captured by 63rd (Naval) Division on 14 November 1916. (Q.4529)

LI and, on the left, a few Essex and King's of 6 Brigade. There were not enough to hold any of the foot-holds but they managed to reach Frankfort Trench, gradually falling back first to Munich Trench and then Wagon Road and Crater Lane.

At 7.30 a.m. 99 Brigade began to move forward and two companies of 23rd Royal Fusiliers were sent two hours later to reinforce 5 Brigade on the first objective. At 9 a.m. the remnants of 6 Brigade were ordered back to the British front line to reorganize.

Twice 99 Brigade were ordered to attack but on both occasions the orders were postponed.

That night 22nd Royal Fusiliers (99 Brigade) were sent to Beaumont Trench as reinforcements. Two sections of 226th Field Company, RE and two platoons of 10th Duke of Cornwall's LI (Pioneers) were sent forward to construct a strongpoint in the first objective. At 8.15 p.m. two battalions of 112 Brigade (from 37th Division) in Corps Reserve, were sent to 2nd Division.

3rd Division

In its attack on Serre this Division also came to grief in the muddy conditions. 8 Brigade was on the right with 2nd Royal Scots and 1st Royal Scots Fusiliers leading, followed by 8th East Yorks and 7th King's Shropshire LI in the second line. On the left were 76 Brigade, 10th Royal Welsh Fusiliers and 2nd Suffolks, with 1st Gordons and 8th King's Own in support with 36 machine-guns. The waist-deep mud soon

turned the attack into a shambles, some of 8 Brigade reaching the German support line but unable to remain, and others losing direction completely. The fate of 6 Brigade was similar and at 6.30 a.m. attempts were made to collect the exhausted men scattered throughout the area. Various plans were made but none came to fruition and, at 4.30 p.m., all operations were cancelled.

XIII CORPS
31st Division

The Division's job was to make a defensive flank with 92 Brigade on a frontage of 500 yards. They attacked with 12th and 13th East Yorks and pushed forward at midnight; Lewis-guns and snipers were to act as close support. At 5.45 a.m. the assault went according to plan and they occupied the front line. To occupy the support line was much more difficult, and bombing counter-attacks from the

south-west along communication trenches in the direction of Star Wood began at about 8 a.m. and lasted all morning. Carrying-parties and two companies of 11th East Yorks were held up by the German barrage on no man's land. At 9.30 a.m. the Germans launched a counter-attack from Star Wood across the open, but a machine-gun group on the left flank stopped it dead. At 5.25 p.m., 3rd Division's attack having been a total failure, 92 Brigade was ordered back, the last parties coming in at 9.30 p.m. after dark.

Tuesday 14 November

Temperature 55°F; overcast

ANZAC
2nd Australian Division

The Division attacked with 25th (Queensland) and 26th (Queensland

and Tasmania) Battalions from 7 Brigade, and 19th Battalion on the right had 1/5th and 1/7th Northumberland Fusiliers (149 Brigade).

The attack was launched just before dawn at 6.45 a.m. The 26th Battalion on the right was stopped by machine-gun fire from the Maze. The 25th Battalion mostly suffered the same treatment. The 19th Battalion, in conjunction with the Northumberlands, took Gird Support. It was found to be waterlogged and they fell back to Gird Trench. The 1/7th Northumberlands appeared to have taken Hook Sap, but they came under severe fire from Butte Trench and nothing more was heard from them.

The day wore on and counter-attacks were fought off. Two companies of 20th (NSW) Battalion attempted a move against the Maze at 4.45 p.m. but were stopped by machine-gun fire. At midnight a detachment of 1/4th and 1/5th North-

umberlands attacked on the other flank and similar results were achieved.

II CORPS
19th Division
At dawn a raid was launched by parties of 9th Welsh (58 Brigade) and 7th South Lancs (56 Brigade) in the vicinity of Stump Road and Lucky Way. The relief of 39th Division began by 19th Division extending its front down to the river, and the task had been completed by 3.30 a.m. on the 15th.

V CORPS
63rd Division
CAPTURE OF BEAUMONT HAMEL

At 6.20 a.m. the attack on Beaucourt Trench was continued by 13th Royal Fusiliers and 13th Rifle Brigade (111 Brigade attached from 37th Division) from Station Road with their right on Redoubt Alley. In the mist they lost direction but partially corrected this under machine-gun fire from Beaucourt village and Muck Trench, their second objective. They did, however, lose momentum. The 13th Royal Fusiliers extended the line of 13th KRRC by 300 yards northwards. The remainder of the Fusiliers and 13th Rifle Brigade stopped 200 yards short of Beaucourt Trench where they waited until 7.45 a.m. and the attack on Beaucourt.

190 Brigade, who were assembled at the station at Beaucourt with some 400 men of HAC and 80 of the 7th Royal Fusiliers, advanced on time, linked up with the mixed force and pushed forward into Beaucourt. The

A halt on the way from the trenches. Near Fricourt, on the Fricourt–Contalmaison Road, November 1916. (Q.4495)

13th KRRC moved south-eastwards through the village. Five hundred prisoners were taken and a line was formed around the eastern edge of Beaucourt. The capture of Beaucourt was reported at 10.30 a.m. By this time 13th Rifle Brigade and 13th Royal Fusiliers had taken Beaucourt Trench and the Rifle Brigade started to bomb down it towards Leave Avenue, but saw no sign of 51st Division.

Two tanks were sent up from Auchonvillers to clear the enemy from the front line which they still held. One got stuck in the mud before the front line, as did the other although when the latter was between the front and support trench it opened fire with its 6pdr gun, and the Germans in and around the Strongpoint surrendered. Some 400 prisoners were taken by 10th Royal Dublin Fusiliers (109 Brigade). The Howe Battalion (188 Brigade) mopped-up the dugouts up to Station Road, taking a further 200 prisoners.

At 1 p.m. the enemy were seen massing at Baillescourt Farm so a bombardment was ordered and dealt with the threat.

That night, 13th KRRC (111 Brigade), the HAC (190 Brigade), a company of 14th Worcesters (Pioneers of 63rd Division) and troops from 189 Brigade consolidated the eastern edge of Beaucourt; the left being taken care of by 13th Royal Fusiliers and 13th Rifle Brigade (111 Brigade) in Beaucourt Trench. The HAC held the railway bridge over the river to the south-east of the village.

51st Division
It had been intended that 152 Brigade attack Munich Trench at 6.20 a.m. when the 111 Brigade (37th Division attached 63rd Division) attacked, but the orders were not received in time by 1/7th Argylls (attached from 154

Brigade) so all they could do was send out strong patrols which were fought off. At 7.30 a.m. two companies moved in to the south end of Munich Trench and, an hour later, it was occupied. Soon after 11 a.m. British heavy batteries started to shell Munich Trench, forcing the Highlanders to evacuate and take shelter in shell-holes back from the Trench. The 1/9th Royal Scots sent one company to bomb forward along Leave Avenue, but with little success. That night 2/2nd Highland Field Company, RE and a company of 1/8th Royal Scots (Pioneers) started to dig a new trench called New Munich. Unbeknown to them, the Germans had evacuated Munich Trench.

2nd Division

At 6.20 a.m. 99 Brigade attacked Munich Trench with the 1st KRRC and 1st Royal Berkshire. They left Beaumont Trench one hour before zero and suffered from the effects of an erratic barrage, losing many men and also their way in the mist. On the right, the Rifles wandered into 51st Division's area and Leave Avenue, thinking it was Munich Trench. Although they realized their error, they could not make any headway on their objective. Some isolated groups stayed on in Leave Avenue for most of the morning, then withdrew to Wagon Road. The Berks, however, reached Munich Trench but with depleted numbers. The result was totally confusing: some Germans wanted to surrender, others did not. On the left, Lager Alley was swept over, the troops not even recognizing it, and went on to extend the hold on Serre Trench. Later in the morning the troops in Munich Trench fell back on Wagon Road where part of 23rd Royal Fusiliers, in support, joined them.

Reporting a message to their officers in a dugout at Eaucourt l'Abbaye, November 1916. Note the kilt aprons, a waterproof cover for the woollen kilt. (Q.4390)

The left of this attack was covered by a barrage that stopped any counter-attack before it started. By dawn 22nd Royal Fusiliers had moved up to hold the flank from south of the Quadrilateral to Lager Alley and linked with the British trench by the Cat Street tunnel. Under the impression that Munich Trench had fallen, 11th Royal Warwicks and 6th Bedfords were to attack Frankfort Trench at 2.45 p.m. They were quite surprised to come under fire from machine-guns in Munich Trench and withdrew to Wagon Road where there was now a mix of units.

Wednesday 15 November

Temperature 46°F

ANZAC

At dawn 19th (NSW) Battalion was relieved by 28th (W Australian) Battalion (7 Australian Brigade), and the Northumberlands were relieved by two companies of 1/4th East Yorks.

II CORPS
39th Division

The Division drove the last of the Germans out of the Schwaben Redoubt, with 4/5th Black Watch, 1/1st Cambridgeshires (118 Brigade) and 17th

KRRC (117 Brigade). The fighting lasted until 11 p.m. The 1/6th Cheshires (118 Brigade) advanced the line on the left. Three counter-attacks made the next day, two with flame-throwers, were repulsed.

V CORPS
37th Division

The major concern of 37th Division, which had begun the relief of 63rd Division, was the linking up with 51st Division on their left. The 13th Rifle Brigade (111 Brigade) bombed up Beaucourt Trench towards Munich Trench before 9 a.m., but it was not until 10 a.m. that the link was established. On the right, Beaucourt was shelled all day. 63 Brigade sent out a patrol and found Muck and Railway Trenches abandoned by the Germans. Muck Trench was found to be full of mud.

51st, 2nd Divisions

The Divisions launched a combined attack at 9 a.m. with two companies of 1/7th Argylls assembled in New Munich Trench, some 500 yards in advance of 2nd Division in Beaumont Trench. The Scots ran into their own barrage; some reached Frankfort Trench but were forced to withdraw under cover of Lewis-gun fire to New Munich Trench.

2nd Division

The Division used the remaining battalions of 112 Brigade (37th Division): 10th Loyal North Lancs and 8th East Lancs under command of 99 Brigade. They lost their way in the mist, suffering heavy casualties, and fell back to Wagon Road.

Meanwhile, on the left 22nd Royal Fusiliers (99 Brigade) improved their position on the left defensive flank by making a strongpoint in the Quadrilateral near the crest of Redan Ridge. Two tanks were supposed to assist but both were stuck in the mud before they could come into action.

After dark the relief of 63rd Division by 37th Division was begun.

Thursday 16 November

Temperature 41°F; clear and cold

V CORPS
21st Division

Little happened during the day, but after dark 8th Somerset LI (63 Brigade) pushed up Ancre Trench and established a post at Bois d'Hollande.

37th Division

The 10th Royal Fusiliers and 13th KRRC (111 Brigade) formed posts at Railway Trench and Muck Trench. The 152nd Field Company, RE were aided by consolidation.

32nd Division

At dawn 14 Brigade (32nd Division relieved the front of 2nd Division) took over the northern defensive flank where they thought the front line was. That night 97 Brigade relieved 112 Brigade in Wagon Road, linking up with 51st Division in New Munich Trench and Leave Avenue. At 3 p.m. on the 16th, a heavy enemy bombardment preceded a strong counter-attack, and at 5 p.m. they re-captured Gird Trench, forcing the British and Australians to withdraw.

Friday 17 November

Temperature 37°F; 2mm rain

V CORPS
32nd Division

The Division with 51st Division were relieved by 97 Brigade which extended their line south and held the front from Leave Avenue to the Quadrilateral.

Saturday 18 November

Temperature 54°F; 8mm rain

FINAL ATTACK

The first snow fell that night and at 6.10 a.m. the attack was launched in whirling sleet which later changed to rain. Visibility was practically nil, objectives were covered in snow

which further obscured the already obscure.

II CORPS
4th Canadian Division

On the right the Canadians were to attack Desire Trench and Desire Support Trench.

On the right of the Pys road, one company of 46th (Saskatchewan) Battalion and two companies of 50th (Calgary) Battalion (10 Brigade) advanced to cover the flank. A certain amount of confusion was caused by the smoke of the barrage laid by No 2 Special Company, RE. 46 Brigade suffered heavily from machine-gun fire and was forced back. The 50th Battalion at first met with little resistance and began to consolidate Desire Support Trench, but later came under heavy machine-gun fire and were forced to withdraw back to Regina Trench.

11 Brigade attacked with two companies each of 75th (Mississauga), 54th (Kootenay), 87th (Canadian Grenadier Guards) and 38th (Ottawa) Battalions. In sleet 75th Battalion swung west by mistake and wandered over the Pys road. Otherwise the assault was successful and patrols of 87th and 38th Battalions went forward into Grandcourt Trench. Early in the afternoon companies of 44th and 47th (British Columbia) Battalions were sent up to reinforce 11 Brigade. The situation was that the Canadians held most of Desire Support Trench and were consolidating. The patrols were recalled from Grandcourt Trench and got back early next morning. They had captured 620 prisoners.

18th Division

The Division attacked with 55 Brigade consisting of 8th East Surreys, 7th Royal West Kents, 7th Buffs and 7th Queen's. They assembled in no man's land, lying in the snow. By 8.10 a.m. 8th East Surreys had occupied the part of Desire Trench next to the Canadians and were consolidating. Seventy minutes later 7th Royal West Kents also reached the objective; there was a gap between them but this was bombed away. The other two battalions were lost—seven runners were sent to find them but they all became casualties. At 10.46 a.m. the Division was informed that 19th Division had failed on its right, west of Stump Road. Later it became clear that the detachment of Queen's detailed to clear the dugouts had been practically annihilated by shellfire. Some of them did make the objective, but few of the Buffs reached that far. The Germans still held Point 66 where the Grandcourt-Courcelette road crossed

The dugouts of an advanced dressing station on a slope at Beaucourt-Hamel, 24 November 1916. RAMC personnel wore the Red Cross brassard. (Q.5798)

the Pozières–Miraumont road, but they were cleared out by the West Kents, which enabled the Buffs to enter part of their objective. At 5 p.m. it was decided to withdraw from west of Point 66, which was consolidated with the help of a section of 92nd Field Company, R.E. A line was dug back to Regina Trench.

19th Division

The Division launched their attack with 57 Brigade on the right. The 8th North Staffords entered the German trenches west of Stump Road and pressed on a considerable distance, but most were cut off and captured. Only 70 managed to escape in small parties, coming up Battery Valley much later. Next to them were 10th Royal Warwicks; they lost direction in the snow but then regained it. The right companies were stopped by uncut wire and suffered accordingly. Some of the left

company managed to enter the Grandcourt line and went forward with 8th Gloucesters on a 300-yard wide front across Battery Valley—the Warwicks and Gloucesters mopping-up after them—and entered the south-western end of Grandcourt. The 7th South Lancs (56 Brigade) advanced two companies along the St Pierre Divion–Grandcourt road and one platoon along the railway to link up with V Corps at Beaucourt. Two companies were deployed to the right of the Hansa Road where the ground was relatively firm, and reached the western end of Grandcourt where they bombed through to join with the Gloucesters.

The left lined up with the platoon that had crossed the river at Beaucourt Mill and moved up the embankment to a point north of the western edge of Grandcourt. Strongpoints were set up by 81st Field Company, RE on the railway and on the road at the entrance to Grandcourt.

The 7th East Lancs (56 Brigade) were to attack Baillescourt Farm in two companies. One was held up by machine-gun fire from Grandcourt, the other went along the railway embankment. Eventually they sent out a patrol which made contact with one from V Corps.

V CORPS
37th Division

To the north of the river, 8th Somerset LI moved up through Beaucourt and by 1 a.m. had formed a line of posts from Bois d'Hollande westward to the Puisieux road and southwards to Ancre Trench. By dawn 8th Lincolns (63 Brigade), 13th KRRC and 10th Royal Fusiliers (111 Brigade) had posts in Muck Trench ready to support 32nd Division after they had captured Frankfort Trench. At zero hour 13th KRRC sent out patrols that met some opposition in Railway Trench. On the left 10th Royal Fusiliers bombed to the junction of Leave Avenue and Frankfort Trench ready to link up with 32nd Division. After various false starts 8th Somerset LI, with bombers and patrols, entered Puisieux Trench and held it as far as the Ancre; 4th Middlesex giving assistance. A patrol made contact with 19th Division on the railway.

32nd Division

The Division was given the job of attacking Munich and Frankfort Trenches between Leave Avenue and Lager Alley. At 6.10 a.m. they advanced through the sleet. The 17th Highland LI on the right were stopped by machine-gun fire. The right of 16th HLI was also held up, but the rest carried on and entered both trenches, but were cut off and suffered heavy casualties, few men

making it back to the British trench. Next on the left, the right of 2nd KOYLI were stopped by a strongpoint in Munich Trench, but held on in no man's land till dusk. The left companies, however, stormed the junction of Lager Alley and down the hill, eventually getting in touch with 2nd Manchesters (14 Brigade).

14 Brigade's task was to take Ten Tree Alley and set up a defensive flank. The 2nd Manchesters started down Lager Alley before zero hour and with three companies left there on Serre Trench, moved down the valley towards Serre. Accompanied by some of the KOYLI, the advance continued and some even reached the

village itself, but during the course of the day all were captured or killed. On the left of the Manchesters, 15 HLI tried to bomb forward but met with machine-gun fire and, by 11 a.m., the failure was known and the rest of the day was spent in rallying the Battalion in Wagon Road and New Munich Trench.

The only gain by 14 Brigade was a slight advance of 15th HLI on the left flank near the Quadrilateral. The 1st Dorsets were sent up to reinforce the Highlanders and replace 2nd Manchesters. The rain which fell on the 19th stopped any further action by II and V Corps, neither of which was fit for any.

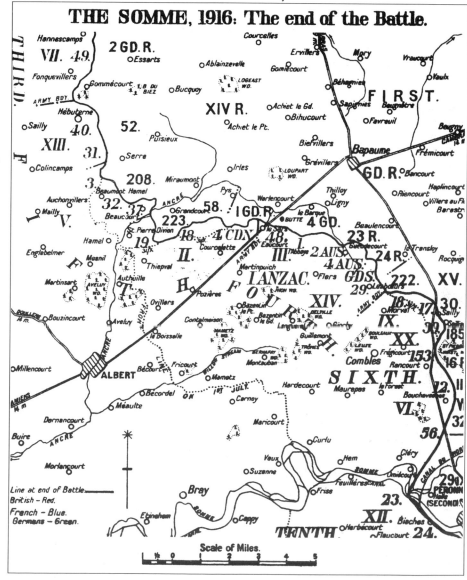

THE SOMME, 1916: The end of the Battle.

Above: Watching over the battlefield. (Q.4143)

Below: Flooded area in the Ancre Valley, November 1916. (Q.1569)

Sunday 19 November

Temperature not known

A gale followed a wet night. Zero hour was set for 11.10 a.m.

II CORPS
19th Division

In chilling rain 7th South Lancs beat off a counter-attack at the western end of Grandcourt. A position was dug from the Ancre up Battery Valley, parallel with and some 500 yards west of Grandcourt Line. The East Lancs, South Lancs, Gloucesters and Warwicks fell back to this line, as the Germans still held the southern end of the Grandcourt Line which overlooked the ground taken. The 10th Royal Fusiliers attempted an attack in the afternoon but were unsuccessful. That night, when 19th Division were withdrawn from Grandcourt, 63 Brigade also relinquished their hold on Puisieux Trench.

POSTSCRIPT

The weather finally brought the Battle of the Somme to a close. The snow was followed by a thaw which turned the entire battlefield into a quagmire. The conditions were rated by some who had experienced both as being as bad as, if not worse than, the conditions encountered in the Ypres Salient the following year. The Official History, with rare candour, describes the appalling conditions:

> Here, in a wilderness of mud, holding water-logged trenches or shell-hole post, accessible only by night, the infantry abode in conditions which might be likened to those of earthworms rather than of human kind. Our vocabulary is not adapted to describe such an existence, because it is outside experience for which words are normally required. Mud, for the men in the line, was no mere inorganic nuisance and obstacle. It took on an aggressive, wolf-like guise, and like a wolf could pull down and swallow the lonely wanderer in the darkness.

The energies of both sides were expended in the endeavour to survive the environment, and it was not until the following year that battle resumed.

An army chaplain tending a soldier's grave, Carnoy Valley, July 1916.
(Q.4004)

APPENDICES

APPENDIX 1
ORDER OF BATTLE, THE SOMME, 1916:
BRITISH AND DOMINION INFANTRY AND PIONEER BATTALIONS

GUARDS DIVISION
1st Guards Brigade: 2/Gren. Gds; 2/Coldstr. Gds; 3/Coldstr. Gds; 1/Irish Gds
2nd Guards Brigade: 2/Gren. Gds; 1/Coldstr. Gds; 1/Scots Gds; 2/Irish Gds
3rd Guards Brigade: 1/Gren. Gds; 4/Gren. Gds; 2/Scots Gds; 1/Welsh Gds
Pioneers: 4/Coldstr. Gds

1st DIVISION
1st Brigade: 10/Gloster; 1/Black Watch; 8/R. Berks; 1/Camerons
2nd Brigade: 2/R. Sussex; 1/L.N. Lancs; 1/Northampton; 2/KRRC
3rd Brigade: 1/SWB; 1/Gloster; 2/Welsh; 2/RMF
Pioneers: 1/6th Welsh

2nd DIVISION
5th Brigade: 17/R. Fus.; 24/R. Fus.; 2/O&BLI; 2/HLI
6th Brigade: 1/King's; 2/S. Staffs; 13/Essex; 17/Middlesex
99th Brigade: 22/R. Fus.; 23/R. Fus.; 1/R. Berks; 1/KRRC
Pioneers: 10/DCLI

3rd DIVISION
8th Brigade: 2/R. Scots; 8/E. Yorks; 1/R. Scots Fus.; 7/KSLI
9th Brigade: 1/North'd Fus.; 4/R. Fus.; 13/King's; 12/W. Yorks
76th Brigade: 8/King's Own; 2/Suffolk; 10/R. Welsh Fus.; 1/Gordons
Pioneers: 20/KRRC

4th DIVISION
10th Brigade: 1/R. Warwick; 2/Seaforth; 1/R. Irish Fus.; 2/R. Dub. Fus.
11th Brigade: 1/Somerset L.I.; 1/E. Lancs; 1/Hampshire; 1/Rif. Brig.
12th Brigade: 1/King's Own; 2/Lancs Fus.; 2/Essex; 2/DWR
Pioneers: 21/W. Yorks

5th DIVISION
13th Brigade: 14/R. Warwick; 15/ R. Warwick; 2/KOSB; 1/R.W. Kent
15th Brigade: 16/R. Warwick; 1/Norfolk; 1/Bedford; 1/Cheshire
95th Brigade: 1/Devon; 12/Gloster; 1/E. Surrey; 1/DCLI
Pioneers: 1/6th A&SH

6th DIVISION
16th Brigade: 1/Buffs; 8/Bedford; 1/KSLI; 2/York & Lanc.

18th Brigade: 1/W. Yorks; 11/Essex; 2/DLI; 14/DLI
71st Brigade: 9/Norfolk; 9/Suffolk; 1/Leicester; 2/Sherwood For.
Pioneers: 11/Leicester

7th DIVISION
20th Brigade: 8/Devon; 9/Devon; 2/Border Regt; 2/Gordons
22nd Brigade: 2/R. Warwick; 2/R. Irish; 1/R. Welsh Fus; 20/Manchester
91st Brigade: 2/Queen's; 1/S. Staffs; 21/Manchester; 22/Manchester
Pioneers: 24/Manchester

8th DIVISION
23rd Brigade: 2/Devon; 2/W. Yorks; 2/Middlesex; 2/Sco. Rif.
24th Brigade:[1] 1/Worcs; 1/Sherwood For.; 2/Northampton; 2/E. Lancs
25th Brigade: 2/Lincoln; 2/R. Berks; 1/R. Irish Rif.; 2/Rif. Brig.
Pioneers: 22/DLI

9th (SCOTTISH) DIVISION
26th Brigade: 8/Black Watch; 7/Seaforth; 5/Camerons; 10/A&SH
27th Brigade: 11/R. Scots; 12/R. Scots; 6/KOSB; 9/Sco. Rif
S. A. Brigade: 1/Regt (Cape Prov.); 2/Regt (Natal & OFS); 3/Regt (Trans. & Rhod.); 4/Regt (Scottish)
Pioneers: 9/Seaforth

11th DIVISION
32nd Brigade: 9/W. Yorks; 6/Green Howards; 8/DWR; 6/York & Lanc.
33rd Brigade: 6/Lincoln; 6/Border Regt; 7/S. Staffs; 9/Sherwood For.
34th Brigade: 8/North'd Fus.; 9/Lancs Fus.; 5/Dorset; 11/Manchester
Pioneers: 6/E. Yorks

12th (EASTERN) DIVISION
35th Brigade: 7/Norfolk; 7/Suffolk; 9/Essex; 5/R. Berks
36th Brigade: 8/R. Fus.; 9/R. Fus.; 7/R. Sussex; 11/Middlesex
37th Brigade: 6/Queen's; 6/Buffs; 7/E. Surrey; 6/R. W. Kent
Pioneers: 5/Northampton

14th (LIGHT) DIVISION
41st Brigade: 7/KRRC; 8/KRRC; 7/Rif. Brig.; 8/Rif. Brig.
42nd Brigade: 5/O&BLI; 5/KSLI; 9/KRRC; 9/Rif. Brig.
43rd Brigade: 6/Somerset L.I.; 6/DCLI; 6/KOYLI; 10/DLI
Pioneers: 11/King's

15th (SCOTTISH) DIVISION
44th Brigade: 9/Black Watch; 8/Seaforth; 8th/10th Gordons; 7/Camerons
45th Brigade: 13/R. Scots; 6th/7th R. Scots Fus.; 6/Camerons; 11/A&SH
46th Brigade: 10/Sco. Rif.; 7th/8th KOSB; 10th/11th HLI; 12/HLI
Pioneers: 9/Gordons

16th (IRISH) DIVISION
47th Brigade: 6/R. Irish; 6/Conn. Rangers; 7/Leinster; 8/RMF
48th Brigade: 7/R. Irish Rif.; 1/RMF; 8/R. Dub. Fus.; 9/R. Dub. Fus.
49th Brigade: 7/R. Innis. Fus.; 8/R. Innis. Fus.; 7/R. Irish Fus.; 8/R. Irish Fus.
Pioneers: 11/Hampshire

17th (NORTHERN) DIVISION
50th Brigade: 10/W. Yorks; 7/E. Yorks; 7/Green Howards; 6/Dorset
51st Brigade: 7/Lincoln; 7/Border Regt; 8/S. Staffs; 10/Sherwood For.
52nd Brigade: 9/North'd Fus.; 10/Lancs Fus.; 9/DWR; 12/Manchester
Pioneers: 7/York & Lanc.

18th (EASTERN) DIVISION
53rd Brigade: 8/Norfolk; 8/Suffolk; 10/Essex; 6/R. Berks
54th Brigade: 11/R. Fus.; 7/Bedford; 6/Northampton; 12/Middlesex
55th Brigade: 7/Queen's; 7/Buffs; 8/E. Surrey; 7/R.W. Kent
Pioneers: 8/R. Sussex

19th (WESTERN) DIVISION
56th Brigade: 7/King's Own; 7/E. Lancs; 7/S. Lancs; 7/L.N. Lancs
57th Brigade: 10/R. Warwick; 8/Gloster; 10/Worcs; 8/N. Staffs
58th Brigade: 9/Cheshire; 9/R. Welsh Fus.; 9/Welsh; 6/Wiltshire
Pioneers: 5/SWB

20th (LIGHT) DIVISION
59th Brigade: 10/KRRC; 11/KRRC; 10/Rif. Brig.; 11/Rif. Brig.
60th Brigade: 6/O&BLI; 6/KSLI; 12/KRRC; 12/Rif. Brig.
61st Brigade: 7/Somerset L.I.; 7/DCLI; 7/KOYLI; 12/King's
Pioneers: 11/DLI

21st DIVISION
62nd Brigade: 12/North'd Fus.; 13/North'd Fus.; 1/Lincoln; 10/Green Howards
63rd Brigade:[2] 8/Lincoln, 8/Somerset L.I., 4/Middlesex; 10/York & Lanc.
64th Brigade: 1/E. Yorks; 9/KOYLI; 10/KOYLI; 15/DLI
Pioneers: 14/North'd Fus.

23rd DIVISION
68th Brigade: 10/North'd Fus.; 11/North'd Fus.; 12/DLI; 13/DLI
69th Brigade: 11/W. Yorks; 8/Green Howards; 9/Green Howards; 10/DWR
70th Brigade:[3] 11/Sherwood For.; 8/KOYLI; 8/York & Lanc.; 9/York & Lanc.
Pioneers: 9/S. Staffs

24th DIVISION
17th Brigade: 8/Buffs; 1/R. Fus.; 12/R. Fus.; 3/Rif. Brig.
72nd Brigade: 8/Queen's; 9/E. Surrey; 8/R. W. Kent; 1/N. Staffs
73rd Brigade: 9/R. Sussex; 7/Northampton; 13/Middlesex; 2/Leinster
Pioneers: 12/Sherwood For.

25th DIVISION
7th Brigade: 10/Cheshire; 3/Worcs; 8/L.N. Lancs; 1/Wiltshire
74th Brigade: 11/Lancs Fus.; 13/Cheshire; 9/L.N. Lancs; 2/Irish Rif.
75th Brigade: 11/Cheshire; 8/Border Regt; 2/S. Lancs; 8/S. Lancs
Pioneers: 6/SWB

29th DIVISION
86th Brigade: 2/R. Fus.; 1/Lancs Fus.; 16/Middlesex; 1/R. Dub. Fus.
87th Brigade: 2/SWB; 1/KOSB; 1/R. Innis. Fus.; 1/Border Regt
88th Brigade: 4/Worcs; 1/Essex; 2/Hampshire; R. Newfoundland Regt
Pioneers: 2/Monmouth

30th DIVISION
21st Brigade: 18/King's; 2/Green Howards; 2/Wiltshire; 19/Manchester
89th Brigade: 17/King's; 19/King's; 20/King's; 2/Bedford
90th Brigade: 2/R. Scots Fus.; 16/Manchester; 17/Manchester; 18/Manchester
Pioneers: 11/S. Lancs

31st DIVISION
92nd Brigade: 10/E. Yorks; 11/E. Yorks; 12/E. Yorks; 13/E. Yorks
93rd Brigade: 15/W. Yorks; 16/W. Yorks; 18/W. Yorks; 18/DLI
94th Brigade: 11/E. Lancs; 12/York & Lanc.; 13/York & Lanc.; 14/York & Lanc.
Pioneers: 12/KOYLI

32nd DIVISION
14th Brigade: 19/Lancs Fus.;[4] 1/Dorset; 2/Manchester; 15/HLI
96th Brigade: 16/North'd Fus.; 15/Lancs Fus.; 16/Lancs Fus.; 2/R. Innis. Fus.
97th Brigade: 11/Border Regt; 2/KOYLI; 16/HLI; 17/HLI
Pioneers: 17/North'd Fus.[5]

33rd DIVISION
19th Brigade: 20th R. Fus., 2/R. Welsh Fus.; 1/Cameronians; 5/Sco. Rif.
98th Brigade: 4/King's; 1/4th Suffolk; 1/Middlesex; 2/A&SH
100th Brigade: 1/Queen's; 2/Worcs; 16/KRRC; 1/9th HLI
Pioneers: 18/Middlesex

34th DIVISION
101st Brigade: 15/R. Scots; 16/R. Scots; 10/Lincoln; 11/Suffolk
102nd (Tyneside Scottish) Brigade:[6] 20/North'd Fus.; 21/North'd Fus.; 22/North'd Fus.; 23/North'd Fus.
103rd (Tyneside Irish) Brigade:[7] 24/North'd Fus.; 25/North'd Fus.; 26/North'd Fus.; 27/North'd Fus.
Pioneers: 18/North'd Fus.[8]

35th (BANTAM) DIVISION
104th Brigade: 17/Lancs Fus.; 18/Lancs Fus.; 20/Lancs Fus.; 23/Manchester
105th Brigade: 15/Cheshire; 16/ Cheshire; 14/Gloster; 15/Sherwood For.
106th Brigade: 17/R. Scots; 17/W. Yorks; 19/DLI; 18/HLI
Pioneers: 19/North'd Fus.

36th (ULSTER) DIVISION
107th Brigade: 8/R. Irish Rif.; 9/R. Irish Rif., 10/R. Irish Rif.; 15/R. Irish Rif.
108th Brigade: 11/R. Irish Rif.; 12/R. Irish Rif.; 13/R. Irish Rif.; 9/R. Irish Fus.
109th Brigade: 9/R. Innis. Fus.; 10/R. Innis. Fus; 11/R. Innis Fus.; 14/R. Irish Rif.
Pioneers: 16/R. Irish Rif.

37th DIVISION
110th Brigade:[9] 6/Leicester; 7/Leicester; 8/Leicester; 9/Leicester
111th Brigade:[10] 10/R. Fus.; 13/R. Fus.; 13/KRRC; 13/Rif. Brig.
112th Brigade:[10] 11/R. Warwick; 6/Bedford; 8/E. Lancs; 10/L.N. Lancs
Pioneers: 9/N. Staffs[10]

38th (WELSH) DIVISION
113th Brigade: 13/R. Welsh Fus.; 14/R. Welsh Fus.; 15/R. Welsh Fus.; 16/R. Welsh Fus.
114th Brigade: 10/Welsh; 13/Welsh; 14/Welsh; 15/Welsh
115th Brigade: 10/SWB; 11/SWB; 17/R. Welsh Fus.; 16/Welsh
Pioneers: 19/Welsh

39th DIVISION
116th Brigade: 11/R. Sussex; 12/R. Sussex; 13/R. Sussex; 14/Hampshire
117th Brigade: 16/Sherwood For.; 17/Sherwood For.; 17/KRRC; 16/Rif. Brig.
118th Brigade: 1/6th Cheshire; 1/1st Cambs; 1/1st Herts; 4th/5th Black Watch
Pioneers: 13/Gloster

41st DIVISION
122nd Brigade: 12/E. Surrey; 15/Hampshire; 11/R. W. Kent; 198/KRRC
123rd Brigade: 11/Queen's; 10/R. W. Kent; 23/Middlesex; 20/DLI
124th Brigade: 10/Queen's; 26/R. Fus.; 32/R. Fus.; 21/KRRC
Pioneers: 19/Middlesex

46th (NORTH MIDLAND) DIVISION (TF)
137th Brigade: 1/5th S. Staffs; 1/6th S. Staffs; 1/5th N. Staffs; 1/6th N. Staffs
138th Brigade: 1/4th Lincoln; 1/5th Lincoln; 1/4th Leicester; 1/5th Leicester
139th Brigade: 1/5th Sherwood For; 1/6th Sherwood For; 1/7th Sherwood For.; 1/8th Sherwood For.
Pioneers: 1/Monmouth

47th (1/2nd LONDON) DIVISION (TF)
140th Brigade: 1/6th London (City of London); 1/7th London (City of London); 1/8th London (P.O. Rif.); 1/15th London (C.S. Rif.)
141st Brigade: 1/17th London (Poplar & Stepney Rif.); 1/18th London (London Irish Rif.); 1/19th London (St Pancras); 1/20th London (Blackheath & Woolwich)
142nd Brigade: 1/21st London (1st Surrey Rif.); 1/22nd London (The Queen's); 1/23rd London; 1/24th London (The Queen's)
Pioneers: 1/4th R. Welsh Fus.

48th (S. MIDLAND) DIVISION (TF)
143rd Brigade: 1/5th R. Warwick; 1/6th R. Warwick; 1/7th R. Warwick; 1/8th R. Warwick
144th Brigade: 1/4th Gloster; 1/6th Gloster; 1/7th Worcs; 1/8th Worcs
145th Brigade: 1/5th Gloster; 1/4th O&BLI; 1/1st Bucks; 1/4th R. Berks
Pioneers: 1/5th R. Sussex

49th (W. RIDING) DIVISION (TF)
146th Brigade: 1/5th W. Yorks; 1/6th W. Yorks; 1/7th W. Yorks; 1/8th W. Yorks
147th Brigade: 1/4th DWR; 1/5th DWR; 1/6th DWR; 1/7th DWR
148th Brigade: 1/4th KOYLI; 1/5th KOYLI; 1/4th York & Lanc.; 1/5th York & Lanc.
Pioneers: 3/Monmouth[11]

50th (NORTHUMBRIAN) DIVISION (TF)
149th Brigade: 1/4th North'd Fus.; 1/5th North'd Fus.; 1/6th North'd Fus.; 1/7th North'd Fus.
150th Brigade: 1/4th E. Yorks; 1/4th Green Howards; 1/5th Green Howards; 1/5th DLI
151st Brigade: 1/5th Border Regt; 1/6th DLI; 1/8th DLI; 1/9th DLI
Pioneers: 1/7th DLI

51st (HIGHLAND) DIVISION (TF)
152nd Brigade: 1/5th Seaforth; 1/6th Seaforth; 1/6th Gordons; 1/8th A&SH
153rd Brigade: 1/6th Black Watch; 1/7th Black Watch; 1/5th Gordons; 1/7th Gordons
154th Brigade: 1/9th R. Scots; 1/4th Seaforth; 1/4th Gordons; 1/7th A&SH
Pioneers: 1/8th R. Scots

55th (W. LANCS) DIVISION (TF)
164th Brigade: 1/4th King's Own; 1/8th King's; 2/5th Lancs Fus.; 1/4th L.N. Lancs
165th Brigade: 1/5th King's; 1/6th King's; 1/7th King's; 1/9th King's
166th Brigade: 1/5th King's Own; 1/10th King's; 1/5th S. Lancs; 1/5th L.N. Lancs
Pioneers: 1/4th S. Lancs

56th (1/1st LONDON) DIVISION (TF)
167th Brigade: 1/1st London (RF); 1/3rd London (RF); 1/7th Middlesex; 1/8th Middlesex
168th Brigade: 1/4th London (RF); 1/12th London (Rangers); 1/13th London (Kensington); 1/14th London (Lon. Scot.)
169th Brigade: 1/2nd London (RF); 1/5th London (LRB); 1/9th London (QVR); 1/16th London (QWR)
Pioneers: 1/5th Cheshire

63rd (RN) DIVISION
188th Brigade: Anson Bn; Howe Bn; 1/R. Marine Bn; 2/R. Marine Bn
189th Brigade: Hood Bn; Nelson Bn; Hawke Bn; Drake Bn
190th Brigade: 1/HAC; 7/R. Fus.; 4/Bedford; 10/R. Dub. Fus.
Pioneers: 14/Worcs

1st AUSTRALIAN DIVISION
1st (NSW) Brigade: 1st Bn; 2nd Bn; 3rd Bn; 4th Bn
2nd (Victoria) Brigade: 5th Bn; 6th Bn; 7th Bn; 8th Bn
3rd Brigade: 9th (Q'land) Bn; 10th (S. Austr.) Bn; 11th (W. Austr.) Bn; 12th (S. & W. Austr., Tas.) Bn
Pioneers: 1st Austr. Pioneer Bn

2nd AUSTRALIAN DIVISION
5th (NSW) Brigade: 17th Bn; 18th Bn; 19th Bn; 20th Bn
6th (Victoria) Brigade: 21st Bn; 22nd Bn; 23rd Bn; 24th Bn
7th Brigade: 25th (Q'land) Bn; 26th (Q'land, Tas.) Bn; 27th (S. Austr.) Bn; 28th (W. Austr.) Bn
Pioneers: 2nd Austr. Pioneer Bn

4th AUSTRALIAN DIVISION
4th Brigade: 13th (NSW) Bn; 14th (Vic.) Bn; 15th (Q'land), Tas.) Bn; 16th (S. & W. Austr.) Bn
12th Brigade: 45th (NSW) Bn; 46th (Vic.) Bn; 47th (Q'land, Tas.) Bn; 48th (S. & W. Austr.) Bn
13th Brigade: 49th (Q'land) Bn; 50th (S. Austr.) Bn; 51st (W. Austr.) Bn; 52nd (S. & W. Austr., Tas.) Bn
Pioneers: 4th Austr. Pioneer Bn

5th AUSTRALIAN DIVISION
8th Brigade: 29th (Vic.) Bn; 30th (NSW) Bn; 31st (Q'land, Vic.) Bn; 32nd (S. & W. Austr.) Bn
14th (NSW) Brigade: 53rd Bn; 54th Bn; 55th Bn; 56th Bn
15th (Victoria) Brigade: 57th Bn; 58th Bn; 59th Bn; 60th Bn
Pioneers: 5th Austr. Pioneer Bn

1st CANADIAN DIVISION
1st Brigade: 1st (Ontario) Bn; 2nd (E. Ontario) Bn; 3rd Bn (Toronto Regt); 4th Bn
2nd Brigade: 5th (Western Cav.) Bn; 7th Bn (1st Br. Columbia); 8th Bn (90th Rif.); 10th Bn
3rd Brigade: 13th Bn (R. Highlanders); 14th Bn (R. Montreal Regt); 15th Bn (48th Highlanders); 16th Bn (Canadian Scottish)
Pioneers: 1st Canadian Pioneer Bn

2nd CANADIAN DIVISION
4th Brigade: 18th (W. Ontario) Bn; 19th (Central Ontario) Bn; 20th (Central Ontario) Bn; 21st (E. Ontario) Bn
5th Brigade: 22nd (Canadien Français) Bn; 24th Bn (Victoria Rif.); 25th Bn (Nova Scotia Rif.); 26th (New Brunswick) Bn
6th Brigade: 27th (City of Winnipeg) Bn; 28th (North-West) Bn; 29th (Vancouver) Bn; 31st (Alberta) Bn
Pioneers: 2nd Canadian Pioneer Bn

3rd CANADIAN DIVISION
7th Brigade: PPCLI; R. Cdn Regt; 42nd Bn (R. Highlanders); 49th (Edmonton) Bn
8th Brigade: 1st Cdn M.R.; 2nd Cdn M. R.; 4th Cdn M.R.; 5th Cdn M.R.
9th Brigade: 43rd Bn (Cameron Highlanders); 52nd (New Ontario) Bn; 58th Bn; 60th Bn (Victoria Rif.)
Pioneers: 3rd Canadian Pioneer Bn

4th CANADIAN DIVISION
10th Brigade: 44th Bn; 46th (S. Saskatchewan) Bn; 47th (Br. Columbia) Bn; 50th (Calgary) Bn
11th Brigade: 54th (Kootenay) Bn; 75th (Mississauga) Bn; 87th Bn (Canadian Grenadier Guards); 102nd Bn
12th Brigade: 38th (Ottawa) Bn; 72nd Bn (Seaforth Highlanders); 73rd Bn (R. Highlanders); 78th Bn (Winnipeg Grenadiers)
Pioneers: 67th Canadian Pioneer Bn

NEW ZEALAND DIVISION
1st NZ Brigade: 1/Auckland; 1/Canterbury; 1/Otago; 1/Wellington
2nd NZ Brigade: 2/Auckland; 2/Canterbury; 2/Otago; 2/Wellington
3rd NZ Rifle Brigade: 1/NZRB; 2/NZRB; 3/NZRB; 4/NZRB
Pioneers: NZ Pioneer Bn

NOTES
1. With 23rd Division until 15 July, in exchange for 70th Brigade.
2. Exchanged with 110th Brigade of 37th Division, 7 July.
3. With 8th Division until 15 July, in exchange for 24th Brigade.
4. Replaced by 5th/6th R. Scots, 29 July.
5. Replaced by 12/L. N. Lancs, 19 October.
6. Attached to 37th Division, 7 July–21 August; replaced by 111th Brigade.
7. Attached to 37th Division, 7 July–21 August; replaced by 112th Brigade.
8. Attached to 37th Division, 7 July–21 August; replaced by 9/N. Staffs.
9. Exchanged with 63rd Brigade, 21st Division, 7 July.
10. Attached 7 July–21 August to 34th Division, q. v.
11. Replaced by 19/Lancs Fus., 6 August.

APPENDIX 2
ORDER OF BATTLE, THE SOMME, 1916: GERMAN INFANTRY

3RD GUARD DIVISION
Guard Fus.; Lehr Regt; Gren. Regt No 9

4TH GUARD DIVISION
5th Gd Ft; 5th Gd Gren.; Res. Regt No 93

5TH DIVISION
Gren. Regts Nos 8, 12; Regt No 52

6TH DIVISION
Regts Nos 20, 24, 64

7TH DIVISION
Regts Nos 26, 27,[1] 165

8TH DIVISION
Regts Nos 72, 93, 153

12TH DIVISION
Regts Nos 23, 62, 63

16TH DIVISION
Regts Nos 28, 29, 68, 69

24TH DIVISION
Regts Nos 133, 139, 179

26TH DIVISION
Gren. Regt No 119; Regts Nos 121, 125

27TH DIVISION
Regt No 120; Gren. Regt No 123; Regts Nos 124, 127

38TH DIVISION
Regts Nos 94, 95, 96

40TH DIVISION
Regts Nos 104, 134, 181

52ND DIVISION
Regts Nos 66, 169, 170

56TH DIVISION
Fus. Regt No 35; Regts Nos 88, 118

58TH DIVISION
Regts Nos 106, 107; Res. Regt No 120

111TH DIVISION
Fus. Regt No 73; Regts Nos 76, 164

117TH DIVISION
Regt No 157; Res. Regts No 11, 22

183RD DIVISION
Regts Nos 183, 184; Res. Regt No 122

185TH DIVISION[2]
Regts Nos 185, 186, 190

208TH DIVISION
Regts Nos 25, 185; Res. Regt No 65

222ND DIVISION
Regts Nos 193, 397; Res. Regt No 81

223RD DIVISION
Regts Nos 144, 173; Ersatz Regt No 29

1ST GUARD RESERVE DIVISION
Gd Res. Regts Nos 1, 2; Res. Regt No 64

2ND GUARD RESERVE DIVISION
Res. Regts Nos 15, 55, 77, 91

7TH RESERVE DIVISION
Res. Regts Nos 36, 66, 72

12TH RESERVE DIVISION
Res. Regts Nos 23, 38, 51

17TH RESERVE DIVISION
Regts Nos 162, 163; Res. Regts Nos 75,[3] 76

18TH RESERVE DIVISION
Res. Regts Nos 31, 84, 86

19TH RESERVE DIVISION
Res. Regts Nos 73, 78, 79, 92

23RD RESERVE DIVISION
Res. Gren. Regts No 101; Res. Regts Nos 101, 102; Regt No 392

24TH RESERVE DVISION
Res. Regts Nos 101, 107, 133

26TH RESERVE DIVISION
Res. Regts Nos 99, 119, 121; Regt No 180

28TH RESERVE DIVISION
Res. Regts Nos 109, 110, 111

45TH RESERVE DIVISION
Res. Regts Nos 210, 211, 212

50TH RESERVE DIVISION
Res. Regts Nos 229, 230, 231

51ST RESERVE DIVISION
Res. Regts Nos 233, 234, 235, 236

52ND RESERVE DIVISION
Res. Regts Nos 238, 239, 240

4TH ERSATZ DIVISION
Regts Nos 359, 360, 361, 362

5TH ERSATZ DIVISION
Landwehr Regts Nos 73, 74; Res. Ersatz Regt No 3

2ND BAVARIAN DIVISION
Bav. Regts Nos 12, 15, 20

3RD BAVARIAN DIVISION
Bav. Regts Nos 17, 18, 23

4TH BAVARIAN DIVISION
Bav Regts Nos 5, 9; Bav. Res. Regt No 5

5TH BAVARIAN DIVISION
Bav. Regts Nos 7, 14, 19, 21

6TH BAVARIAN DIVISION
Bav. Regts Nos 6, 10, 11, 13

10TH BAVARIAN DIVISION
Bav. Regt No 16; Bav. Res. Regts Nos 6, 8

6TH BAVARIAN RESERVE DIVISION
Bav. Res. Regts Nos 16, 17, 20, 21

BAVARIAN ERSATZ DIVISION
Bav. Res. Regts Nos 14, 15; Ersatz Regt No 28

89TH RESERVE BRIGADE
Res. Regts Nos 209, 213

MARINE BRIGADE
Marine Regts Nos 1, 2, 3

NOTES
1. Replaced by Regt No 393 for second tour.
2. Reorganized for second tour, composition being Regts Nos 65 and 161 and Res. Regt No 28.
3. Left division before second tour.

APPENDIX 3
THE SOMME, 1916: VICTORIA CROSS AWARDS

1 July	T/Maj. S. W. Loudoun-Shand	10/Green Howards		Capt. N. G. Chavasse	RAMC (att. 1/10th King's)
	Sgt J. Y. Turnbull	17/HLI			
	Pte W. F. McFadzean	14/R. Irish Rif.	11 Aug	Pte M. O'Meara	16th Bn AEF
	Lt G. S. Cather	9/R. Irish Fus.			
	Pte R. Quigg	12/R. Irish Rif.	3 Sept	Sgt D. Jones	12/King's
	Cpl G. Sanders	1/7th W. Yorks		Lt J. V. Holland	3/Leinster (att. 7/Leinster)
	Drummer W. Ritchie	2/Seaforth			
	Capt. J. L. Green	RAMC (att. 1/5th Sherwood For.)		Pte T. Hughes	6/Conn. Rangers
				Capt. W. B. Allen	RAMC
3 July	Pte T. G. Turrall	10/Worcs	9 Sept	Pte L. Clarke	2nd Bn CEF
	Lt-Col Carton de Wiart	8/Gloster	15 Sept	Lance-Sgt F. McNess	1/Scots Gds
5 July	2/Lt D. S. Bell	9/Green Howards		Lt-Col J. V. Campbell	3/Coldstr. Gds
	Lt T. O. L. Wilkinson	7/L. N. Lancs		Sgt D. F. Brown	2/Otago
14 July	Sgt W. E. Boulter	6/Northampton	16 Sept	Pte J. C. Kerr	49th Bn CEF
15 July	Pte W. F. Faulds	1/Regt (Cape Prov.)	25 Sept	Pte T. A. Jones	1/Cheshire
20 July	Pte A. Hill	10/R. Welsh Fus.	26 Sept	Pte R. E. Ryder	12/Middlesex
	Pte J. J. Davies	10/R. Welsh Fus.		Pte F. J. Edwards	12/Middlesex
	Maj. W. La T. Congreve	76 Bde	27 Sept	2/Lt T. E. Adlam	7/Bedford
	Pte T. W. H. Veale	8/Devon	30 Sept	Capt. A. C. T. White	6/Green Howards
23 July	Pte J. Leak	9th Bn AEF			
	2/Lt A. S. Blackburn	10th Bn AEF	2 Oct	Lt-Col R. B. Bradford	1/9th DLI
25 July	Pte T. Cooke★	8th Bn AEF	4 Oct	2/Lt H. Kelly	10/DWR
27 July	Sgt A. Gill	1/KRRC	8 Oct	Piper J. C. Richardson	16th Bn CEF
29 July	Sgt C. C. Castleton	5th MG Corps AEF	23 Oct	Sgt R. Downie	2/R. Dub. Fus.
30 July	Pte J. Miller	7/King's Own			
	Coy Sgt-Maj. W. J. G. Evans	18/ Manchester	5 Nov	Lt E. P. Bennett	2/Worcs
			13 Nov	Lt-Col B. C. Freyberg	Hood Bn RND
6 Aug	Pte W. H. Short	8/York & Lanc		Pte J. Cunningham	12/E. Yorks
9 Aug	2/Lt G. G. Coury	3rd S. Lancs (att. 1/4th S. Lancs)			

★Posthumously awarded

168

BIBLIOGRAPHY

Bean, C. E. W., *Official History of Australia in the War of 1914–1918*, University of Queensland Press (1982). Reprinted as mammoth paperbacks, these volumes have enabled a wider range of the public to gain access to the mine of information on the AIF.

Charlton, P. *Pozières*, Leo Cooper/Secker & Warburg (1986). A study of the battle, well written from the Australian point of view.

Coombs, E. B., *Before Endeavours Fade*, After the Battle (1990). A guide to the First World War, still one of the best.

Edmunds, Brigadier-General Sir J., *British Official History*, Vol. 1916, Macmillan (1932, 1938). Often criticized for a pro-Haig stance, but as a source of information it has no rivals: the facts are not in doubt.

Gliddon, G., *When the Barrage Lifts*, Gliddon Books (1987). A topographical history and guide, with a strong literary bias; a 'must' for anyone interested in the Somme.

———, *VCs of the Somme*, Gliddon Books (1991). If you have an interest in the VC this is a useful volume.

Holt, T. and V., *Battlefield Guides: The Somme*, T. & V. Holt, (1986). A pocket guide to the Somme battlefield. Very good value for money.

Hughes, C., *Mametz*, Gliddon Books (1990). A well-researched and informative book about the unfortunate 38th (Welsh) Division.

Keegan, J., *The Face of Battle*, Jonathan Cape (1976). The start of current thinking: an important book.

Macdonald, L., *The Somme*, Michael Joseph (1983). The story of the battle, told in personal accounts.

Middlebrook, M., *First Day on the Somme*, Allen Lane (1971). The book that put the Somme back on the map. Should be read by anyone interested in the First World War.

Middlebrook, M. and M., *The Somme Battlefields*, Viking (1991). A guide to the Somme in 1916 and 1918, particularly good on the cemeteries in the area.

Norman, T., *The Hell They Call High Wood*, William Kimber (1984). A good account of the battle.

Simkins, P., *Kitchener's Army*, Manchester University (1988). While not about the battle, it *is* about the men who fought it.

Travers, T., *The Killing Ground*, Allen & Unwin. A study of the British Army during the First World War. Modern thinking at its best—a 'must' to read.

Uys, I., *Delville Wood*, Uys Publishers (1983). The South Africans' account of the Battle of Delville Wood.

MATTERS OF RELATED INTEREST

The Western Front Association publish a journal called *Stand To!*, available free to members. Membership Secretary: Mrs M. Arthur, Greenwood Lawson Leas, Barrowby, Grantham, Lincs NG32 1EH.

Tours

Flanders Tours are the appointed tour operator for the Western Front Association. Lieutenant-Colonel G. Parker OBE, c/o 4 Spencer House, 45a Crystal Palace Road, East Dulwich, London SE22 9EX.

Major & Mrs Holt's Tours, Golden Key Building, 15 Market Street, Sandwich, Kent CT13 9DA.

Martin Middlebrook's Battlefield Tours, 48 Linden Way, Boston, Lincs.

INDEX